Rabba, Maharat, Rabbanit, Rebbetzin

Rabba, Maharat, Rabbanit, Rebbetzin

Women with Leadership Authority According to Halachah

Daniel Sperber

Afterword by
Rabbanit Dr. Michal Tikochinsky

מהרת
maharat

Urim Publications
Jerusalem • New York

Rabba, Maharat, Rabbanit, Rebbetzin:
Women with Leadership Authority
According to Halachah

by Daniel Sperber

Afterword by Rabbanit Dr. Michal Tikochinsky
Index by Marc I. Sherman

Printed in Israel

First Edition

ISBN 978-965-524-246-1

מהרת
maharat

Urim Publications
P.O. Box 52287
Jerusalem 9152102
Israel

www.UrimPublications.com

Cover art by Andi Arnovitz

Description: "If Only They Had Asked Us" by Andi Arnovitz is a paper garment. Like a robe of judgment or a mantel of leadership, comprised of thousands of rolled scrolls from old pages of the Gemara, this vest suggests a future when women will be included in the "conversation" and Halachah will be more vibrant.

Library of Congress Cataloging-in-Publication Data

Names: Sperber, Daniel, author.
Title: Rabba, Maharat, Rabbanit, Rebbetzin : women with leadership authority according to halachah / Daniel Sperber.
Description: First edition. | Jerusalem ; New York : Urim Publications, [2020] | Includes bibliographical references and index.
Identifiers: LCCN 2016055438 | ISBN 9789655242461 (hardcover : alk. paper)
Subjects: LCSH: Women in Judaism—History. | Leadership—Religious aspects—Judaism. | Orthodox Judaism. | Jewish law.
Classification: LCC BM729.W6 S635 2020 | DDC 296.6/1082—dc23 LC record available at https://lccn.loc.gov/2016055438

אשרנו מה טוב חלקינו,
ומה נעים גורלנו,
ומה יפה ירושתנו!

This volume is dedicated to

Belda Kaufman Lindenbaum
and Marcel Lindenbaum

by their children, grandchildren
and the students and alumnae
of Yeshivat Maharat.

Their devotion to women's scholarship and leadership
was an inspiration and a call to action.

יהי זכרם ברוך

"The woman of valor . . ." – *Eshet Hayyil*

She opens her mouth with wisdom;
and in her tongue is the law of kindness.
Strength and honor are her clothing;
And she shall rejoice in time to come.
Give her the fruit of her hands;
 and let her own works praise her in the gates

– Proverbs 31:25, 26, 31

"And she shall rejoice in time to come" and she will receive her reward in time to come, even though she is doing what she is not obligated to do [i.e., wearing a *tallit* and laying *tefillin*, cf. verse 25], nonetheless, she will receive a reward . . . And her wisdom stood her in good stead, that she did not ask the Sages whether to do this, but acted on her own accord. And she made the benedictions [over them], and not in accordance with their rulings, but of her own will . . .

(R. Yisrael Yaakov Algazi, 1680–1756 in his commentary to *Eshet Hayyil*, apud Yom Tov Algazi – his son – *Kedushat Yom Tov*, Jerusalem, 1843.)

CONTENTS

PREFACE

On Thursday evening, June 2, 2016, I attended the ordination ceremony of three new Orthodox female rabbis. They had been rigorously trained in Yeshivat Maharat in Riverdale, New York, under the directorship of Rabba Sara Hurwitz and the Rosh Yeshivah, Rabbi Jeff Fox. This was the fourth such event, and to date fourteen ladies have been ordained, all of whom have leadership positions in various Orthodox communities. The moving spirit behind this new phenomenon is, of course, Rabbi Avi Weiss, of the Hebrew Academy of Riverdale, who has pioneered this rapidly developing movement.

At that event I made the following brief speech which I quote word for word:

> Dear Friends,
>
> Once again we are celebrating the rabbinic ordination of women. A relatively short while ago such an occasion within an Orthodox setting would have seemed to be impossible, almost hallucinatory. Yet what was so recently a dream has now become a reality. What was once implausible has now become almost a norm, at least within a certain segment of the modern Orthodox community. What was once revolutionary has now become evolutionary. There are now institutions in the United States and Israel where women from a variety of countries are being trained stringently and exhaustively in all aspects of rabbinic leadership. Of course, there are those critics and denigrators

who would seek to drive us beyond the bounds of Orthodoxy. But this was to be expected, and indeed understandable, given the traditionalist inability to recognize the dynamic nature of halachah. For they are grounded in dogmatism, while we strive after dynamism.

Our movement is growing, and ordained women are finding their place in Orthodox communities. They are holding positions of influence and authority, and giving overt expression to their wisdom and learning. I see in the not-too-distant future a situation where we will no longer be a peripheral phenomenon, while at the same time our antagonists shrink to a minority position. We see an ever-increasing number of women who are willing to devote themselves to many years of intensive study, and to commit themselves to a career of spiritual and halachic leadership. They will be adding that additional component of feminine sensitivity to the halachic process, and responding to the needs of our contemporary society in accordance with the requirements of these times.

May the thus-far ordained continue to grow in learning and practice in their various communities. Their work is truly *melechet kodesh*. May the present ordainees be blessed with a future of success. And may our students, the future cadre, gain encouragement and hope from what has happened so far.

And what has happened so far is only due to the courage, commitment and persistence of certain individuals without whose heroic activism none of this could have taken place. They are the pioneer trailblazing visionaries of the current radical changes. I am, of course, referring to such well-known "earth-shakers" as Rabbi Avi Weiss, Rabbi Shlomo Riskin, Dr. Blu Greenberg, and others, known and lesser-known, who have made such significant contributions to this development.

Finally, I personally feel deeply gratified and honored to have been granted the opportunity to play if only a small part in this historic process, a process which, with the help of God, is changing the landscape of modern Orthodoxy.

At the end of that presentation, I somewhat whimsically added the following thought.

> This is indeed a most joyous occasion, both for the ordinees, their families and friends, as well as their teachers, and indeed all who are attending this very special ceremony. It has taken place on the fortieth day of *Sefirat ha-Omer*. Surely the period of *Sefirah* is one of mourning, in which we are told to minimize all forms of joyful celebrations! Should an event of this nature not have been delayed till after Shavuot? On further contemplation, however, I thought that this was a wholly suitable time for the event. For traditional sources tell us that the reason for this period of mourning is in memory of the twelve or twenty-four thousand disciples of R. Akiva, who during the period between Pesach and Shavuot, all died, smitten by the plague of *ascara*, primarily because they did not pay sufficient respect to one another. In effect, a whole generation of future rabbis was decimated by this plague. The Maharat ordination ceremony, on the other hand, serves to expand the horizon of rabbinic leadership, adding a new component of true respect for the achievements of these very special women rabbis. It is, therefore, truly a *tikkun*, and most suited to be celebrated with joy and pride during the *Sefirah* period.

This was on Thursday evening in New York. On Tuesday evening of the following week I attended a *hag ha-semichah* in Jerusalem, where over twenty rabbis were ordained, all pupils of Rabbi Daniel Landes, among them some eight women ordainees! So this is indeed a growing, nay, a flourishing phenomenon, which is going to have a real impactful change on the landscape of Orthodox Jewish communal life.

In effect, this study argues for the complete halachic legitimization for this new role for Orthodox women. It is an innovation grounded, as we shall argue, in tradition, drawing upon ancient rabbinic sources, reinvigorating our Orthodox communities.

The next decade will reveal to us the extent to which this innovation is accepted in the Orthodox world. I personally am convinced that future generations will come to see this as a perfectly normal practice, so that indeed, in Rav Kook's words, החדש יתקדש – "innovation will be sanctified."[1]

1. Clearly the future of this trend, or movement, will be largely dependent on the reactions and responses of the various elements in the Orthodox Jewish community. And in this connection, it is interesting to observe the varying responses already evident, as revealed in the findings of the new research file of "American Modern Orthodox Jews" from *Nishma* (September 28, 2017), as was recently brought to my attention: https://bit.ly/2yDL7x6.

The question addressed was: Should women have expanded roles in the clergy? The responses are as follows:

How much support is there for women with expanded roles in the clergy and a title signifying their "rabbinic authority"? Overall, 19% strongly support this, another 19% somewhat support this, and 62% do not support this.

How strong and widespread is the support for women with expanded roles in the clergy and titles signifying "rabbinic authority"? Overall, 19% strongly support this – more women (25%) than men (14%) – with sharp differences across denominations: this is the issue that most divides the left (strongly supportive) from the right (strongly opposed).

This then gives us a picture of its current state of affairs in the U.S. Orthodox Jewish community. The future will tell the directions in which these figures will change and develop.

ACKNOWLEDGMENT

I HAVE ALWAYS CLAIMED THAT I AM NOT A FEMINIST, BUT rather a halachist. The general response to my claim is usually: But you have seven daughters and only three sons. So you are bound to be "prejudiced" in favor of women. Maybe so, but not with conscious awareness. For I fully believe that the halachah has to respond actively and positively to the burning challenges of the times, and, in our days, high on these priorities is the status of women in Judaism. Hence, I have written copiously on women's role in the synagogue, also on the *Agunah* issue, and it was only natural that I should become involved in the discussion on women's ordinations and its practical implementations.

In all these issues I have been graced with the full support of my family, and foremost among them, my dear wife Chana, who has had to bear the burden of my studies and communal activities. Without her unfailing aid and encouragement I would not have been able to achieve whatever I may have managed to achieve.

For to Chana I owe a worthy portion, for Chana I love.

– Daniel Sperber

PRELIMINARY CLARIFICATION

When we use the term Rebbetzin, the intention is to women with rabbinic authority, rather than wives of Rabbis. Here we may point out that the concept of a learned woman, *Ishah Hachamah*, is to be found in our classical sources. Sometimes the formulation is *ke-Man de-Kari ve-Tani*, like one who has read (Torah) and studied (Mishnah). See the discussion in the *Rosh* to *Ketubot* 2:6; and R. Shimon Levi's article, "*Kibud Talmid Hacham, Rav ve-Zaken*," *Shematin* 28/104–105, pp. 44–46. R. Levi's conclusion (ibid., p. 46) is as follows:

> Nonetheless, a woman who is wise in the wisdom of the Torah, and even if just in those laws which obligate women, her halachic status is as that of a wise man (*hacham*), and one is duty-bound to respect her, and to rise before her, and [her status is such that] one is commanded to honor and rise before her (*hiddur ve-kimah*).[1]

---

1. The above is, of course, contrary to the view of R. Eliezer in *B. Yoma* 66b, *Y. Sotah* 3:4; *Numbers Rabba* 9:48, Rabbeinu Bahye to *Exodus* 35:25. On the other hand, see the views of Ben Azai in *B. Sotah* 21b and *Tosafot* ibid. etc.

Marc B. Shapiro (referred to below ch. 2 note 3) notes the use of the term "Rabbanit" as "a title of respect." He points out that Flora Sassoon (1859–1936), who was an extremely learned woman, and whose husband was not a rabbi, was called Rabbanit in a *derashah*, published by R. Joel Herzog, in his *Imrei Yoel*, vol. 3, London, 1923, pp. 204–206. (See on her also below note 41.) Shapiro brings other examples of women called Rabbanit (ibid., note 13).

1 INTRODUCTORY REMARKS

In a volume I wrote entitled *The Importance of the Community Rabbi* the discussion centered exclusively around the "Rabbi," i.e., it has a definite male-gender orientation. This, of course, is due to the nature of the sources used, drawn as they are from a broad spectrum of rabbinic writings. However, in recent years the question has been raised as to whether women can also play a significant role in rabbinic leadership positions – and this taking into account the profound societal changes that have taken place over the past few generations in the status of women. And if they can play such a role, to what extent, and are there limitations or special areas of rabbinic activity in which they cannot participate.

This study seeks to examine these questions, and while not giving answers to all of them, at least opens the way to suggesting partial solutions. And irrespective of the choice of titles that may be accorded such women, *Maharat, Rabba, Rebbetzin, Yoetzet Halachah, Poseket, Baalat Heter Horaah*, *Morat Horaah*, *Manhigah Ruhanit* (the latter being the exact and specific title used by Ohr Torah Stone and Rabbi Shlomo Riskin for graduates of their "women clergy"), etc., the precise mode of address, will, I believe, be more a socio-political issue, rather than a halachic one. Presumably each congregation will choose its own formulation in accordance with her "job description," i.e., the duties it wishes to impose on its elected "lady-leader."

We have also included a somewhat expanded version of my

essay first published in *Meorot* 8, 2010, pp. 1–12, that analyzes the halachic issues regarding women assuming positions of communal leadership and serving as rabbis. It examines in detail Maimonides' halachic ruling restricting communal appointments to adult Jewish males, citing pre-modern and modern halachic decisors and arguing with R. Moshe Feinstein (among others) that Maimonides' ruling was his own innovation and is a "rejected ruling." Maimonides' prohibition of women in communal leadership is also not borne out historically. We conclude that while allowing women rabbis is an innovative step in the Orthodox community, there is no normative halachic bar to women being ordained or functioning as Jewish communal leaders.

Following that are comments on and responses to a number of essays written on the subject, and a refutation of the position of the RCA and R. Hershel Schachter, and leading authorities of the RCA.

There are those who argue that our whole halachic system is skewed with a overwhelming bias towards males: it is wholly "androcentric." As a consequence it should be completely deconstructed and then reconstructed in an egalitarian fashion given the contemporary status of women.[1] I find this view unacceptable. I have always thought in terms of the normative tradition of classical halachah, and believe that we have a sufficiently rich legal heritage to be able to confront the majority of challenges that modernity presents, and find for them solutions within the

1. As to the "male-gender orientation" of rabbinic writings mentioned, I do not wish within the context of this study to enter into the vast realm of feminist polemic literature; suffice it to mention Ronit Irshai's recent volume entitled *Fertility and Jewish Law*, Waltham, Mass., 2012, pp.12–18, on "The Maleness of Halakhah," with copious bibliographic references, and, of course, Tamar Ross' classic *Expanding the Palace of Torah: Orthodoxy and Feminism*, Waltham, Mass., 2004, throughout. And cf. below note 5.

parameters of classical halachic thinking.[2] And even when it might appear that we may have to reject hallowed precedent and tradition, a careful examination of the relevant sources will demonstrate that this is not necessarily the case. Rather we may circumvent and/or reinterpret them so that the apparent precendental sources actually present no threat or contradiction to contemporary needs. This, I believe, may be done, without straying beyond the parameters of the normative halachic process. Here I shall try to demonstrate this by examining the question of the possibility of granting women elements of rabbinic status and communal authority.

Indeed, already in our early sources we hear of learned women. Thus, the Midrash in *Numbers Rabba* 21:12 informs us that the daughters of Tzelofhad knew the law (regarding inheritance\ that Moshe Rabbeinu did not know (referring to *Numbers* 27:5). (See parallels listed in M.M. Kasher, *Torah Shelemah* to *Pinhas*, vol. 43, Jerusalem, 1992, p. 83, notes 23 and 24. See also the complex discussion in *B. Baba Batra* 189b, and cf. ibid., 108a, 110b.)

This issue recently became a *cause célèbre*, triggering an acute controversy, when a woman was given a form of ordination and a title suggestive of rabbinic authority. I am, of course, referring to the highly publicized episode in 2012 of Ms. Sara Hurwitz, who after exhaustive examinations by a number of rabbinic authorities, was granted the title of "Maharat," an acronym denoting a position of halachic, spiritual and Torah leadership.[3] Shortly

---

2. I stress this point because my view on this matter was misunderstood by the correspondent of the "Forward," Debra Nussbaum, in her report of March 16, 2010, misconstruing what I expressed at the JOFA conference on that date.

3. In point of fact a number of women had already been granted some sort of "*Semichah*" long before. Thus, Haviva Ner David was given an Orthodox ordination by Rabbi Arie Strikowsky (2009). Rabbi Yonathan Chipman ordained Evelyn Goodman Tau (2010), and three anonymous Orthodox rabbis (including Reb Shlomo Carlebach) granted *Semichah* to Mimi Feigelson (Jerusalem Post Magazine, March 20, 2010, p. 41). And though I have no firsthand knowledge of the nature of those ordinations and on what level of knowledge they were based, they seem largely to have escaped the notice of would-be detractors.

afterwards her title was changed to "Rabba," which sparked an even more vehement and acrid response on the part of the ultra-Orthodox Agudat Yisrael and the Moetzet Gedolei ha-Torah of America, and also the so-called centrist Rabbinic Council of America (RCA). Many contended that the RCA buckled under to the extreme right-wing pressure. But be that as it may, the juggernaut of opposition forced a partial retraction from the title of "Rabba," which in any case was probably politically ill-advised. But while the *title* seemed to be the main source of

---

More recently in 2013 nine women have been ordained within the framework of *Yeshivat Maharat* (and see below).

Earlier on there was a great public controversy over the appointment of a woman on a rabbinic municipal council – *moetzah datit.* I am referring to the "Leah Shakdiel affair" (1990). See on this Yehezkel Cohen, *Nashim be-Hanhagat ha-Tzibbur: Ha-Mahloket al Haverut Nashim be-Moetzah Datit*, Jerusalem, 1991, which was published by *Ha-Kibbutz ha-Dati and Neemanei Torah ve-Avodah.* There he examines carefully the religious-ideological and political elements in this controversy, and includes additional articles by a number of authorities. The history of the affair is fascinating from a sociological aspect.

As to the "Maharat Affair," see the illuminating socio-halachic analysis of Alan J. Yuter, "Orthodox Judaism Today: Ordaining a Female Rabbi and the Critique of R. Avi Weiss," *Keren* 1, 2013, pp. 114–132. See also M.J. Broyde and S.M. Brody, "Orthodox Women Rabbis, 2nd edition, Tentative Thoughts that Distinguish between the Timely and the Timeless," *Hakira* 11, 2011, pp. 25–58. Among the prime "objecters" are R. Avi Shafran and R. Hershel Schachter (see further ibid., pp. 121–130), but there were many other signatories to their condemnation (ibid., p. 115, note 3, for a list – to which later on others no doubt agreed).

Actually already in 1935 (on December 27), Regina Jonas was ordained as the first woman rabbi (*Rabbinerin*) in Berlin by a liberal Orthodox rabbi, Meir Max Dienemann. See Elisa Klapheck, *Fraeulein Rabbiner Jonas: Kann die Frau das rabbinische Amt bekleiden??*, Teetz, 1999, and most recently, Margalit Shlain, Regina Yonas: Roah Ruhanit La-Tzibbur ha-Yehudi be-Berlin u-be-Gheto Terezenstadt, Teetz 13, 2017, pp. 187–219. On Haviva Ner-David, see her Life on the Fringes: A Feminist Journey Toward Traditional Rabbinic Ordination, Needham, Mass., 2000; Jonathan Chipman, "May a Woman Be Ordained as Rabbi?" apud Li-heyot ishah Yehudiah: divrei ha-kenes ha-beinleumi ha-sheni, Jerusalem, 2003, English section, pp. 9–24.

Most recently, in May 2018, Rabbi Shlomo Riskin ordained three women, refraining from calling them rabba, but conferring upon them the title "spiritual leader and halachic teacher" (Jerusalem Post, Wednesday, May 23, 2018, p. 13).

the controversy, the actual *function* was largely ignored. For there had already been women in similar functional positions, but under different titular definions, such as "intern," "educational director," "Rosh Kehillah," or "Scholar-in residence" on more or less a permanent basis. And so Sara Hurwitz continues, and will continue, in her authoritative function, while the title-controvery rages, and hopefully will eventually wane.

The heated argument was more recently reignited by the rabbinic ordination of a number of women: two from Harel Bet Midrash in Jerusalem, more than six from Yeshivah Maharat in New York, and shortly after two more from Michlelet Lindenbaum in Jerusalem were granted *heter horaah*. In all these cases the title is a subject of serious debate. While some will call themselves "Rabba," others will decry the use of this term and seek to delegitimize them. Hopefully, with the passage of time, the polemic will morph into a non-issue.

After all, Deborah the Prophetess was a judge, and Beruriah, the wife of R. Meir was a *Tannait* whose ruling in *Tosefta Kelim Baba Metzia* 1:6 was accepted by R. Yehoshua. Similarly in *Tosefta Baba Kama* 4:17, R. Yehudah ben Bava accepts her ruling rather than that of her brother, Yehoshua ben Haninah (ben Taradion). (It appears that Beruriah was indeed R. Haninah ben Taradion's daughter, see *B. Avodah Zarah* 18a.) However, we should note that in *M. Kelim* 11:4, Beruriah's view, referred to above (from *T. Kelim B.M.* 1:6) is here assigned to the authorship of R. Yehoshua, who in the *Tosefta* ibid, had praised her for her eloquence. Perhaps we have here evidence of that male gender orientation mentioned above.[4]

At the time when the issue of some sort of ordination for a

---

4. On this see Tal Ilan, *Integrating Women into Second Temple History*, Tübingen, 1999, 2nd ed. Peabody, Mass., 2001, pp. 181–194.

See further idem, *Mine and Yours are Hers: Retrieving Women's History from Rabbinic Literature*, Leiden, 1997, pp. 58, 72–73; Marc B. Shapiro, *Changing the Immutable*, Oxford, Portland, Oregon, 2015, pp. 45–47, on internal Talmudic censorship, with several examples.

woman was being raised, I was asked to write a responsum on the subject. I readily consented to do so, and did not really make any significant innovation, since the subject had been carefully discussed by a number of prominent authorities and scholars.[5]

I was perhaps able to add some additional elements, and here I give a somewhat expanded version of the argument that I put forward in my responsum. It was entitled "Question as to whether a woman may give halachic decisions," which is one of the important functions of a rabbi, though, of course, not the only one.

---

5. To give but a selection of examples:

Women Who Would Be Rabbis: A History of Women's Ordination 1889–1985, by Pamela S. Nadel, Boston, 1998.

The Ordination of Women as Rabbis: Studies and Responsa, ed. Simon Greenberg, New York, 1988 (a Centennial Publication of the Jewish Theological Seminary of America); the Conservative approach (though Prof. Israel Francus' views are more Orthodox and largely negative).

Chanah Henkin, "Women and the Issuing of Halakhic Rulings," apud *Jewish Legal Writings by Women*, eds. Micah D. Halpern and Chana Safrai, Jerusalem, 1998/5758, pp. 278–287; David Golinkin, *The Status of Women in Jewish Law: Responsa*, Jerusalem, 2012, pp. 286–307, a chapter entitled "Women as Poskot," with additional bibliography.

Avi Weinrot, *Feminism ve-Yahadut*, Israel, 2001, pp. 84–117; A. Frimer, "Women in Public Positions in the Modern Period," *Afikei Yehudah*, ed. I. Warhaftig, Jerusalem, 2005, pp. 330–354 [Hebrew]; Aliza Bazak "Women Judges: An Analysis after Sources of the Law and its Examination in the Light of the Rulings on Judges and Officeholders throughout the Generations," *Lihyot Ishah Yehudiyah*, ed. T. Cohen and A. Lavi, Jerusalem, 2005, pp. 88–99 [Hebrew]; H. Hirshensohn, *Malki ba-Kodesh*, vol. 2, Hoboken, 1941, pp.182–192; 2nd edition, Jerusalem, 2013, pp. 393–408. And see below ch. 4 notes 1, 3; Irit Bartov, "Ha-Im Ishah Yecholah le-Chahein ke-Dayyenet," apud *Mah She'elatach Ester ha-Malkah Teshuvat Hilchatiot she-Nichtevu al-Yedei Musmachot ha-Machon*, Jerusalem (n.d. c 2014?), pp. 37–65.

Most recently, Noam Stadlan published a detailed essay on the subject, entitled "Gender Roles in Ordination, Leadership and the Public: An Analysis of the OU Paper," *Conversations* 31, 2018, pp. 87–129. Much of his discussion touches on points analyzed in this book. The essay reached me too late to be able to give it fully deserved references throughout this study.

2 WOMEN IN RABBINIC POSITIONS

QUESTION: CAN A WOMAN ANSWER HALACHIC QUESTIONS, that is to say, be a halachic decisor?

RESPONSE: In *Mishnah Niddah* 6:4 it is said: Whosoever is eligible to judge is eligible to bear witness. And in *Yerushalmi Yoma* 6:1 it seems to be explicitly stated that since a woman may not bear witness she cannot judge. [1] The *Tosafot* (*Niddah* ibid. 50a)

1. I wrote "seems to be" because recently the Tosafot's interpretation of the *Yerushalmi* was called into question by R. Ahiah David , in his article entitled "*Ishah Psulah la-Dun?*" in *Hemdat ha-Aretz* 5, 2007, pp. 61–66, who argues persuasively that "*Mei-atah ein ha-ishah danah*," is a question rather than an affirmative statement. And indeed, this is predominantly the case in the *Yerushalmi*, as shown by Leib Moskovitz, in his *Ha-Terminologiah Shel ha-Yerushalmi: Ha-Munahim ha-Ikarrim* (*The Terminology of the Yerushalmi: The Principal Terms*), Jerusalem, 2009, pp. 447–448, and especially note 525, ibid., referring to our *Yerushalmi* text. See further Zachariah Frankel, *Mevo ha-Yerushalmi*, 2nd edition, Jerusalem, 1967, 12a, s.v. *mei-ata*; Moshe Assis, *Otzar Leshonot Yerushalmiim*, New York, 2010, vol. 2, pp.1070–1072. From the context David Ovitz also suggests that "*dana*" in that phrase does not mean "judges" but is a "litigant" or "plaintiff." He also examines the parallels in Y. *Sanhedrin* 3:9 and Y. *Shevuot* 4:1. His conclusions were called into doubt by R. Daniel Katz, ibid., pp. 67–72, but Katz's arguments are not persuasive. See also Yisachar Tamar, *Alei Tamar Jerushalmi Moed*, vol.1, Alon Shvut 1991, pp. 370–371, who shows the text is corrupt and suggests a reconstruction of it based on manuscript sources, parallels and early testimonies.

We may also refer the reader to R. Moshe Ehrenreich's article in *Hemdat Ha-Aretz*, pp. 29–43, entitled "*Kol ha-Pasul le-Ha'id Pasul la-Dun*," who con-

asked: How then did Deborah the Prophetess serve as a judge? For in Judges 4:4–5 it is stated: "And Deborah, a prophetess, the wife of Lapidoth, she judged Israel at that time . . . and the children of Israel came up to her for judgement." And one of their answers is that what the Mishnah means to teach us is only that he who is eligible to give witness may judge, i.e., that he who for some specific reason is ineligible to bear witness, may not judge. That does not mean that there is an overall prohibition against a woman acting as a judge just because in some instances she is ineligible to bear witness. (But see below, note 11.)

This answer takes no account of the *Yerushalmi*'s formulation, which would appear to give an overall prohibition against women acting as judges.

In an additional answer offered by the Tosafot, ibid., it is stated: "She [Deborah] did not herself give judgement, but taught [the judges] the laws; and the *Yerushalmi* declares that women are ineligible to judge. From this answer we learn that a woman may give halachic rulings, for that is the real meaning of teaching halachah to others."

Yet another solution to this apparent contradiction is found in the *Ritba* to *Kiddushin* 35a (ed. A. Dinin, Jerusalem, 1985, p. 373), and in the *Rashba* to *Bava Kama* 15a. (ed. A. Lichtenstein, Jerusalem, 1987, p. 21), namely that the statement in *Niddah* refers only to a man, meaning that only a man who is unfit to bear witness is unfit to give judgement. But women, though they are (sometimes) unfit to bear witness, may act as judges, as we learn from Deborah the Prophetess.

Quite a different reply is given by the *Ran* (R. Nissim) to *Shavuot* 30a (13a in the *Rif's* pagination), and the *Rashba* to *Shavuot* ibid. Concerning Deborah's position as a judge they write, in their second response:

---

cludes, inter alia (p. 43), that there are views among the Tosafists that see no parallel identity between the law of testimony and that of judgement, and which according to this view (both) women (and blind people) are qualified to act as judges.

> ... Or perhaps she did judge and did give rulings, because they accepted her, just as a person can accept one of his [close] relatives [as a judge, even though a close relative is legally disqualified from being a judge].

What the *Ran* is saying is that just as one can take upon oneself to accept the ruling of one who is legally disqualified from serving as a judge, such as a close relative or a non-Jew, so too, since "the children of Israel came up to her for judgement" agreeing to accept her ruling, her rulings were binding upon them. Hence, if a woman is approached for a halachic ruling, it may be presumed that the questioner will accept her reply as authoritative.

Further proof for this, if at all necessary, may be found in R. Ovadiah Yosef's discussion in *Yabia Omer*, 2nd edition, vol. 1, Jerusalem, 1986, *Orah Hayyim* sect. 41:16, p.146. He refers us to R. Yonatan Eibeschutz's *Tiferet Yonatan*, Lvov 1860, to *Yitro* (*Exodus* 18:16) who raised the question how could Deborah give judgement alone. Surely we have learned from R. Yishmael be-R. Yossi, "Judge not alone, for none may judge alone save One" (*M. Avot* 4:8). His answer is that many *poskim* wrote that when the plaintiff comes to the judge requesting his judgement, a single judge is permitted. This is also his ruling in *Urim ve-Tumim*, Warsaw, 1882, to *Hoshen Mishpat* 3:5. R. Ovadia strengthened this position by referring us to *Y. Sanhedrin* 1:1, where we read as follows:

> R. Abbahu sat in judgement alone in Kenishta Maradeta in Caesarea. His disciples asked him, "Rabbi, did you not teach us not to give judgement alone?!" He replied to them, "Since they see me sitting alone in judgement, and [nonetheless] they come to me, they are as those who have accepted upon themselves [a solitary judge]." And so indeed have we learned: When are we referring to that [one may not judge alone]? When the plaintiffs did not accept [such an arrangement]. But if they did accept

> [such an arrangement] upon themselves, even a single judge may give judgement.[2]

To the above we may add what we find in *Ruth Rabbah* 1:1, according to which both Deborah and Yael were judges (see *Redal*, R. David Luria's note ad loc.). Likewise, *Ecclesiastes Rabbah*, commenting on the verse in *Ecclesiastes* 2:8 עשיתי לי שרים ושרות, explains: דיינים זכרים ודיינות נקבות, male and female judges.[3]

Furthermore, even a blind person, who according to many

---

2. See on this passage, Yisachar Tamar, *Alei Tamar, Nezikin*, Israel, 1983, pp. 75–76, on the differences of opinions on this issue, referring to *Deuteronomy Rabba* 1:10, *Shach, Hoshen Mishpat* 3:10, according to the *Maharshal*, responsum 35, *Tosafot Yom Tov* to *Avot* ibid., basing themselves on Rav Huna's actions, in the *Yerushalmi*, ibid. And see earlier on in that *Yerushalmi sugya* the other rulings of R. Abbahu. See further on the legitimacy of the acceptance of non-qualified judges in Rabbi Yitzhak Ha-Levi Herzog, *Tehukah le-Yisrael al-pi ha-Torah*, vol. 1, Jerusalem, 1989, p. 43.

See further the very detailed discussion of R. Ovadiah Yosef in his *Yabia Omer* vol. 2, 2nd edition, Jerusalem, 1986, *Even ha-Ezer* 13:3, p. 246, who brings a wealth of evidence to prove that *gittin*, bills of divorce, can be granted by a court of *hedyotot,* laymen – needless to say laymen who have learned the basic law of divorce, but are not necessarily ordained as *dayanim* – judges. Indeed, the *Beit Yosef* in *Hoshen Mishpat* 8 cites the Rashba as saying "that in villages where there are no individuals who know even a single letter, . . . one should appoint judges in accordance with the understanding of the local authorities," referring to *B. Sanhedrin* 23a, etc. See his conclusions that it is sufficient that one know how to carry out the process of divorce in accordance with the books [which one has learned and assimilated].

3. Again see Redal ad loc. who interprets that text differently. See also *Numbers Rabbah* 10:17, where it is asserted that women may not serve as judges. See Marc B. Shapiro's post of March 2, 2012, in the *Seforim blog*, entitled "Answers to Quiz Questions and Other Comments, part 2," who discusses the *Eccles. Rab.* text in detail, referring, inter alia, to R. Yisrael Beeri, in his *Ha-Midrash ke-Halachah*, Nes Tziona, 1960, p. 317, who suggests that Solomon not only had female courts, but also "co-ed" *batei-din*. Similarly, R. Hayyim David ha-Levi, in his *Asei le-cha Rav*, vol. 8, pp. 247–248, deals with this text, suggesting that it is operating under the assumption that there was no problem in appointing women *dayanim*, or alternatively that Solomon and his council accepted the authority of the women, and therefore this was permissible. See the continuation of Shapiro's very learned discussion.

Rishonim is not qualified to act as a judge, since he cannot give evidence (cf. *Niddah* ibid.), and so rules the *Shulhan Aruch, Hoshen Mishpat* 7:2, nonetheless, if he is accepted by the community or the plaintiffs, he may do so, and the defendant can even force the plaintiff (claimant) to accept his judgement, since the defendant has the upper hand in these matters.[4]

And returning to our main subject, even according to those who do not follow the lines of interpretation we have cited above, there are numerous areas in which a woman is indeed eligible to give testimony, such as in the cases of *Yibum* and *Halitzah* (*Shulchan Aruch, Even ha-Ezer, Seder Halitzah* 21–24. Rambam, *Hilchot Yibum ve-Halitzah* 4:31), issues between a man and his wife (Rambam, *Ishut* 21:10), establishing that a captive woman was not raped and is permitted to marry a *Cohen* (Rambam, *Issurei Biah* 18:17), establishing ownership (*Baba Kama* 104b), issues both monetary and otherwise (*Ketubot* 85b, *Responsa Rivash* 182), in cases where the testimony of a single witness suffices (Rambam, *Edut* 5:3), *Kashrut,* separating *hallah*, Shabbat, and menstrual purity and impurity – *Niddah* (Responsa *Tzitz Eliezer*, vol. 4, 20), everything that a person can of his own accord correct (*Shulhan Aruch, Even ha-Ezer* 17:3, based on M. *Yevamot* 16:7), etc.[5] It follows that in all these areas a woman is eligible not merely to give testimony, but also to give judgement.[6]

---

4. Shapiro in an article in the *Seforim blog*, Tuesday, February 9, 2016, p. 14, note 12, also refers us to R. Jonathan Eliasburg, *Darkei Horaah*, Vilna, 1884, part 2, chapter 8, where he thinks that a woman can be a *dayan*, but she cannot be a *dayan* together with men.

See e.g., R. Hayyim Benveniste, *Knesset ha-Gedolah* to *Hoshen Mishpat* 7:2 (vol.1, Izmir 1660); and his *Bai Hayyai ,Hoshen Mishpat* , Saloniki, 1788, vol.1, sects. 5–6. And see the numerous sources cited by Aryeh Rodrigez, in his *Sefer ha-Suma,* Jerusalem (n.d. but c. 2000), pp. 483–490.

5. See most recently Eliezer Hadad, "*Hishvah ha-Katuv Ishah ke-Ish": Al Maamadan Shel Nashim be-Vatei Din Rabbaniim* (*Mehkarei Mediniut* 100), Jerusalem, 2013, pp. 32–82; Idit Bar-Tov, "Ha'Im ha'Ishah Yecholah le-Khahein ke-Dayyenet?" apud *Mah She-elatech Ester ha-Malkah ve-Te'as,* Jerusalem (n.d. c. 2014), pp. 60–65, who brings additional examples.

6. Hardly any of this was taken into account in R. Moshe Meiselman's apol-

ogetic chapter on "Women as Witnesses," in his *Jewish Women in Jewish Law*, New York, 1978, pp.73–80. He does note some situations in which women's testimonies may be accepted, such as monetary issues "where male witnesses are not readily available"(*Rema, Hoshen Mishpat* 35:14; cf. Rambam, *Sanhedrin* 24:1). "However," he adds, "this does not mean that their statements are raised to the level of witnessed testimony; it only means that where witnessed testimony is not available, we rely on their credibility" (ibid., pp. 77–78).

He then discusses the basic question as to "why this technical disqualification was imposed upon women," arguing "it might be arbitrary or it might have deeper implications. . . ."

He continues (pp. 78–79):

> I am unaware of any authoritative or semi-authoritative statement regarding the possible involvement of implicit principles in the disqualification of women as witnesses. Hence, any search for such principles is highly speculative, and the following material is nothing but my own private speculation and should be regarded as only that. . . .
>
> To *require* all women to testify at all times might very possibly contradict their private role in Jewish life, which we discussed earlier. In a similar vein, the requirement that a litigant must appear himself in court, rather than appoint an attorney to appear in his stead, is waived for women because of the verse "The entire glory of the daughter of the king lies on the inside" [*B. Shevuot* 30a and *Tosafot* ad loc.; *B. Ketubot* 74b]. The technical disqualification of women in Jewish law may also be due to a feeling that it would be improper to subject women to the indignity of intense cross-examination in court. Hence, the reasons for the disqualification of women and kings would be similar.
>
> There are many possible reasons for the technical disqualification of women, and no one really knows for sure. The only clear facts are that the ability to testify is neither a right nor a privilege, but an obligation from which women have been excused. The disqualification of women is a technical rule, rather than an expression of lack of credibility. Thus, women's statements are acceptable whenever credibility is required rather than witnessed testimony. Women's statements are not considered witnessed testimony. A woman's oath is acceptable in court, as is the oath of any credible person.

(We should point out that there is a biblical requirement for one who witnesses a prohibited act to give testimony before the authorities; see *Leviticus* 5:1, Rambam, *Hilchot Eidut* 1:1, etc.)

But returning to R. Meiselman's argument, my response to the above would be to refer the reader to R. Yehudah Henkin's discussion in his *Shut Bnei Banim* vol. 1, Jerusalem, 1981, no. 40, pp. 136–138. There he relates to Rambam, *Hilchot Ishut* 13:12, where he limits a married woman's right to go out of the house to visit to her father's house, to a mourner, to involve herself in acts of charity etc., but not to regularly stroll in the streets. Furthermore, the Rambam limits the wife's excursions to once or twice a month, in accordance with the relevant needs. To this R. Henkin responded that the Rambam was only referring to unnecessarily excursions. But when they have a positive purpose, or constitute a *mitzvah*, even the Rambam argues they are permissible. Clearly, the concept of a "positive purpose" is much broader nowadays, and would include shopping, visiting friends, and even entertainment which is good for a person's mental and emotional health.

To the above we may also add the remarks of R. Eliezer Yehudah Waldenberg, in his *Tzitz Eliezer* vol. 9, no. 50, that:

> In older times women were not wont to walk about in the streets, but would sit at home. Consequently walking behind a woman would more likely lead to intimate thoughts (*hirhur*). But this is not the case in our days where the reality is not so . . . and [men] are used to seeing women in the streets, and hence "their failure (*kalkalatan*) is in their savior (*tikunan*), and there is no danger of intimate thought in walking behind a woman as there was then. . . .

He is referring to the Talmudic rule not to walk behind a woman, which I discussed in detail in my article in *JOFA Journal* 7/2, 2007, pp. 7–9, to which I refer below. But here again we see that the sociological change in the status of women, and their "release" from being limited to staying indoors, directly affects the *halachah*. (See also R. Yitzhak Yosef, *Shulhan ha-Maarechet*, vol. 2, Jerusalem, 2010, p. 729, who comes to a similar, if perhaps a nuanced, conclusion).

As to the ruling of the *Shulhan Aruch, Hoshen Mishpat* 96:6 in the Rema, and 124, that "our precious women, for whom it is not dignified to come to a court, we send them clerks of the court, and they can make their claims before them . . . ," R. Henkin refers us to the beraita in *B. Shevuot* 30a, where it becomes clear that women can come to court, and it is only when women are [or perhaps were] not used to going out and felt it impugned their dignity of the principle of "the glory of the daughter of the King lies inside" (*kol kvudah bat melech pnimah*).

(See also most recently the article by Mordechai Akiva Friedman, in *Shenaton ha-Mishpat ha-Ivri* 25, 2014–2015, pp. 229–238, entitled "*Ha-Agunah, ha-Dayyan ve he-Hacham* . . .", on whether a married woman has to come to court, in a responsum probably of the *Rif*, R. Yitzhak Alfasi.)

However, this is hardly the case nowadays, as so cogently and forcefully argued by R. Henkin, in his chapter "The Significant Role of Habituation in Halachah," in his book *Understanding Tzniut: Modern Controversies in the Jewish Community*, Jerusalem, New York, 2008, pp. 73–84 (and see his additional comments ibid., pp. 85–91). I also related to this issue in my brief article in *JOFA Journal* 7/2, 2007, pp. 7–9, entitled "The Human Element in the Commandments: The Effect of Changing Community Norms on Halakhic Decisions." Gershon Holzer, in his Hebrew article in *Sinai* 67, 1970, pp. 94–112, which deals with women's testimony in Jewish Law, marshaled a considerable list of cases where, by the rabbis' own evidence, women's testimonies could be accepted. Tal Ilan, in her *Jewish Women in Greco-Roman Palestina*, Peabody, Mass., 1996, pp.164–166, brings additional instances (e.g., *M. Ketubot* 2:3, etc.).

The principle *Kol Kvudah Bat Melech Pnimah* was discussed by Meir Shoresh in a series of articles published in *Shmatin* nos. 60, 64–68, and afterward in a booklet with that title published in Jerusalem, 1983. On pp. 9–12 he also discusses in detail the ruling cited above from the *Shulhan Aruch*, with its sources and implications, also noting, on pp. 10–11, the fact that this ruling on occasions goes against a different rule, called "*Shamoa bein Achichem*" (*B. Sanhedrin* 7a), citing the *Beit Yosef* at the end of *Hoshen Mishpat* 124.

For the Islamic background to Maimonides limiting women's "outdoor activities," see, for example, the passage in Sheyekha Nefzani, *The Perfumed Garden*, translation Richard F. Burton, New York, 1964, p. 97:

> An ideal woman, speaks and laughs rarely and never without a reason. She never leaves the house, even to see neighbours of her acquaintance. She has no women friends, gives her confidence to nobody, and her husband is her sole reliance. She accepts nothing from anyone, excepting her husband and her parents. If she sees her relatives, she does not meddle in their affairs. She is not treacherous, and has no faults to hide, nor bad reasons to proffer. She does not try to entice people. If her husband shows his intention of performing the conjugal rites, she agrees to satisfy his desire and occasionally provokes it. She assists him always in his affairs, and is sparing in complaints and tears; she does not laugh or rejoice when she sees her husband moody or sorrowful, but shares his troubles, and wheedles him into good humour, till he is quite content again. She does not surrender herself to anybody but her husband, even if abstinence would kill her. Such a woman is cherished by everyone.

See Asghar Ali Engineer, *The Rights of Women in Islam*, London, 1992, pp. 147–148, and the whole of chapter 7, "Islam and the Individual Dignity of Women," pp. 144–153. According to Colville, in the introduction to his translation of Nefzani, he lived in the 12 cent. Others say this is a 15 cent. work.

And while we are discussing the admissibility of women giving testimony, we should take yet another issue under consideration. For R. Uziel was asked concerning the admissibility of the testimony of a non-Jew. His responses, with its detailed argumentation to be found in his *Mishpatei Uziel*, vol. 4, 2nd edition, Jerusalem, 2010, *Hoshen Mishpat* 17, pp. 86–88. He is dealing specifically with testimony in monetary cases and torts. First he argues that in

Incidentally I would like to bring a quotation from the responsa of R. Eliyahu Katz, of Beer Sheva, in his *Beer Eliyahu*, vol. 3, Beer Sheva, 1961, *Even ha-Ezer* no. 2, pp. 11–12:

> Those people for whom there was evidence from kosher witnesses, *in the testimony of a woman*, in accordance with the law of the Torah, whose wives were sent by the accursed [Nazis], may their names be erased, to the left [i.e., to the extermination centers], and it is close to certainty that they did not survive, permission is granted to the *Beit Din* in their city, or to that which is close to their city, after hearing testimonies and clarifying them and arriving at an opinion, to permit them to get married, and loosen their enchainedness (*igun*) from their first

---

our pluralistic, i.e., multi-religious, society, we cannot respond negatively, for this would be neither just nor civil. "Did we not complain bitterly when we were disqualified in the lands of our exile." And even though it is an explicit ruling that non-Jews are disqualified from bearing testimony even in monetary affairs (*B. Baba Kama* 15a, and *Shulhan Aruch, Hoshen Mishpat* 34:16), and so too Rambam (*Hilchot Edut* 9:4), he nonetheless finds a way of declaring the admissibility of their testimony, thus:

> Since in our times the gentiles that live amongst us are educated in law and science and commerce, and they fear their conscience and [for betraying] the truth, even according to their own laws, and they would, according to their own legal system be punished for false testimony and [it would be accompanied by] dishonor, all of this suffices to [persuade us] of their veracity and prove that they are [careful as to the] accuracy of their statements, and they would not steep so low as to lie. [Therefore], according to Rashi, Rabbenu Yakar, the Tashbatz, we can rely upon their honesty, even according to Torah law. . . .

He further argues that the community has the power to institute profitable reforms, which are appropriate to the requirements of the law, declaring the admissibility of their testimony.

See further his article "*Be-Hagdarat Psulei Eidut*," *Ha-Maor* 1953–1954, on the power of establishing new *takanot*. See further on his position on this issue in Zvi Zohar, *He'iru Penei ha-Mizrah*, Tel Aviv, 2001, pp. 251–284; and for a brief overview of this whole issue, see Akiva Sternberg, *Ha-Halachah ve-ha-Maaseh: Perakim be-Toldot ha-Halachah ve-Yisumah*, Jerusalem, 2010, pp. 263–266. Cannot these same arguments be applied to women?

> wife, as is expounded in the *Kuntres ha-heter* of the Rabbi of Riskeve. . . and the Rabbi of Brashov [my grandfather, R. David Sperber, of blessed memory]. [My emphasis, D.S.]

This is merely to highlight the eligibility of women giving testimony in certain cases, and even extremely serious ones.[7]

According to the above opinions, the upshot of the passage in *Bavli Niddah* is that a woman may give halachic rulings. This, indeed, is how one must understand a statement in *Sefer ha-Hinuch* (158),[8] where we read concerning the prohibition that one who is inebriated may not give judgement: "[This prohibition] prevents giving judgement in any place and at all times on the part of males *and of a wise woman who is suited to give rulings* [emphasis added]." That is to say, "a wise woman who is suited to give rulings" may not do so if she is inebriated, but indeed may do so if she is not inebriated. And this is how the *Hida* (R. Hayyim Yosef David Azulai) in his *Birkei Yosef*, *Hoshen Mishpat* 7:12, (and thence in *Pithei Teshuvah* ibid., sect. 5) understood the situation:

> Namely, that a woman is ineligible to judge; however, a wise woman may give rulings. So is it apparent from one of the Tosafot's answer, namely that Deborah taught them the laws. And see that this is so in *Sefer ha-Hinuch*, for in sect. 83 he agreed that a woman is ineligible to judge,[9] while in section 158, concerning

7. See also *Pit'hei Teshuvah* to *Even ha-Ezer* 17:104; and my grandfather's *Afracasta de-Anya,* vol. 3, Brooklyn, 2002, p. 261, etc.

8. So in Chavel ed., Jerusalem, 1952, p. 227. In Ahavat Shalom ed., Jerusalem, 1998, with commentary of R. David Pipano, *Me'il ha-Efod.* It is in vol. 1, no. 152, p. 253, and see note 14 ad loc. For an extensive discussion on the authorship of *Sefer ha-Hinuch*, see now R. David Metzer's introduction to the Machon Yerushalayim ed. of the *Minhat Hinuch*, vol. 1, Jerusalem, 1988, pp. 16–19, who concludes that he was a disciple of the Rashba.

9. No. 77, in Ahavat Shalom ed., vol. 1, p. 125.

> drunkards he wrote: "and so a wise woman who is suited to give rulings. . . ."[10]

Furthermore, the Rambam in *Hilchot Yesodei Torah* chapter 4 ad fin., wrote of:

> the need to understand the forbidden and the permitted and the rest of the commandments . . . which constitute the great goodness the Lord bestowed [upon us] to the betterment of this world so that we may merit the World to Come, for these are subjects that all have to know. And they may be known to all – old and young, *man and woman*, one with a broad heart and one with a narrow one." [My emphasis, D.S.]

From here we infer that an adult woman, with a broad heart, may well "understand what is forbidden and what is permitted." Indeed, states the Rambam, "the crown of Torah stands waiting for all, as it is said 'Moses commanded us a law, even the inheritance of the congregation of Jacob' (*Deut.* 33:4) – everyone who wishes may come and take" (*Talmud Torah* 3:1).

On the basis of these sources several great authorities of recent times agreed that a "wise woman," who took upon herself to study the Torah in depth, and who could be said to be crowned

---

10. And cf. *Shaarei Teshuvah* to *Orah Hayyim* 461:17.

See further the Hida's *Shem ha-Gedolim ha-Shalem* vol. 1, s.v. *Rabbanit*, (ed. Brooklyn, N.Y., 1965, p. 172) who lists seven learned women, and those women he seems to regard as rabbis; idem, *Tov Ayin*, Husiatin 1904, sect. 4 (Jerusalem, ed. 1961, 4b–5a), and Marc Shapiro's comments, (cf. above note 3). (See also in *Shem ha-Gedolim* ibid., *Sheerit Tziyyon* p. 251, *resh* sect. 86, where additional information is brought.) Of relevance is also the introduction of R. Yosef Yospe to his *Derishah* for a description of his wife; *Shach* to *Yoreh Deah* 326:4, R. Yair Bachrach's introduction to his *Havat Yair*, etc. See also S.D. Goitein, *A Mediterranean Society* vol. 2, Berkeley, Los Angeles, London, 1971, p. 184 that the daughter of Samuel ben Eli, the Gaon, or head of the Jewish academy in Baghdad during the years 1164–1193, was so learned that she was able to teach her father's students not only the Bible, but also the Talmud (S.W. Baron, *History of the Jews*, vol. 5, p. 323, note 89).

with the "crown of Torah," and who achieved a standard of learning such that she could give halachic rulings, may indeed do so. Rav Yitzhak Isaac Herzog *z"l* (in his *Tehukah le-Yisrael al-Pi ha-Torah*, vol. 1, Jerusalem, 1989, p. 110), and Rav Bakshi-Doron (*Binyan Av*, Jerusalem, 1982, 65:5, p. 287), wrote that women can be "of the great ones of the generation and serve as decisors, teaching Torah and halachic rulings, for which the authority stems from personal abilities."

And this, indeed, is the conclusion of R. Meshulam Roth, in his responsum in *She'elot ve-teshuvot Kol Mevasser*, vol. 1, Jerusalem, 1955, sect. 12, p. 29b.[11]

And because of the clarity of Rav Bakshi-Doron's formulation, it is worth citing his summation in full:

> From all that has been said above it appears that a woman (and a convert) can serve in leadership positions, and even as the great ones of the generation for the power of their leadership mandates the authority. A woman (and a convert) can serve as decisors and teach Torah and halachic rulings. Positions the authority of which is determined by the candidate's qualifications and this authority is based on those qualifications – such positions may be filled by a woman (and a convert.) They can judge without coercion. There is some doubt whether they can accept authority though a democratic vote, which has the halachic status

---

11. Referred to briefly in R. Yaakov Ariel's *Halachah be-Yameinu: Morashtah, Limuda, Horaatah ve-Yissumah*, Ashkelon-Jerusalem, 2010, p. 222, note 1.

See also R. Yaakov Ariel, "The Women's Study Hall" [Hebrew], apud Y. Arzoni, ed., *Halachic and Philosophical Issues in Jewish Women's Education* [Hebrew], Kiryat Arba 2003–2004, pp. 205–219, who can envision women issuing halachic rulings; however it would appear from the tone of his comments that he would not view such a development as positive. See further Yoel Bin Nun, "Women Will Rule for Themselves" [Hebrew], *Nequdah* 268, 5764, pp. 40–43; so also R. Shlomo Riskin, in his article "Women as Halakhic Decisors" [Hebrew], apud *Ayin Tovah . . . Sefer Yovel le-Tovah Ilan*, ed. Nahem Ilan, Tel Aviv, 1999, pp. 698–704.

> comparable to their acceptance of by the congregation. In the opinion of many authorities this *is* permitted. Therefore, in the case of a woman one should rule leniently in this direction, since the actual prohibition is the subject of controversy among the *Rishonim*. In all such positions one must make a clear distinction between the power of authority and the power of leadership.[12]

We stated above that if a woman is approached for a halachic ruling, it presumes that the questioner will accept her reply as authoritative, and if the congregation appoints her, accepts and trusts her, its acceptance gives her position legitimacy – *kabbalah mehania*.[13] Indeed trust and acceptance are obviously key elements in leadership.[14]

In actual fact, many questions put before a rabbi are of a technical nature, and the questioner could easily find the answer in a halachic book, if he were competent to deal with such literature.

---

12. However, Marc B. Shapiro, in his article in the *Seforim blog*, Feb. 9, 2016, p. 6, cites a letter written by R. Bakshi-Doron to the RCA from 26/6/15, in which he strongly rejects the notion of woman rabbis, seeing this as a Reform innovation. He admits that women can function as *poskot*, as he had written in his responsum, but rejects the idea that they can be appointed in any official way which would give them authority (*serarah*), and rules that one may not grant them the [Reform] title Rabba. He adds that this also entails lack of modesty in our permissive age. His letter came as a "clarification" requested by Rabbi Leonard A. Matanky, president of the RCA, who had written to him on 3rd Tammuz (=June) 2015. (Shapiro, ibid., p. 5).

The issue of the status of the convert is only of partial relevance to our discussion, and therefore is not dealt with here. But see the recent summarizing analysis of Zev Farber, in his article "The Ger as a Judge and Public Figure," in *Keren* 1, 2013, pp. 133–245. See also ch. 5 note 2, and *A Concise Code of Jewish Law for Converts*, by Michael J. Broyde, Jerusalem and New York, 2017.

13. This principle does not apply to capital cases. See *B. Niddah* 50a, *Tosafot* ibid. s.v. *Kol ha-Kasher*, *B. Baba Kama* 15a, *Tosafot* s.v. *Asher*; *Minhat Hinuch Mishpatim* no. 77:7, note 8, ed. Mechon Yerushalayim, vol. 1, Jerusalem, 1988, p. 327.

14. This notion of "acceptance" legitimizing the use of almost any judge was already mentioned by R. Yaakov Lewinson, in his *Shivyon ha-Nashim mi-Nekudat ha-Halachah*, New York, 1920, pp.12–16, 22.

And so in many cases, the rabbi's answer is almost the equivalent of opening a book, but for some people easier and more readily available.[15] Clearly, the element of trust again comes into play, and the answer is much in the nature of a testimony. And since the answer can always be checked out, such a class of testimony is acceptable from a woman too.

Furthermore, this position would seem to be borne out by an early responsum of *Ri Migash* (R. Yosef Ibn Megas, 1077–1141), Jerusalem, 1959, sect. 114 (fol.17ab). He was asked:

> What would you say, Our Master, about a man who has never in his life studied *halachah* under a Rabbi, and does not know the way of *halachah* and its ways of interpretation, on how to read [such literature], but he saw many responsa of the Geonim and books of regulations (*dinim*)?

The answer he gives is as follows:

> Know that this person is more suited to be given permission to give rulings than many other people who have given themselves authority to give rulings in our time; for most of them have neither of two requirements, that is to say: an understanding of *halachah*, and a knowledge of the opinions of the Geonim. And those who think they can rule out of their own study of *halachah* and because of the strength of this study of Talmud, it is they who should be prevented from [giving rulings], as in our times there are more individuals who are worthy of this, and [even] one who has reached the wisdom of the Talmud may not rule out of the results of his personal study unless he be acquainted with the view of the Geonim. But, on the other hand, he who

15. And today halachic books are more or less the equivalent of rabbis (see *Sheelot u-Teshuvot Shvut Yaakov*, by R. Yaakov Reischer, vol. 2, Offenbach, 1719, sect. 64, R. Ovadiah Yosef, *Yabia Omer*, vol. 3, 2nd edition, Jerusalem, 1986, introduction).

> rules out of a knowledge of the Geonim and relies upon them, even if he does not understand Talmud, he is more suitable and praiseworthy, than he who thinks he knows Talmud and relies upon himself.

This remarkable statement clearly expresses the preference for one acquainted with the writings of the authoritative sources, to one who relies on his own judgement but does not base himself on the authorities. In our days, the authoritative sources are readily available in books and other media, so that, provided the answers given are based on and consonant with those sources, they may be given even by a less learned individual.

See further *Shut Maharshdam* (R. Shmuel de-Medina, Salonika, 1506–1589), *Hoshen Mishpat* 1:

> ... In our days the scholar only rules in accordance with the book. And if we see that he is expert and experienced in studying [the sources] and has a healthy sense of reason (*u-baal sevara yodea daat u-meivin*), it is obvious that he can give rulings ... even when there is someone greater [in learning] than him in his locale.[16]

16. See Avi Sagui, apud *Rabbanut: Ha-Etgar*, Jerusalem, 2011, vol. 2, p. 716, and note 24, ibid., for additional material on this issue. And see *Entziklopedia Talmudit*, vol. 8, s.v. *Horaah*, 489–490, on the various opinions on ruling from books; but there is a consensus that one may rule in accordance with the *Shulhan Aruch*, and its super-commentaries; see *Pithei Teshuvah* to *Yoreh Deah* 242:8. And see *Entziklopedia*, ibid., 491–494, and especially ibid., note 109, that women may give rulings if they are sufficiently well educated (*ishah hachamah*).

The importance of books is already mentioned in mediaeval rabbinic sources. See, for example, the statement of the Tosafist, R. Moshe of Evreux, who stated that:

> From the time the Jewish people was exiled from its land, when our Temple was destroyed ... the law that reverence for a teacher must be like reverence for God no longer applies, and all the rules regarding the relationship between disciple and master are abrogated. This is because

> the books, the treatises, and the commentaries are masters, and everything depends on intelligence and logic.

See further R. Ovadiah Yosef, *Yabia Omer*, vol. 4, *Hoshen Mishpat* 1:6, that this phrase "the books . . . are our masters" mandates that all books must be examined prior to rendering a *psak*. See A. Yehuda Warburg, *Rabbinic Authority: The Vision and the Reality*, Jerusalem and New York, 2013, pp. 39 (especially note 63), 47–49, on *sifrei psak*.

Further, on the importance of books, see *Pithei Teshuvah* to Yoreh Deah 242:3, in the name of R. Yaakov Reischer, the *Shvut Yaakov*, that the books which have been disseminated and accepted among [the Rabbis of] Israel are our Sages. See also M.M. Shklarsh, *Hayyei Moshe* to *Yoreh Deah*, Bnei Brak, 2001, p. 257, note 16, citing the *Urim ve-Tumim* to *Hoshen Mishpat* 72, that one should study books and come to rulings on their basis, and also ibid., p. 258, note 22, on the need to study the book even of the most contemporary authorities.

The issue of the importance of books and their use in *psak* has also been discussed by R. Ovadiah Yosef in his *Maor Yisrael*, vol. 3, *Tabaat ha-Melech al ha-Ramban*, vol. 1, Jerusalem, 2005, p. 17 (to Rambam *Hilchot Talmud Torah* 5:4). There he quotes the *Radbaz*, vol. 5, sect. 2 (2147), that:

> . . . . Nowadays, since there are several works on halachah and response of the Geonim, anyone who has reached the stage of being able to adjudicate (*higia le-horaah*) even if he is not yet aged forty, can rule according to the books, because he will be able to understand what the Geonim have clarified.

This is also cited in the *Beit Yosef* to *Hoshen Mishpat* 10:7, and similarly in the response of the *Maharshdam*, *Hoshen Mishpat* 1, etc. However, the *Rema* in *Yoreh Deah* 242:31, wrote that before the age of forty no one should make halachic rulings, and so too the *Mabit* sect. 280. And on the basis of the *Rema*'s ruling R. Eleazar Fleckeles, in his *Teshuvah me-Ahavah*, Prague, 1709–1721, sect. 375, writes that at the order of the *Noda bi-Yehudah* (R. Yehezkel Landau), a notice was publicized in Prague that since there has been an inflation of new books on *Shas* and *poskim* of relevance to practical halachah, and they have spread all over the world creating a stumbling block, because local Rabbis do not distinguish between [the different types] and think that anything published may be relied upon in *pesak* – therefore one must insist that someone who has not reached the age of forty may not publish his halachic novellae, and only after the age of forty may he be permitted to do so. This notice was signed by the *beit din* of Prague, which also included R. Michael Bachrach, R.S.Z. Amrich, and R. Eleazar Fleckles. However, R. Ovadiah Yosef concludes that this applies to those who only follow the opinion of the *Rema*. But we (Sefardim) who follow the *Beit Yosef* allow one who has reached the stage of

However, it must also be borne in mind that one has to choose the books upon which one bases one's ruling with the utmost care. One must be clear as to the status of the author, and the accuracy of the traditions cited, etc.[17]

One should further take note of the fact that the institution of *Semichah*[18] (ordination) was suspended, or even abolished, close to one thousand seven-hundred years ago, and as a result the notion and character of ordination underwent a radical change.[19] From that time onwards the practice is that a learned scholar, rich in experience and accepted by his congregation, after becoming

---

being able to adjudicate, even if he is less than forty, to publish his novellae, and we will give them our approbation (*haskamah*). And see, in greater detail his responsum in *Yabia Omer*, vol. 4, 2nd edition, Jerusalem, 1986, Hoshen Mishpat no.1:4–5, pp. 378–379. We see here, on the one hand, the importance of halachic works and their value, but on the other hand, the care to be taken in distinguishing between significant and reliable ones and those less so, before making use thereof. A balanced discussion on the parameters of the use of books for *psak* (including the well-known controversy on the use of the *Shulhan Aruch*, or indeed the Rambam for *psak*, see Yaakov Yosef Neischlass, *Meishiv ka-Halachah*, Brooklyn, 2008, no. 18.

We may further add that it is told of the wife of R. Eliyahu Mani (1818–1899, Chief Rabbi of Hevron) that when people came to the house with questions of *issur ve-heter*, and he was not available, she would go to the library, find the relevant book and give the answer. (See Yehiel Michel Stern, *Sefer Eshet Hayyil*, vol. 2, Jerusalem, 2014, p. 366.) So she gave the *psak* on the basis of books, no doubt with the acquiescence of her husband.

17. See Yitzhak Yosef, *Maarechet ha-Shulhan* vol. 2, Jerusalem, 2010, pp. 412–420.

18. On this institution, see J. Newman, *Semikhah (ordination) A Study of its Origin, History and Function in Rabbinic Literature*, Manchester, 1950; Jacob Katz, "Rabbinic Authority and Authorization in the Middle Ages," apud *Studies in Mediaeval Jewish History and Literature*, ed. I. Twersky, Cambridge, Mass. and London, 1976, pp. 41–56. And on the importance of *sevara*, see A.H. Rabinowitz, *The Jewish Mind*, Jerusalem, 1978, pp.149–165. But cf. ibid., pp.151–161, on the limitation of ruling from codices without a true understanding of the underlying source and principles involved, i.e., *Sevara*. (Compare Yitzhak Yosef, *Shulhan ha-Maarechet*, vol. 2, Jerusalem, 2010, p. 614.)

19. See R. Moshe Isserles, in his *Darkei Moshe* to *Tur Yoreh Deah* 242:14, Machon Yerushalayim ed., pp. 599–600; cf. his responsum no. 24, ed. A. Ziv, Jerusalem, 1970, p. 147.

acquainted with a candidate for ordination, and examining him in one way or another, gives him a "document of ordination" (*ketav hasmacha*)[20] which bears witness to his knowledge and competence in certain areas of *halachah* (either *Orah Hayyim* and *Yoreh Deah* – "*Yoreh Yoreh*" or *Hoshen Mishpat* and *Even ha-Ezer* – "*Yadin Yadin*"). This does not constitute a transfer of authority, but rather a testimony as to the candidate's abilities and suitability to respond to questions in specific areas of *halachah*.

Indeed this was very clearly elucidated by Blu Greenberg, in her article in *Moment*, December 1992 (pp. 50–53, 74), entitled "Is Now the Time for Orthodox Women Rabbis?" There she wrote:

> A close look at the convention of ordination reveals that it is not the conferral of holy status nor a magical laying of hands to transmit authority. Nor does the process uniquely empower a rabbi to perform special sacramental functions that a knowledgeable layperson, cannot. Ordination is the confirmation of an individual's mastery of texts (largely from the Talmud and codes); familiarity with precedents; the ability to reason analogically and apply precedents to contemporary questions. Conferring the title "rabbi" is a guarantee to the community that this person has been judged fit by a collective of rabbis or by a single great scholar to give guidance on matters of *issur v'heter,* the forbidden and the permitted, primarily as it concerns the laws of *kashrut*, Shabbat and family purity. The *smicha* process assumes but does not even test for personal piety, good character or spiritual bent. The formal criteria are almost wholly intellectual.[21]

20. This is sometimes called *Hatarat Horaah*. The certificate carries with it the right to the title "Rabbi," or, as in some communities *Morenu,* or *Harav*. See Newman, ibid., pp. 171–172. A discussion of the history of these titles is beyond the scope of this study.

21. See further her article in *Judaism* 33/1, 1984, pp. 23–33, "Will There

More recently, in certain communities there have been established a series of examinations, not necessarily individually tailored, but formalized and covering a broad spectrum of halachic issues. These are offered by institutions which prepare and vet them, and then give documents of ordination which are widely accepted by their communities. Such is the case of the Israeli rabbinate and Yeshiva University in New York, etc. But, as stated above, this is a relatively modern phenomenon. Even up to the present day the traditional practice that has been in use for so many generations since the abolishment of the original *semichah*, has been the granting of a testimony of competence given by a rabbi who was ordained, and accepted by the community as a decisor (*posek, baal horaah*), to one whom he has personally examined in a detailed, systematic manner. (See what I wrote in my introduction to *The Importance of the Community Rabbi.*) The document specifies and defines the areas of competence. Thus the nature of such ordination and the ultimate source of authority for the ordained person is the level of competence he has demonstrated. Today, such competence is not gender limited, and may well be demonstrated and proven by women as well as by men.

Indeed, there is now an accepted institution of women who are qualified to act as pleaders in rabbinic courts (*toanot rabbaniyot*)[22] and there are women advisors on halachic issues concerning *niddah*, etc., (*yoatzot hilchatiyot*). The latter are, in effect, offering halachic rulings. The authority and recognition of such women is based on their proven competence.

Furthermore, there are additional examples of women giving *piskei halachah*. The *Magen Avraham* in *Orah Hayyim* 263:5, in note 12 cites the view of the mother of the *Derishah* that on *Yom Tov* a woman should bless the candles and only afterwards light them. "And so is written at the end of *Sefer ha-Derishah*,

---

be Orthodox Women Rabbis?" and Ben Greenberg in *First Things*, September 2009, "Women Orthodox Rabbis: Heresy or Possibility?"

22. See Hadad, ibid., pp. 83– 86.

by R. Yehoshua Falk (1550–1614), on *Even ha-Ezer* (in the *Derishah*'s son's introduction), in the name of his mother" (i.e., the *Derishah*'s wife, Baila). It is true that the *Magen Avraham* rejects this ruling, adding that "there is no wisdom in a woman [except regarding the spindle]" (Y. *Sotah 3:3 B. Yoma* 66b), ruling that Shabbat and *Yom Tov* candles should be lit in an identical fashion; however, that same son, R. Yosef Yuzpa Falk accepts her ruling, adding "and her counsel is blessed and her reason is excellent, and I decided to print this in a book in her name, and cry 'beautiful beautiful' to her" (*Zechariah* 4:7; preface to *Tur Yoreh Deah*, Lublin, 1596, nowadays printed at the beginning of *Tur Orah Hayyim*). So too, R. Yehezkel Landau, in his *Dagul Mi-Revavah* to *Orah Hayyim* 263, accepted her ruling, adding "she is a woman who excelled in wisdom." (Cf. *Exodus* 35:26; see Golinkin, ibid., pp. 288–289, 301–302, and see ibid. for additional examples.)[23]

23. Shlomoh Ashkenazi, in his *Ha-Ishah be-Aspaklariat ha-Yahadut*, Tel Aviv, 1953, vol. 1, pp.115–137, gives a long list of learned women, such as Rachel, daughter of Rashi who wrote *halachot* and responsa in his name (ibid., p.118); Miriam the daughter of Rivan, son-in-law of Rashi, whose practices served an early *Rishon* to clarify a halachah (ibid); the mother of R. Mattiyahu of Treibish (born 1305), was greatly respected by the *Tashbatz* (Shimon ben Tzemah Duran, 1361–1444), and cites her in his responsa (vol. 3, no. 78; ibid., 118–119); Havah Bachrach (1585–1652), mother of R. Shimon [1600–1670], who when he came to Vermaiza (Worms) to serve as its Rabbi, she came with him, and helped him solve halachic problems; her grandson R. Yair Hayyim Bachrach (1639–1702), author of *Havat Yair*, quotes many of her *hiddushim* in his writings (ibid., 123). The title of his book *Havat Yair* was in her memory, as he relates in his introduction, etc.

Furthermore, Rabbenu Tam's wife, Miriam gave halachic rulings in her city (ibid, 131); Gittel the wife of R. David Schwerdscharf from Bilgurai (Poland) has several of her *hiddushei Torah* and responsa published in *Petach ha-Bayit* in the beginning of *Beit Yehezkel*, and in *Har ha-Bayit* at the beginning of *Pinot ha-Bayit*.

Shapiro, in his article in the *Seforim blog*, Feb. 9, 2016, pp. 8–11, refers us to the *Leket Yosher* (by R. Yosef be R. Moshe, c. 1460), ed. Machon Yerushalayim, vol. 2, Jerusalem 2013, *Hilchot Niddah* 19–20, pp. 35–37, where we see "a *yoetzet* in action." A woman sent a question to R. Israel Isserlein's wife. The wife inquired from her husband, and then replied to the questioner. Shapiro remarks

These are but some of the women listed by Shlomoh Ashkenazi.

---

that "had she already known the answer she would not have had to ask her husband." He adds, "This is exactly what *yoatzot* do in the 21st century." He further refers us to *B. Niddah* 13b, where we learn of a deaf woman who not only "checked herself, but also neighbors would come to show her [the *niddah* cloths]." There, she served as a *yoetzet*.

We might add biblical Naomi. For in *Ruth Rabba* 2:22, on the verse in *Ruth* 22:17, which reads, "And Ruth said: 'Entreat me not to leave thee or to return from following after thee . . . ,' the Midrash asks, 'What is "Entreat me not . . .'?"

The answer given is as follows:

> "You cannot force me to leave you. In any case it is my intention to convert. And it is preferable that this be done by you rather than anyone else." And as soon as Naomi heard this, she began to set out [before Ruth] the laws of conversion . . .

See the continuation of this Midrash for examples of how she taught Ruth. Additionally, we might take note of the Mishnah in Negaim 3:1, which rules:

> All are qualified to inspect leprosy-signs, but only a priest may pronounce them unclean or clean. They [that are skilled] say to a priest, "Say Unclean," and he shall say "Unclean," or [they say to him], "Say: Clean" and he shall say: "Clean!" . . .

The *Mishnah Aharonah* ad loc. explains that "all are qualified to inspect" – לראות – means "to rule on the laws of leprosy (להורות דיני נגעים)." "All" includes women, who may therefore rule in such cases, even though the final practical application of their ruling is dependent upon the declaration of a *Cohen*. Nonetheless, clearly the initial inspection and opinion of the woman – in this case – is very consequential. Since, for example, all the contents of a leprous house become impure, and this obviously also has economic implications.

And in *Midrash Tanhuma, Tazria* sect. 6, we read of a *Cohen* who wishes to leave the land of Israel because of his poverty, and wished to teach his wife the laws of leprosy so that in his absence she could deal with any queries on this subject. (Ct. *Midrash Aggadah, Tazria* to *Lev* 13:2, ed. Buber vol. 2, p. 33, for parallel with slight variations.) This Midrash supports the view that women have the right to make such "recommendations," a view that was, however, by no means universally accepted. Thus, the *Minhat Hinuch, Mitzvah* 169, and the *Tiferet Yisrael* to *Negaim* 2:5, etc., are of the opinion that women may not do so. Others would link this question to an earlier controversy among the *Rishonim*, as to whether "Aaron and his sons" always excludes females from a priestly family or not. (See Z.W. Zicherman, *Otzar Plaot ha-Torah*, vol. 3, Brooklyn, 2016, pp. 563–564.)

It should be noted that already in 1942 Ashkenazi had published (in Tel-Aviv) a small booklet entitled *Nashim Lamdaniyot* (*Skirah Historit*). It is somewhat more extensive than the material in that section of his *Ha-Ishah* etc. In his concluding remarks (p. 69) he wrote that we may learn from his list that there were Jewish woman "who were learned, and with book-knowledge, who at times reached the status of *Roshat yeshivah* and preachers (*darshaniyot*) and those who gave halachic rulings (*poskot sheelot*)." So there are precedents for women in positions of halachic authority.

We may further add a comment by Cecil Roth in his article "Outstanding Jewish Women in Western Europe," which appeared in R. Leo Jung's anthology, *Women: The Jewish Library*, London and New York, 1970, note 2 to pp. 152–153. He writes as follows:

> In this connection, the present writer may be excused for mentioning a family legend relating to his grandmother, Miriam, daughter of Rabbi Joseph Lissa and wife of Rabbi David Roth. It is recounted that on one occasion, when she was a girl, a dispute arose in the *Bet Hamidrash*, and she was asked to go fetch her father, the rabbi of the town, to decide it. She replied that it was not worth while to trouble him about it, as the solution was quite simple; her explanation was afterwards confirmed by her father. Another time, she is said to have heard one of the local scholars give an inaccurate opinion about some complicated question. She told him, in all humility, that her father would not have concurred, as indeed he did not. It is obvious, from these anecdotes, that knowledge of the *Talmud* was no male prerogative.

3 WOMEN IN POSITIONS OF COMMUNAL AUTHORITY

As to the question of whether a woman can serve in a position of communal authority, the view of the Rambam (*Melachim* 1:5) is well known, forbidding women from having any position of authority.[1] However, later authorities stated that

---

1. This matter requires much further elaboration, and therefore I have addressed it below.

Most recently Prof. Abraham Grossman, in an article entitled "*Ishah u-Mishpahah be-Haguto shel R. Avraham ben ha-Rambam*," in *Dinei Yisrael* 26–27, 2009–2010, p.123, pointed to the ambivalent attitude of the Rambam to women. He refers us to *Hilchot Teshuvah* 10:1, where women's worship of God is categorized as of those of ignoramuses and children; *Iggeret ha Shemad* (*Iggerot ha-Rambam*, ed. Y. Shilat 1. Jerusalem, 1987, p. 30): ". . . even women lacking in brains . . ."; *Hilchot Avodat Kochavim* 11:16: "those senseless idiots, and among them women and children, who lack understanding" (my translation, D.S.). On the other hand, the Rambam, Grossman points out, was concerned for the rights of women (see ibid.).

More recently Marc Shapiro, in his book *Changing the Immutable: How Orthodox Judaism Rewrites Its History*, Oxford, Portland, Oregon, 2015, p. 64, discussed Maimonides' attitude towards women. He writes that he is not to be placed in the category of the misogynists:

> It is true that he often places women together with children and the ignorant, and in some of these passages it is clear that he did not think women had much religious sophistication. [See the list of passages in A. Melamed, "Maimonides on Women: Formless Matter or Potential Prophet," apud A. Ivry ed., *Perspectives on Jewish Thought and Mysticism*, Amsterdam, 1998, pp. 119–122, and add: *Hilchot Avodah Zarah* 11:16, where women and children are said to have "undeveloped intellects."] When it comes

they know no source for this opinion (*Igrot Moshe, Yoreh Deah*, vol. 2, 44–45), and that it is "a rejected ruling "(*Mishpetei Uziel*, vol. 3, *Hoshen Mishpat* 6). In addition Rav Uziel wrote (in *Piskei Uziel* 44, p. 232):

> This ruling only refers to an appointment by the Sanhedrin. But when the appointment is by the consent of the community, where through a majority vote the public voices its opinions, the agreement and trust of the public in its appointees, who will be supervising their communal affairs – in such a case even the Rambam would agree that there is no hint of a prohibition [i.e., for a woman to so serve].

> to the study of Torah, he writes: 'Our Sages commanded that one should not teach his daughter Torah, because most women cannot concentrate their attention on study, and they transform the words of Torah into nonsensical matters due to their lack of understanding [*Hilchot Talmud Torah* 1:13]. Nevertheless, Maimonides should not be placed with other medieval figures who speak negatively about women. In fact, he is actually one of the most progressive medieval Jewish writers when it comes to views on women.

Shapiro continues that though Maimonides was greatly influenced by Aristotle, who believed women are defective by nature (see his references in note 113) he, however, broke with Aristotle when it came to the latter's view of women. He writes:

> For Maimonides, any judgement to be made about the intelligence of women is due to their social circumstances, living in what was a Taliban-like society. However, they are not inherently inferior to men. Maimonides, in fact, asserts that women too are required to obtain knowledge of God and that this is necessary to fulfil various commandments. [*Sefer ha-Mitzvot* positive commandments nos 1–6; *Hilchot Yesodei ha-Torah* chapters 1–4; Warren Zev Harvey, "The Obligation of Talmud on Women according to Maimonides," *Tradition* 19, 1981, pp. 122–130.] They are inferior because they have received no education, but this is not something "hardwired" into them. In the words of Menachem Kellner, according to Maimonides the position of women "was a function of sociology, not of ontology." Seen in the context of medieval times, when negative views of women's nature were standard, Maimonides' alternative perspective can be seen as a "radical egalitarian stance."

In other words, since the appointment of the leader of a community, be it in a position of spiritual leadership (or administrative, financial and/or political) is dependent upon the congregation's agreement, or that of their elected representatives, the authority vested in such a leader stems from the community which has the halachic right to vest its authority in its leaders.[2]

---

2. See A. Yehuda Warburg, *Rabbinic Authority: The Vision and the Reality*, Jerusalem and New York, 2013, pp. 39–42, who discusses the notion of the *mara de-atra*, and the degree of autonomy of individual synagogues within a particular locale, explaining that, in such circumstances:

> ... the synagogue's autonomy is defined by having its own rabbi, conducting daily prayer services with its own liturgical practices, and maintaining governance by its lay membership. If the synagogue is construed as a *kahal*, the elected rabbi, contingent upon possessing the requisite scholarship, is to be viewed as the *mara de-atra* of the synagogue.

Menachem Friedman, "Halachic Rabbinic Authority in Modern Open Society," apud J. Wertheimer ed., *Jewish Religion Leadership: Image and Reality*, New York, 2004, pp. 765, termed this "Voluntary Community" to distinguish between the traditional Jewish community that existed in Europe up to the eighteenth century. . . . The development of the Voluntary Community became possible from the moment that the leadership of the Jewish Community no longer had the power to enforce the observance of the traditional Jewish way of the members of the community.

Warburg continues to explain as follows:

> The synagogue's *mara de-atra* will either be "an authority" or "in authority" to the same degree as any communal *mara de-atra* is. Synagogue acceptance of the *mara de-atra* is either actualized through the adoption of a *takanot kahal,* synagogue bylaws, and/or the adoption of a *ketav rabbanut*, a rabbinic contract. . . .

See continuation. And in note 80, ibid, he states that the *takanot kahal* promulgated by duly elected and representative members of a particular town, as found in *Shulhan Aruch, Orah Hayyim* 153, can be equally extended to the general membership and/or board of a synagogue.

We may add that from the mediaeval period onwards, the majority of Rabbis were "democratically" appointed by all the (paying) members of the congregation, or their elected representatives, as is evidenced by the many protocols of congregations (*pinkasei ha-kehillot*), referred to by Y.Y. Bronstein, in his *Avnei Gazit,* Jerusalem, 2002, pp. 419–420.

This view may find further support from the following discussion:

The *Tosafot Yom Tov* in his commentary to *Mishnah Avot* 1:10, raises the following question related to Rambam's statement (in his introduction to his commentary in the Mishnah), namely that Shemaya and Avtalion were converts and rose to be *Nasi* and *Av Beit Din* (head of the court). But surely we have learned (*Mishnah Sanhedrin* 4:2 and *Horayot* 1:4) that converts cannot receive such appointments! His reply is that they themselves were not converts, but perhaps born of a non-Jewish father and a Jewish mother (from "*kehal gerim*"). However, the *Hida* (in his *Birkei Yosef*, *Hoshen Mishpat* 7:6; quoting R. Hayyim Benveniste [1603–1673, Chief Rabbi of Smyrna] in his *Knesset ha-Gedolah*) has a different solution. He asserts that "*kabbalah mehania*" – acceptance has legal effect, "as we have learned from Shemaya and Avtalion. . . . In every case where the community accepts and is satisfied with an appointment, the appointee can judge even on matters of authority and enforcement (*be-milei de sevarah u-kefiah*)." And this indeed is the explicit ruling of the Rema in *Shulchan Aruch Hoshen Mishpat* 8:1.

There is, as it were, a contract of agreement that the congregation accept the rulings of its appointee, similar to the case of court arbitration, *borerut*. And when a great and accepted authority appoints an individual to such a position of leadership, the community assents to such appointment.

Moreover, we see that R. Feinstein (*Igrot Moshe Yoreh Deah*, vol. 4, sect. 24) states that a woman is in no way prohibited from accepting a position of authority. Indeed, he permitted a woman to serve as a *kashrut* supervisor, even though this is a position of communal authority and can have serious financial implications, should she, for example, annul a *kashrut* certificate from a given institution, as R. Moshe explicitly states. (*Igrot Moshe,Yoreh Deah*, vol. 2, 44.)

Rav Herzog went even further (*Tekumah le-Yisrael al-pi ha-Torah*, vol. 1, Jerusalem, 1989, ibid., p. 111), stating that the women of our generation, especially those who have been put forward as candidates for parliament, have a very broad education, and are successful in business, run charitable institutions, etc. Accordingly, they are surely fit to serve in leadership positions in the community, even as members of parliament. And, he argues, the Rambam would agree with this, and his remarks were made given the cultural state of women in his time (cf. above note 1). And as to the *acceptance* of women on the part of a congregation, as judges as opposed to their *nomination*, see his, albeit reserved, view, ibid., pp. 43–46, where Rav Herzog finally agrees that it is permitted (p. 45).

And this indeed is what the *Sefer ha-Hinuch* says (*Mitzvah* 77) says.[3] For after citing the Rambam's position, and raising the question of Deborah the Prophetess, the author first gives the answer offered by earlier authorities, namely that she did not give the final ruling, but:

> they would discuss with her matters of *issur ve-heter* and *dinim*, and therefore it was said that "she judged Israel."

The author of the *Sefer ha-Hinuch* then continues to offer a second alternative solution, namely that:

> since the leaders of Israel accepted her authority, for with acceptance (*kabbalah*) everyone is certainly fit to give rulings, since on conditions regarding monetary issues (*tenai she-be-mammon*) everyone's ruling has validity. However, all that I have stated that they do not judge, is only according to some of the *Aharonim* and the *Yerushalmi* (*Sanhedrin* 3:9), where this is explicitly stated. However, according to some of the commentators, they [women] may judge [without conditions].

R. Hayyim David ha-Levi, in his *Asei le-cha Rav*, vol. 8, Tel-Aviv, 1988, cites the *Hinuch* and adds that there may be an indication in *Ecclesiates Rabba* (to Eccles 2:8), a text we have already referred

3. In Ahavat Shalom ed., vol. 1, p. 125; in Chavel ed., No. 83, p. 141.

to above, that there were women judges. For this *Midrash* (also found in *Yalkut Shimoni* Ecclesiastes 968), explains the verse ". . . I made men singers and women singers, *shiddah ve-shiddot*" which latter words the homilist explains as "*dayanim zecharim* ve-*dayanot nekeivot*," male and female judges.

And should one suggest that a woman's serving in a central position of authority in a community, and especially in the synagogue, constitutes a breach of modesty (as indeed does R. Yaakov Ariel, in his *Halachah be-Yameinu: Morashtah, Limmudah, Horaatah ve-Yissumah*, Ashkelon-Jerusalem, 2010, p. 190, although he agrees that in principle women may serve in leadership positions), and perhaps even involves the prohibition against "the voice of a woman being unchaste," Rav Uziel already determined (*Piskei Uziel* 44):

> It is common sense that in any serious meeting and meaningful conversation there is no question of lack of modesty. . . . And sitting in the proximity [of women] when involved in communal affairs, which is work of holiness, does not lead to lightheartedness [i.e., immodesty]. For all Israel are holy people, and her women are holy, and are not to be suspect of breach of modesty and morality.

Morever, latter-day authorities stated that wherever the awe of the *Shechinah* is present, we need not concern oneself with this rule (R. Zvi Elimelech of Dinov, *Bnei Yisaschar* [Zolkiev-Lvov 1846] Kislev-Tevet 4, 123, in the name of the *Hida* [*Rosh David*, Mantua, 1776], 56d., *Be-Shalah*).

See further *Sefer Yad Sofer*, by R. Yaakov Hayyim Sofer (in his *Knesset Hayyim*, Jerusalem, 1993), p. 54, who quotes the Hida in his *Rosh David* (*Parshat Be-Shalah* 54:4), who wrote:

> When we pay attention to the song that the prophetess Miriam sang with all the women following her, and surely we hold that a woman's voice is *ervah* – unchaste, and how could this

> have taken place in such a holy situation! And early authorities answered in accordance with that which is found in *B. Niddah* 14 [read 13a] that where there is fear of the *Shehinah* (*beiatuta de-Shehinta*) there is no suspicion of sexual distraction, and here at the Red Sea surely the fear of the Divine Presence hovered over them, and hence there was no chance that this would lead to suspicion of inchastity. Hence, it was completely acceptable for the women to sing. This is what he stated. Such are the words of the Hida.

Furthermore, in *Hemed le-Mareh* (by R. Nissim Avraham Raphael Ashkenazi, *Zeraim*, Saloniki, 1732) to *Y. Halah* 180a, we read that concerning a woman's carrying out a verbal *mitzvah* for an individual, there is an issue of *kol be-ishah*; but when she does so for a congregation (*rabim*), one does not raise this issue, because of the "fear of the *Shehinah*."[4]

---

4. See Akiva Moshe, *Ha-Keriyah ba-Torah ve-Hilchotehah*, Jerusalem, 2009, p. 294, note 2, ad fin.

And to this we may add the comment of R. Yisaschar be-R. Yisrael Leizer Eilenburg, in his *Tzeidah la-Derech*, Prague, 1623, to Rashi on *Leviticus* 1:3 (cited by R.M.M. Kasher, in his *Torah Shelemah* vol. 23, Jerusalem, 1969, p. 122), namely that when a Cohen took the *minhah* offering of a *Sotah* (adulterous woman) from her, he raised it up before God (see *Numbers* 5:25). According to *Y. Sotah* 3:1 he would place his hand under that of the *Sotah*, and so lifted it up. The *Yerushalmi* there asks: Is this not unseemly (*ki'ur*), i.e., immodest? And the reply given is that he brings a napkin and places it between their hands. The *Yerushalmi* continues to ask: Surely this constitutes an intervening object (*hatzitzah*)? And the answer given is that one uses an elderly Cohen, who is unlikely to have immodest thoughts, or alternatively, if it be with a young Cohen, we do not assume that he has immodest thoughts for such a brief time (*she-ein yeitzer ha-ra matzui le-shaah*). The *Tzeidah la-Derech* adds two words to the Yerushalmi's answer; after *le-shaah*, he adds: *be-shaat mitzvah*, meaning that it was not because of the brevity of the moment that he was unlikely to have immodest thoughts, but because, since he was engaged in a *mitzvah*, the evil inclination would not trouble him. His addition is his interpretation, and is not – to the best of my knowledge – based on an alternative version.

However, his suggestion is surely problematic. For the Rabbis explained the use of the brazen laver made out of looking glasses (*Exodus* 38:8), so that the Cohen, when he offers a woman's sacrifice, and she is present at the time of the

Further proof for this position may surely be inferred from the passage in *Torat Kohanim* to Leviticus 7:2 (*Tzav* 5:3), where it is stated that the sacrifice of the *asham* (sin) offering may be carried out by women. (So too, ibid., *Nedavah* 4:2; and cf. *M. Zerahim* 3:1, *B. Zerahim* 31b–32a.) And we learn from that passage in *Torat Kohanim* that the sacrifice of the *asham*, as well as that of the *hatat*, was offered at the north of the altar, i.e., in the innermost sanctum of the temple itself. And women were also allowed *semichah*, that is to say, the placing of the hands upon their sacrifice. So their presence in the inner sanctum of the Temple was completely permissible, and apparently, there was no fear of a breach of modesty.

To the above we may add the ruling of the *Rema* in *Even ha-Ezer* 21:5 that:

> There are those who say that any such actions that are not carried out as a form of affection (*derech hibah*) but for the sake of heaven, are permitted, and therefore they ruled leniently in such matters (referring to *Tosafot Kiddushin* 82a s.v. *Ha-Kol le-Shem Shamayim* [ruling like Shmuel, ibid.].

And furthermore, the *Sdei Hemed* (*Maarechet kof, klal mem-beit*) cites the view that wherever the singing is not songs of lust (*shirei agavim*, i.e., sexually provocative ones), and the listeners do not

---

offering, he need not look at her directly, but only see her in the reflections of the laver. (See e.g., Menachem Recanati, to *Exodus*, ibid., and the many sources cited by Kasher, ibid. pp. 132–133.) But surely he was engaged in a *mitzvah*, and according to the *Tzeidah la-Derech* he should not be forbidden to glance at her (in order to identify that it is her offering that is being sacrificed). Perhaps the sacrificial process took longer than the raising (*tenufah*) act, and we should take the Yerushalmi's response at its straighforward meaning – i.e., brevity of time. Or, alternatively we might suggest, supporting the *Tzeidah la-Derech's* interpretation, that the Kohanim put strict impositions upon themselves wherever it was possible. In the case of the *Sotah*, there was no legitimate alternative to touching her hand. (And perhaps this is also the meaning of *Kohanim zerizin hem* in *B. Shabbat 20a*, etc., see Rashi, ibid.)

intend to enjoy [the feminity of her voice] when she intones songs of praise to God, the issue of *kol ishah* is not relevant. See R. Yehiel Weinberg, *Seridei Eish*, vol. 2, Jerusalem, 1962, pp. 16–17, who permits women to participate in Shabbat *Zemirot*, adding that any such a prohibition would be seen as an insult and an act of exclusion. (See my essay, "Women and Public Torah Reading: A Halachic Study," apud *Women and Men in Communal Prayer: Halakhic Perspectives*, Jersey City, 2000, pp. 100–102.)

All the above surely applies to women leading (parts of) the service in the synagogue.[5]

This may also be deduced from the straightforward reading of the *beraita* in *Megillah* 23a; and R. Ovadia Yosef (*Yehaveh Daat*, vol. 4, Jerusalem, 1981. sect. 15 ad fin, and his note on p. 78), as well as Rav Herzog (ibid., p. 98), write that they see no problem concerning matters of immodesty, for "surely women appear in our law courts. . . . and we have never heard that anyone has cast doubt on such behavior. And if we were to take such a stringent position, life would no longer be liveable."

In actual fact, the issue of modesty is largely irrelevant. For R. Yehuda Henkin, in his *Understanding Tzniut: Modern Controversies in the Jewish Community*, Jerusalem and New York, 2008, pp. 72–84, has convincingly demonstrated that because we are so used to seeing women in a broad variety of roles and situations, this no longer causes sexual distraction – *hirhur*. Thus, for example, among the several sources he cites, we read that the *Levush*, at the end of his *Minhagim* stated that:

---

5. So too the *Hida* in his *Nahal Kedumim*, Lvov, 1879, *Be-Shalah* 14; idem, *Meirat Ayin*, Livorno, 1804, to *Niddah* 13a; Y. Hayyim Sofer, *Yad Sofer*, vol. 2, apud *Knesset Hayyim*. Jerusalem, 1993, p. 54; Akiva Meller, *Ha-Keriyah ba-Tora ve-Hilchotehah*, Jerusalem, 2009, p. 294, note 2 ad fin., etc.

On a related issue, see Yisachar Rabinowitz, *Alei Tamar, Nashim*, Givataim 1981, p. 196, on dancing at a wedding with the bride being permitted (by some). See *Bach* (*Bayit Hadash*) to *Tur Even ha-Ezer* ibid, ad fin., referring to the *Maharshal* (R. Shlomoh Luria) in his commentary to the *Smag* (*Sefer Mitzvot Gaddol*), sect. 126.

> We do not take care about [avoiding] mixed seating, because nowadays women are very common among men, and there are relatively few sinful thoughts about them. . . . (ibid., 81–82)

Indeed, this was the basis of R. Yosef Messas' remarkable ruling permitting married women to appear in public without hair covering. At the end of his responsum he writes:

> It is certainly understood. . . that since nowadays all women uncover all their hair. . . this being so usual it is not considered immodesty (*peritzut*). . . . and any man is personally aware that in seeing thousands of women day by day passing before him with an uncovered head, he does not even notice them, and certainly has no *hirhur*, for uncovered hair [no longer] excites sexual distraction. (*Otzar ha-Michtavim*, no. 1484, vol. 3, Jerusalem, 1975, p. 211)

(However, see most recently a critique of Messas' opinion in an article by Michael Avraham and Rinat Ankri, in *Derishah* 1, 2006, pp. 54–84.)

More recently, R. Mosheh Lichtenstein, in his article entitled *Shirat Nashim le-Lo Kiruv ha-Daat, Tehumin* 32, 2002, pp. 291–299, reached much the same conclusion with regard to listening to a woman's singing, that where there is no likelihood of sexual distraction (*hashash hirhur*) there is no reason to forbid it, and in the reality of our social situation, this indeed is the case.

TO SUMMARIZE: From the time of our ancestoral mothers, such as Sarah, Yael, Deborah the Prophetess, Beruriah the wife of R. Meir, Yalta the wife of Rav Nahman, there were learned women who dealt in *halachah*, and gave halachic rulings. See, for example, *Teshuvot Maimoniyot* to *Maachalot Asurot* 5; *Tosafot Shabbat* 111 b; *Raviah, Evel*, sect. 841; *Or Zarua*, vol. 2, 256; Responsa *R. Hayyim Or Zarua* 101, 146, etc. Madame Bailah the wife of the *Sma*, was famous and was described by his son,

R. Yosef Jospe ha-Cohen (in his introduction to the *Derishah* on *Tur Yoreh Deah*, part 2) as being learned. R. Avraham Gombiner (the *Magen Avraham*) disagreed with two of her *hiddushim*, but R. Yehezkel Landau wrote of her "that in my humble opinion the law is according to his mother. . . . And so would I rule like the wife of the *gaon* the *Derishah*, who is a lady whose heart rises up in wisdom."[6]

There is even a tradition brought by R. David Conforte, in his *Koreh ha-Dorot*, (Venice 1746, 25b, Jerusalem, 2008, p. 93) that "a wise woman wrote" the anonymous Kol Bo, a famous mediaeval book of *halachah* (though he himself, probably quite rightly, rejects this attribution).

Here it is interesting to take note of a most unusual comment of R. Efraim Shlomoh Luntshitz (Lenczyca, Poland, 1550–1619), in his *Klei Yakar* to *Numbers* 13:2, "Send thou men [that they may search the Land of Canaan which I give unto the children of Israel, of every tribe of their fathers shall ye send a man, every one a ruler among them]":

> For the Sages said that they hated the Land of Israel, and said, "Let us make a captain, and let us return to Egypt" (*Numbers* 14:4), while the women loved the Land, and said [i.e., the daugh-

6. Shlomoh Ashkenazi, in his book *Ha-Ishah be-Aspaklariat ha-Yahadut*, vol. 1, Jerusalem, 1953, pp. 115–130, lists over seventy learned Jewish women, several of whom had leadership positions (e.g., the daughter of Rabbenu Nissim of Kairuan, the wife of R. Yosef ha-Nagid 1031–1066, who after her husband's death led the community of Luciena, Ashkenazi, p.118), and gave halachic rulings (e.g., the wife of R. Yehoshua Walk, 1550–1614, Bailah, ibid., p.122, or the wife of R. Avraham of Falaise, ibid. p.119). See further M. Kayserling, *Jüdische Frauen*, Leipzig, 1879; Shlomoh Ashkenazi *Nashim Lamdaniyot: Skirah Historit*, Tel-Aviv, 1993; A. Neubauer and M. Steinschneider, *Zur Frauenliteratur*, ed. A.M. Habermann, Jerusalem 1968. On Madam Bailah, see also *Entziklopedia le-Toldot Gedolei Yisrael*, ed. M. Margaliot, vol. 3, Jerusalem, 1943, col. 710. See also the remarks of R. Hayyim David ha-Levi in *Asei Lecha Rav*, vol. 2, Tel-Aviv, 1978, p.193, who refers us to the *Hida* (Shem ha-*Gedolim* s.v. Rav, – *Rabbanit*, who cites R. Shimshon who surprisingly found a woman Tannait who in *Tosefta Baba Metzia* 1, was, of course, Beruriah.

ters of Tzelofhad] "Give unto us therefore a possession among the brethren of our father" (ibid. 27:4). Therefore, the Holy One blessed be He said, "In my opinion, seeing the future, it would have been better to send women who love the Land [to spy it out], for they would not speak badly of it. But you [Moses] think these people are suitable, so send them." And from these words one could conclude that women could serve in public positions of authority.[7]

7. See *Sifrei Zuta Pinhas* 27:1; *Sifrei Pinhas* no. 133, etc.; *Torah Shelemah*, by R.M. Kasher, vol. 39, Jerusalem, 1985, pp. 45–46, no. 30.

The homiletic stress is on the word *lecha* (literally yourself), of the words *shlach lecha* – literally send *yourself*, i.e., on your own responsibility, not Mine (God's). (Compare *Genesis* 12:1, "*Lech Lecha*," literally "send yourself," and Rashi ad loc., "For your benefit and your good." Cf. *Zohar* 1:77b, 2:32a; see *Torah:Ariel: Rashi ha-Shalem, Bereishit*, vol. 1, Jerusalem, 1986, p. 122, note 1.)

We find this same claim in R. Gedaliah ibn Yihya's brief essay in praise of womanhood, cited in A. Neubauer's Zur *Frauenliteratur, Israelietische Letterbode* 10, 1884–1885, p. 147:

> And so will you find that Israel on the advice of the spies refused [to go to] the Land of Israel, but in advance the daughters of Tzelofhad asked for their portion in the land. And it was for this reason that they were not subject to the decree of the spies, for they did enter the Land, as it is said, "And there was *not left a man of them*, save Caleb the son of Jephuneh and Joshua the son of Nun" (*Numbers* 26:65). ["Not left a man of them"], but the women were left.

The following verse (*Numbers* 27:1) is "Then came the daughters of Tzelofhad . . .", and it is from the juxtaposition of these two verses that the Rabbis derived this homiletic position. The source is in *Numbers Rabba* 21:10, and parallels. (Cf. *Midrash ha-Gadol* to *Numbers* 26:65, ed. Tzvi Meir Rabinowitz, Jerusalem, 1967, p. 463.)

Gedaliah ibn Yihye's essay is in response to a misogynist poem by Abraham of Sarteano, and others, published by Neubauer, in *Israelitische Letterbode* 10, 1884–1885, pp. 115–116, and see the other polemic poems brought by Neubauer, ibid., pass. (They were collected in a small booklet by A.M. Habermann, under the title *Zur Frauenliteratur*, Jerusalem, 1968, pp. 1–50.)

We might further point out that R. Gedaliah ibn Yihye had great respect for the wife of R. Yom Tov, author of the *Magid Mishneh* (otherwise known as Don Vidal di-Tolosa from Catalonia). He relates (in his *Shalshelet ha-Kabbalah*, Warsaw, 1877, p. 79) that he was told in the name of Maharam Padua that R. Yom Tov had a wife, and when she was widowed, the author of the *Migdal Oz*

It is true that this interpretation of the *Klei Yakar* was rejected by R. Eliyah Katz in his *Beer Yaakov* (vol. 3, Jerusalem, 2003, no. 15, p. 32); however, whether his refutation be correct or not, clearly R. Efraim Luntshits saw a place for women in public leadership positions, and sought to find some source in the canonic texts.

IN CONCLUSION: From the above sources, the *Tosafot* in *Niddah*, the *Ran* in *Shevuot*, the *Rashba* and the *Ritba* to *Bava Kama*, the *Sefer ha-Hinuch*, the *Hida* in *Birkei Yosef*, and a number of latter-day authorities, it emerges that "a wise woman," a God-fearing one, who studied Torah intensively and *halachah* systematically in depth and in breadth from truly learned scholars, and who was examined by them and/or by an experienced rabbi, and who gained practical experience in the areas of *halachah* by being in constant contact with true authorities – *shimush*, she is certainly worthy to be crowned with the crown of Torah, and rightly to be considered eligible to give halachic responses and practical ruling, in those areas in which she was examined and found competent. And may the Lord guard over her that she make no error, and lead no one astray, but guide her congregation along the pathway of Torah and the fear of God.

(Shem Tov be-R. Avraham ibn Gaon) came to her requesting her in marriage. Her reply to him was, "The last *Yom Tov* compared to the first was declared by the Rabbis as secular." (This is a clever paraphrase of Rav Ashi's statements in *B. Beitzah* 6a that "the Second Yom Tov with regard to a dead person was declared by the Rabbis as secular, meaning that one buried a dead person on the second day of Yom Tov and one does not delay the burial, even if there is no fear of the corpse's putrefaction.) This was her clever formulation for rejecting Shem Tov over Yom Tov. (See Shlomoh Ashkenazi, *Nashim Lamdaniyot* (*Skirah Historit*), Tel-Aviv, 1942, p. 36.)

4 CAN WOMEN SERVE IN POSITIONS OF AUTHORITY?

I ALREADY BRIEFLY ALLUDED TO THE RAMBAM'S POSITION on this issue, and here I should like to address it further in depth. It is well-known that the Rambam rules in *Hilchot Melachim* 1:5, that in "all positions of authority in Israel (כל משימות בישראל) one appoints only men," and clearly this rabbinic position is one which carries with it considerable authority. The apparent source of this ruling is the biblical verse in *Deut.* 17:9. "You shall surely appoint over yourself a king," upon which the *Sifrei* ad loc. adds, "a king and not a queen." The Rambam, ibid., follows the ruling of the *Sifrei*, however, expanding it to exclude a woman from having any position of authority, as we have just seen. R. Moshe Feinstein (in his *Igrot Moshe, Yoreh Deah* 2, sect. 45) writes, "I do not know, in my ignorance, of any source for his words, and we must assume that this was his personal opinion." R. Hayyim David Halevi (*Tehumim* 10, 1989, p. 121) also thought this was the Rambam's personal opinion, but was troubled by the fact that usually when the Rambam expresses his own view he prefaces it with the words "it would appear to me" (ויראה לי), and therefore he finally concludes that the Rambam must have had a source which has been lost to us. (This is also the conclusion of R. Halevy, in his article in Yehezkel Cohen's *Nashim be-Hanhagot ha-Tzibbur*, Jerusalem, 1991, p. 89.)

In point of fact, R. Ben Zion Hai Uziel (in his *Piskei Uziel be-Sheelot ha-Zeman*, Jerusalem, 1977, sect. 43, pp. 224 et seq.)

claims to have found Rambam's source in a homiletical exposition on *Deut.* 17:15, "You cannot place upon yourself a gentile [as King]" – from here they learned that one appoints a man as *parnas* (community leader) over the community, but one does not appoint a woman as *parnasah* over the community" – a source discovered by R. Shlomo Aharon Wertheimer. See *Midrash Lekah Tov, Shoftim*, p. 58. Earlier on R. Yaakov Levinson, (in his *Shivyon ha-Nashim mi-Nekudat ha-Halachah*, New York, 1920, chapter 3, p. 18), pointed to the passage in *Midrash Lekah Tov* to *Shoftim* (p. 58), where the author adds: "A man and not a woman . . . this is a negative commandment [!] that one may not appoint a '*parnasah*' (female community leader) over the community." One can also point to *Midrash Shoher Tov, Psalm* 22:20 (ed. Buber, p.192), where it is stated: חסיך דרא דאיתתא דברייתא "Woe to the generation where a woman is its leader."[1] R. Uziel,

1. Marc Shapiro, in his article in the *Seforim blog*, Feb. 9, 2016, pp. 6–8 notes that this phrase was quoted by R. Bakshi-Doron in his letter of 26/6/15 to the RCA (cf. above ch. 2 note 4), in a slightly different form. He points out that this phrase was also used by R. Yisrael Zeev Mintzberg, in his *Ve-Zot Hukat ha-Torah*, Jerusalem, 1920, p. 33, which is devoted to demonstrating that women are not permitted to vote. His position was strongly attacked by R. Hayyim Hirschensohn (*Malki ba-Kodesh*, vol. 2, St. Louis, 1921, p. 172) who also referred to the *Midrash Shoher Tov* text where he goes so far as to say that according to R. Mintzberg he would not even permit a woman to be a woman! On the other hand, R. Shlomoh Zalman Ehrenreich (in *Devar Hevron: Hashkafah ve-Inyanei Emunah*, Kiryat Arba, 2011, p. 232) uses this text to argue that it means: women were not created to bring others to Torah, but rather their role is to enable their husbands to reach perfection.

See also R. Yonah Dovrat, in his article "*Behirat u-Minui Nashim le-Tafkidei Tzibbur, Ha-Kibbutz ba-Halachah*, Shalavim, 1984, p. 299, who discusses Rambam's source, and R. Yisrael Rosen, *Nashim be-Tafkidim Tzibburim, Tehumim* 19, 1998, pp. 18–19; Avi Weinrot, ibid,. p. 107, note 12, with additional references. He also refers us to a discussion between R. David Tzvi Hoffmann and Dr. Ritter, as the Status of Shlomtzion ha-Malkah, who Hoffmann argues received her royal authority by right of inheritance from her late husband Yannai. He further argues that there was no prohibition involved, merely halachic policy. Ritter for his part held that there was no prohibition involved because the appointment was not by the people, but by King Yannai. See *Ha-Kibbutz ba-Halachah*, ibid., pp. 286–290; Weingort, ibid., pp. 107–108, note 14. See further on this point the responsum of the *Nodah bi-Yehudah, Mahadurah Kama, Hoshen Mishpat*, sect. 1; *Minhat Hinuch* 497:1; Y. Rosen, ibid., pp. 20–21, for a further discussion of this point with additional bibliography.

As an aside it is interesting to hear of the Moslem position on this issue. In "The Tale of Salim, the Youth of Khorasan," as related in Richard F. Burton's *Supplemental Nights* to the book of the *Thousand Nights and a Night*, vol. 1, 1886 (facsimile ed., Denver, 1900), p. 350, we read that Salma says: "But now Allah hath deigned reunite me with my brother, and it is no longer lawful to me that I be king and Sultan over the people, and I a woman; because there is no Sultanate for women, when men are present." To which Burton adds a note (1):

> There is no Salic law among Moslems; but the *Rasm* or custom of Al-Islam, established by the succession of the four first Caliphs, to the prejudice of Ayishah and other masterful women would be a strong precedent against queenly rule. It is the reverse with the Hindus who accept a Ravi as willingly as Rajah, and who believe with Europeans that when kings reign women rule, and *vice versa*. To the vulgar Moslem feminine government appear impossible and I once was asked by an Afghan, "What would happen if the queen were in childbed?"

However, there were women leaders in the Modern world. This is clearly pointed out by S.D. Goitein, in his magisterial *A Mediterranean Society*, vol. 3, Berkeley, Los Angeles, London, 1978, p. 357:

> Al-Hākim's (966–1021) sister, Sayyidat al-Mulk ("The Mistress over the Kingdom"), was suspected of having engineered his murder and she ruled the country after his death for four years. The Sudanese mother of the Caliph al-Mustansir (1036–1094), who originally had been a slave girl in the possession of the Jew Abū Sa'd al-Tustari (who later became her "vizier"), held power while her son was a minor. Al-Mustansir himself, on his deathbed, put the Imamate, the religious and temporal leadership of the empire, into the hands of his sister, who then swore allegiance to al-Musta'lī, the youngest and therefore, most amenable, of the seven sons of her dead brother. Al-Mu'izz, the most splendorous ruler of Zirid Tunisia (1016–1062), was brought up by his aunt Mallāl, also known in the Geniza papers as al-Sayyida, "The Mistress," or "The Ruler," who acted as regent until her death in October 1023, and there were other prominent women of the Zirid court. The role of women at the courts of eleventh-century Egypt and Tunisia was so conspicuous that Ibn 'Idhārī, the noted historian of the Muslim West, dedicates a special chapter to the topic.

See ibid., pp. 506–507, notes 207–210. And Shapiro (ibid., p. 8) relates that recently a Moslem member of Knesset, Issawi Frej, journeyed to Bnei Brak to try to convince some leading rabbis to support the appointments of women

when discussing the Rambam's view (ibid., p. 230) expresses doubt as to whether he intended this prohibition because of the disqualification of womanhood (פסול האשה) or perhaps because it might constitute an affront to the dignity of the community (כבוד הציבור). The difference being, that when the appointment is not that of the Sanhedrin, but is made by the community itself, if it reflected an innate disqualification of womanhood, the disqualification would nonetheless remain in force. But if it is a matter of the "dignity of the community," when the community itself makes the appointment, obviously they do not see this as an affront to their dignity. Hence, in such a case, even the Rambam would agree to the legitimacy of such an appointment.[2] Indeed, this is R. Uziel's conclusion, namely that if a woman is elected by the public "even the Rambam would agree that there is no hint of prohibition" (ibid., p. 232).

---

qadis (i.e., judges). But Yahadut ha-Torah bloc strongly opposed this move. However, this subject is beyond my area of competence.

2. This issue of "the dignity of the community" has been discussed by me in considerable detail in the essay entitled "Congregational Dignity and Human Dignity: Women and Public Torah Reading," apud *Women and Men in Communal Prayer: Halakhic Perspectives*, Jersey City, 2010, pp. 27 et seq. There I pointed to the sources that state clearly that a community can absolve themselves of that dignity, i.e., can declare that they do not see a particular action as demeaning their honor. This is the view of the *Riaz* (R. Yishayah di-Trani ha-Aharon) in his rulings to *B. Megillah* 24a, cited by the *Shiltei Giborim* ad loc.; *Magen Avraham*, *Orah Hayyim* 53:9; *Aruch ha-Shulhan*, ibid., 144:8; *Beit Yosef, Orah Hayyim* 53; *Knesset ha-Gedolah*, *Orah Hayyim* 90; R. Ovadiah Yosef, *Hazon Ovadiah*, *Moadim Noraim,* pp. 344–345, etc.

There I also discussed the *halachic* status of the dignity of the individual, and I cited the relevant bibliography, to which I now add a succinct summary of the subject in an article by Eliezer ben Shlomoh, "*Kevod ha-Adam le-Umat Shalom ha-Tzibbur" Shmatin* 97–98, 1989, pp. 92–93. To this we should also add: Nahum Rakover, *Gaddol Kevod ha-Briyot: Kevod ha-Adam Ke-Erech-Al,* Jerusalem, 1998.

We may point out that recently R. Aharon Lichtenstein expressed the view that there should be a greater stress on the well-being of a *tzibbur* in several of his studies. See e.g., "The Human and Social Factor in Halakha," *Tradition* 36/1, 2002. p. 20; "'Mah Enosh': Reflections on the Relation between Judaism and Humanism," *The Torah U-Madah* Journal 14, 2006–2007, pp. 30–43, etc.

This too is the position of R. Hayyim David Halevy (ibid., p. 90). He further brings the words of the *Hida* (*Birkei Yosef* to *Beit Yosef*, *Tur Hoshen Mishpat* 7) who relates that he "found written in a manuscript that Deborah acted like a queen – *manheget ke-din malkah*." Ha-Levi explains that:

> His intention was to say that she was not actually a judge, as one might understand from the biblical texts . . . , but rather, with the meaning of all the judges of Israel who came after Joshua to lead the people, and this is what he meant by *ke-din malkah*, namely having national leadership.

However, continues Halevy, the *Hida* is then troubled by the Rambam's position, asking how could she have ruled like a king/queen. In response to this question he cites the *Rashba* (*Shevuot* chapter 4, ad init.) who states as follows:

> One may say that she was not actually a judge, but a leader, just like the judges who ruled Israel. And even though we say "put on yourself a king," and not a queen, in her case they did not appoint her, but regarded her as if she were a queen.

From the above, concludes Halevy, even according to the *Sifrei* there is no prohibition to appointing a woman as a queen, or to another position of leadership, if one accepts that position of leadership and follows her judgements. He argues that, in his opinion, the Rambam too would accept such a view, finding indications of this in the Rambam's careful formulation.

We have already mentioned that R. Moshe Feinstein did not accept the Rambam's ruling, arguing that numerous early authorities disagreed with it.[3]

---

3. E.g., the *Hinuch*, *Rashi*, *Ran* to *Kiddushin* 76b, *Tosfot Sotah* 41b, etc.; *Igrot Moshe Yoreh Deah*, part 2, sect. 45.

Here we may also add the opinion of R. Yitzhak Nissenbaum, who wrote in the second conference of the Mizrahi, which took place in Warsaw in April 1919 (see *Hagut: Maasaf le-Mahshavah Yehudit*, pp. 80–81, cited by Menahem Elon, in his *Maamad ha-Ishah: Mishpat ve-Shiput, Masoret u-Temurah, Arachim shel Medinah Yehudit ve-Demokratit,* Tel-Aviv, 2005, pp. 60–61; and see the whole chapter [1] on the Leah Shakdiel affair, Bagatz 153/87):

> It is true that the *Sifrei* expounds, "Place upon yourself a king – a king and not a queen," and the Rambam, ruling in accordance with the *Sifrei,* expands the implications, saying, "and all kinds of authority in Israel are appointed only to a man" (*Hilchot Melachim* 1).
>
> [However,] this ruling of the Rambam was also unclear to the Sages of France and they did not give an absolute ruling, namely that "a woman is ineligible to rule." (See *Tosafot* to *Baba Kama* 15, *Niddah* 50, etc.) And from the words of these Sages we may also learn that a woman is eligible to be elected to those learned people who clarify the laws, and even to those who establish them. That is what they meant by saying concerning Deborah the judge, that "she used to teach them, the judges. . ." And therefore, she is eligible according to all opinions, or because "the children of Israel accepted her."

He concludes that this acceptance gives her authority not only over those who accepted her, but also over those who did not. See Elon's comments ad loc.

This is, of course, part of a much broader discussion on women's voting rights, to which, for example, Rav Kook objected.

See the two manifestos which he signed, a *Gilui data* ("declaration") from 1920, and an open letter from 1926 (*Maamrei ha-Reiyah*, 189; *Igrot ha-Reiyah*, pt. IV, 50–53), brought by Moshe Yehiel Tzuriel, *Otsrot ha-Reiyah*, pt. IV, Shaalavim (n.d.) pp. 123–124. And see also M.Z. Nehorai, "Some Notes on Rav Kook's Approach to *Pesikah*" [Hebrew], *Tarbiz* 59 (1990), pp. 498–502; Menahem Friedman, *Hevrah ve-Dat* (Jerusalem, 1978) 162; and, recently, Haggi Ben-Arzi's doctoral dissertation, "*Ha-Reaya Kook ke-Posek* (2003), pp. 299–302 (Hebrew University). And see Blidstein's comments, *op cit.*, p. 180; Yehoram Kirsch, *Mahapechot ba-Halachah*, Israel, 2002, pp. 49– 55; Yehezkel Cohen, "The Controversy between Rabbis Kook and Uziel on Women's Rights to Vote" [Hebrew], in *Sefer Peninah*; *Ha-Ishah ha-Yehudit be-Hevra, ba-Mishpahah uva-Hinuch*, Jerusalem, 1989 (*P. Herzog Festschrift*), pp. 51–62. More recently, Prof. Margalit Shilo called my attention to a tract by Rav Menahem Mendel Kasher entitled *Da'at Rabbanim,* a collection of articles against franchising women, which includes, on pp. 6–7, a "decision of the congress of the Rabbis of Eretz Yisrael with the approval of Rav Kook." And cf. Yisrael Zeev Mintzberg, *Ve-Zot Hukat ha-Torah* (Jerusalem, 1920). Rav Herzog also opposed this issue in principle, as did R. David Zvi Hoffman, in an article in *Yeshurun* 6, 1919, p. 262, in which he came to a favorable conclusion. See Rav Herzog's *Tehukah le-Yisrael al-Pi ha-Torah,* pt. I, Jerusalem, 1989, p. 95. The article by Hoffman was translated by Samuel Daube and appended to

Furthermore, historically speaking we know there were women in leadership positions. We have already mentioned Deborah the Prophetess, have alluded to Queen Shlomtzion (above note 1), and there are a number of inscriptions from the Roman and Byzantine period referring to women as *archisynagogos* or *presbytera*. We even know of a Rufina, who was a Jewish woman and an *archisynagogos*.[4] And in modern times we may add that Dame

---

Yosef Efrati, "Female Members in a Local Council in a Collective Settlement" [Hebrew], in *Ha-Kibbutz be-Halachah*, Shaalavim, 1984, p. 272 (as noted by I. Warhaftig in his note in *Tehukah le-Yisrael,* ibid.). And cf. R. Hayyim Hirschensohn, *Malki ba-Kodesh*, vol. 2 (St. Louis, 1921), pp. 12–15, 171–209 (in the second ed. David Zohar, Jerusalem, 2013, pp. 72–85, 372–436) on women's right to vote and be elected; R. Yehiel Ya'akov Weinberg, *Teshuvot Seridei Esh*, pt. I, 286; R. Bakshi-Doron, *Teshuvot Binyan Av*, pt. I, p. 284; and R. Yaakov Lewison, *Shivyon Nashim mi-Nekudat ha-Halachah*, New York, 1920, pp. 24–32, whose attitude towards women's voting rights is definitely positive.

See what I wrote in my article "Congregational Dignity and Human Dignity: Women and Public Torah Reading," apud *Women and Men in Communal Prayer: Halachic Perspectives*, ed. C. Trachtman, Jersey City, NJ, 2010, p. 77, and now add Menachem Elon, ibid., pp. 51–101, for a summarizing discussion.

4. There is some debate in the professional literature as to whether women served in leadership positions in the synagogues of ancient times, but the preponderance of evidence is that they did. There are at least four inscriptions from the Roman and Byzantine period referring to women as *archisynagogos* or *presbytera*. See B.J. Brooten, *Women Leaders in the Ancient Synagogue: Inscriptional Evidence and Background* (Chico, Cal., 1982), pp. 41–46; D. Noy, *Jewish Inscriptions in Western Europe; Vol.1* (Cambridge, 1993), pp. 59, 62, 163. But there are others who question this interpretation of the documents. See D.D. Binder, *Into the Temple Courts: The Place of the Synagogues in the Second Temple Period* (Atlanta, 1997), pp. 372–379 (with abundant bibliography, ibid., p. 372. n. 58). These issues were recently summarized by W. Marburg in *The Cambridge History of Judaism*, vol. 3 (Cambridge, 1999), pp. 389–401, and by Lee I. Levine in his comprehensive book, *The Ancient Synagogue: The First Thousand Years* (New Haven and London, 2000), pp. 482–483. Levine tends to accept Brooten's thesis that the majority, if not all, of the titles appearing in more than twenty inscriptions from outside of Palestine indeed indicate that women held official positions in the synagogue. On Rufina, see P.W. van der Horst, *Ancient Jewish Epigraphy: An Introductory Survey of a Millennium of Jewish Funerary and Epigraphy* (300 BCE–700 CE) (Kampen, 1996), pp. 70, 105–109, who brings testimony concerning the offices of *archisynagogissa, prytanis, gymnasiarchos, agonothetes, mater synagogue, pateressa*, and *mater*

collegii, all of which indicate that women served in positions of leadership both inside and outside the synagogue.

To the above we may also add the discussion in J. Reynolds and R. Tannenbaum, *Jews and Godfearers at Aphrodisias*, Cambridge, 1987 (Cambridge Philological Society-Supplementary Volume 12), where in the stone inscription (face a, col. 9, on p. 5) we find *Iael prostates*. On p. 41, the authors discuss this name writing:

> Jael may be a woman's name [as in Judges 4:18]: the title is no obstacle to its being so here, since women are often given titles of high synagogue or community office in the diaspora [a full listing of reference and bibliography on p. 71 note 130]; but it is more probably a man's name. . . .

Op. 101 (34) they further discuss this name as follows:

> *Iael* . . . ; transliterated biblical name in the form used by the Septuagint (Josephus has *Lala* for the feminine and would presumably have used *Lalos* for the masculine). At first sight it evokes the woman Jael of Jdg. 4:18f., and has been taken as a woman's name by Brooten, 151; but although some women were highly honoured in diaspora communities, see p. 41, the lists here are otherwise demonstrably and consistently masculine; since the Septuagint uses the same form for a man at *IV Ezra* 10:43, cf. also at 10:26, we believe that the feminine should be rejected in favour of the masculine here. No other example found in use.

I find the argument against regarding *Iael* as a woman quite unconvincing. As to the term *prostates* they write as follows (p. 41):

> Philo usually employs *prostates* and *prostasia* in the sense of the title or office of the 'president' of a community, which it could have here. But the word can also apply to the patron of a pagan Hellenistic religious society, i.e., one who represents and defends its interests; that a woman can fulfil such a function is suggested by St Paul's reference [Romans 16:2] to Phoebe as *prostatis*, presumably because she has looked after the interests of the Christians and of the apostle at Rome. The position of *prostatis*, if it refers to patronage of the community, would be similar to that more usually designated by *pater-synagoges* if, as here, to the protection of a particular Jewish confraternity, the position would be similar to that of the patrons/patronesses of Hellenistic cult societies.

I personally prefer to understand them as "president" or "presiding officer"; see Liddell & Scott, *A Greek-English Dictionary*, new ed., Oxford, 1940, p.1526b, s.v. *prostateia*, III/II 3; (but cf. F.W. Danker, *A Greek-English Lexicon of the New Testament and Other Early Christian Literature*, 3rd ed., Chicago and London, 2000, p. 885a svv. *Prostates, prostatis*; Moulton and Milligen, *The Vocabulary of the Greek Testament*, Glasgow, 1930, p. 551 s.v. *prostatis*).

Flora Sassoon (1859–1936) was appointed in the year 1924 as the chairperson of the Rabbinic seminary in London, i.e., Jews College, and in that year delivered a learned Talmudic discourse there. (See Shulamit Pflaum, *Bat Yisrael Nodedet*, Jerusalem, 1935, p. 328, for a description of her Torah erudition. See also Shlomoh Ashkenazi *Ha-Ishah be-Aspaklariat ha-Yahadut*, vol. 1, Tel-Aviv, 1953, p. 133.)[5]

Of course, the reason the editors of the Aphrodisian inscriptions preferred to regard *Yael* as the name of a man, is because *prostates* is masculine, and the feminine form is attested as *prostatis* (as indicated above). However, we do find a vowel interchange between *eta* and *iota* in unaccounted syllables, especially in a final position as in the case in *prostates*. (See F.T. Gignac, *A Grammer of the Greek Papyri of the Roman and Byzantine Periods*, Milan, 1975, vol. 2, pp. 235–236; e.g., *despoti* for *despote,* PHermRees 7.1 (4 th cent.), 49.6 (6th cent.) etc.; similarly S.B. Psaltes, *Grammatik der Byzantinischen Chroniken*, 2nd edition, Göttingen, 1974, pp.113–114, no. 224.) The inscription is probably from the early 3rd cent. C.E., (pp. 21–22) and is one of a number of Jewish inscriptions (cf. pp. 24–77, 124–140).

The gender of *Yael* remains uncertain, although, as mentioned above, I would opt for feminine.

5. However, the Council of Young Israel in the U.S.A. in their Constitution, which was ratified on Oct. 6, 1997, and amended in May 21, 2013, do not permit women to function in high positions of their synagogues.

Thus, Sect. 4.3 states explicitly:

> The offices of President, Chairman, 1st Vice-President and Second Vice-President shall be filled by *male delegates only*. [My stress, D.S.]

In Section 4.7, the duties of these positions are described, especially the power of the President "to remove all chairman and members of the standing and temporary committees . . . [and] to act in all cases of emergency . . ." etc. This position is also that of R. Hershel Schachter, one of the leading authorities of the RCA. In his Torah Online, Shiur 43, he rules that a woman may not serve as president of a synagogue "unless there is absolutely no other choice."

This clause in the constitution caused a furor in 2010, when a Young Israel Synagogue in Syracuse elected two women consecutively as Presidents, Joan Pottersen and Beverly Marmor. Eventually, in 2013, Young Israel changed their rules, permitting the Syracuse synagogue to leave the organization.

There is a considerable literature on the subject which was widely covered by the local press, such as: *The Jewish Week* June 30, 2010, Nov. 1, 2010; *The Jewish Star*, June 24, 2010, July 28, 2015; *Jewish Philanthropy*, July 1, 2010, etc.

CAN A WOMAN BE A PRESIDENT OF A SYNAGOGUE?
By Rabbi Ben Hassan

The following excerpt was originally published on the blog, Ask Rabbi Hassan, at http://askrabbihassan.blogspot.com/2014/12/can-woman-be-president-of-synagogue.html, on Dec. 8, 2014.

I felt that in the last twenty years since the passing of Rav Soloveitchik things have evolved a great deal. Synagogue boards work differently. President does not make decisions unilaterally. There is no discretionary power, all decisions are made by committees or boards and not by individuals. I felt it was important to talk to a major posek, a halakhic decider of complicated meta-halakhic issues.

I contacted Rav Gedalia Dov Schwartz, the Av Beit Din of the Rabbinical Council of America he indicated to me that he believes that the issues raised by the Rambam are not applicable to the position of synagogue president, and that, consequently, there is no halakhic prohibition. He added that it would be better if there was a woman who wished to be president but did not say that it was essential.

Rabbi Nahum Rabinovitch, head of Yeshivat Birkat Moshe in Ma'ale Adumim, Israel and a well known modern orthodox posek, felt that there was good reason to allow a woman to serve as a synagogue President, since to his mind serara is the right to exercise discretionary authority. This does not exist in

On the internet there were numerous discussions pro and con, analyzing whether these positions constituted the Rambam's *serarah* – authority, i.e., control, or respect. (They refer to R. Moshe Feinstein's response in *Igrot Moshe* 4.26; *Hoshen Mishpat* 2:34, as to whether a convert can serve as a *Rosh Yeshivah* or *Mashgiah*. See above ch. 2 near note 11, and below ch. 5 note 2 on the status of the *Ger*.) But, as we have seen in the formulation, the President does have controlling authority. Nonetheless, since he/she is *elected*, according to the sources we cited above, she should halachically be able to serve – rule as president.

synagogue presidencies as every decision is reviewed by the Board and members.

To the question of changing the status quo and what the Orthodox Jewish community is comfortable with, there are a number of orthodox organizations in Seattle that have Female presidents or leaders both currently and in the past. There are also many orthodox synagogues outside of Seattle with female presidents.

To those who are concerned about the slippery slope, Rabbi Frimer writes the following "Rav Nahum was, however, concerned about the cohesiveness of the community. In the 50s, 60s and 70s there was a real justified fear of the slippery slope, of the inroads made by Conservative Judaism. But in 2007, things have, to his mind, changed radically. Orthodoxy is vibrant and the Conservative movement is weak. Nevertheless, one can't dismiss the fears and concerns of those who want to be stringent. But these fears and concerns may well dissipate in 10 years from now."

My definitive halakhic ruling is that women can serve as vice president or president of SBH. Despite Rabbi Maimon supporting the view of his illustrious teacher Rabbi Solovetichik, both Rabbi Maimon and Rabbi Benzaquen have made it clear to me that they support the process I went through and that I asked a major posek. Whatever, the membership decides on Sunday, I hope that this does not become a divisive issue. I feel that I have shown through the halakhic sources that it is permitted to have women serve in the positions of vice-president and president. It is now up to the membership to vote.

Are we to assume that all these historical precedents have no halachic significance? Or rather, shall we follow the reasoning offered by several authorities that the Rambam's ruling is irrelevant to the contemporary situation, and that he himself would agree to the appointment of women elected by a democratic process to leadership positions, or alternatively appointed by a select committee with the agreement of, and the satisfaction of, the community.[6]

6. This is clearly the view of the *Yam shel Shlomoh, Baba Kama* 10, sect. 34, and the *Mishpetei Shemuel,*, by R. Shemuel Kalai, Venice, 1599–1560, sect. 92, "that when the communities accepted them [as community leaders], even if they are relatives, it is patently simple . . . that there can be no claim [of disqualification] against them."

Perhaps we should also take cognizance of what the *Beit Yitzhak* (*Yoreh Deah* 257:5), citing the *Mordechai* (to *Baba Batra* sect. 488) says, namely that when a community wishes to appoint someone as its treasurer, he is duty bound to acquiesce to their request. The *Mordechai* refers us to *Yerushalmi Peah* 8:1, when the appointment of treasurers, or collectors of charity, is discussed by R. Yitzhak and R. Haggai. This is also cited by the *Darkei Moshe, Yoreh Deah* 256:2, and this ruling is accepted by the *Hochmat Adam* 147:29. A treasurer (*gabbai tzedakah*) was a position of considerable authority, for he could bring much pressure upon those reluctant to pay their dues, forcing them to do so. And since we are discussing appointments made by a community, in effect the community is requesting the individual to assume a position of authority and leadership; hence, it would be halachically problematic for the individual to decline such a request.

5 CONCLUSION

I HAVE TRIED TO DEMONSTRATE THAT A CAREFUL STUDY of the relevant sources leads us to the conclusion that there is no halachic impediment to a woman's appointment to a leadership position. This, indeed, was the ruling of Supreme Court Judge Menahem Elon in the famous case of Leah Shakdiel, who was elected to the membership of a religious Municipal Committee (מועצה דתית), an appointment which evinced aggressive opposition on the part of the ultra-religious establishment.[1] Nor yet should there be any halachic problem in the case of a woman appointed to a position of halachic authority within a congregation, which welcomes her and heartily accepts her leadership.[2]

---

1. See Elon, *Maamad ha-Ishah . . .* , Tel-Aviv, 2005, chapter 1, pp. 51–101; *Bagatz* 153/87. There, pp. 80–82, he also discusses R. Moshe Feinstein's ruling on women *mashgichot kashrut* that we mentioned above.

2. It is true that there may be congregational functions which she cannot carry out; see Francus' remarks referred to above ch. 1 note 5; but they too are not altogether convincing and require further examination. However, all in all, they are few and far between and leave her sufficient areas of fertile rabbinic activity.

Just to add a further layer of complexity to the whole discussion, we should point to the *sugya* in *B. Yevamot* 102a, discussing whether a *ger* – convert – can act as a judge. In monetary matters anyone can act as a judge (Rashi, ibid., referring to *B. Sanhedrin* 32a). To what sort of positions one can appoint a convert is a matter of controversy among the *Rishonim:* some say one may not ask an appointment which empowers him to enforce his opinion upon others (*be-milei de-kefiah*), but other appointments are permitted, while others forbid all manners of appointments. (See *B. Yevamot* 45b, Rashi *Tosafot* and

After all, we have, and have had, women police, women judges – even supreme court judges! – a woman prime minister, women members of cabinet, women in command positions in the army, etc., etc. Would we say all this is not permitted by the *halachah*? These we have readily accepted. But a woman "rabbi" not!?[3]

Rosh ad loc.) However, it might follow that if the appointment was, as it were, democratically effected, this would constitute acceptance even of that form of empowerment. Such an argument can then be transferred to a woman judge. But this is speculative, and perhaps even far-fetched. See Elisha Alterman, *Binyano shel Olam*, Jerusalem, 2010, pp. 75–76.

3. In order to fit this argument into a broader cultural perspective, I shall quote the "Draft Resolution: Women in Federation Policy – and Decision-Making" from August 29, 1975. I cite this from Steven M. Cohen, Susan Dessel and Michael Palavin's article entitled "The Changing (?) Role of Women in Jewish Communal Affairs: A Look into the UJA," apud *The Jewish Women: New Perspectives*, ed. Elizabeth Koltun, New York, 1976, pp. 200–201:

> In carrying out a policy of nondiscrimination, selection of persons for highest Jewish communal responsibilities must be on the basis of ability. Women should neither be chosen nor denied such positions because they are women.
>
> While we applaud the efforts of a number of communities to utilize women in the highest policy-making and decision-making roles in Federations, on Agency Boards, in the campaign structure, and in all aspects of Jewish community life, we must again call attention to the fact that as yet the potentials for the involvement of women are far greater than have been realized.
>
> The facts collected by CJF reveal that one of every twenty Federation presidents, one of six vice-presidents, one of six members of executive committees, one of five board members, one of four members of allocations and planning committees, one of three chairmen of these committees or their subcommittees are women.
>
> The pressing tasks at home and abroad which lie before our entire community demand the fullest commitment on the part of each man and woman volunteer in Jewish life. It is essential therefore that the talent of individuals as individuals be recognized and utilized. Women remain our greatest untapped resource.
>
> In the realm of Jewish professional service, we also urge that Jewish women be accorded equal treatment both in employment opportunities and in remuneration by Federations and by member agencies. We endorse and support the policy of equal pay for equal work.
>
> August 29, 1975

In the above discussion we have not in any way deconstructed classical *halachah*, nor have we ignored or rejected the views of dominant authorities. We have shown them to have referred to different situations from those we are dealing with in our present-day society, and believe that the most reverant of authorities could agree with our conclusions when being apprised of the contemporary situation. Admittedly such moves are innovative, and many of our leading authorities fear any kind of innovation. But we follow the motto of the sainted R. Kook, who expressed his credo thus: "May the old be renewed, and the new be sanctified": הישן יתחדש והחדש יתקדש.

I would end by quoting Chanah Henkin in the final sentence of her very cogently argued study referred to above, ch. 1 note 5, writes as follows:

> "When we create new role models for women's religious leadership, we must ensure that they represent not only great learning but also personal piety, commitment to family and to *chesed*, and excellence in *middot* as well." [And I would add that these are basic requirements for male religious leadership as well. DS]

The statistics (from 1975!) surely demonstrate how out of synch we are in our various Orthodox institutions. Perhaps the "halachists" will see this as irrelevant!

A clear expression of the changing status of women may be found in R. Moshe Malka's *Mikveh Mayyim*, Jerusalem, 1961–1971, vol. 3, *Yoreh Deah*, sect. 21, who writes as follows:

> In our days women play a great role in [all] walks of life, they penetrate to the depths of secular wisdoms, they fill the benches of the universities, they manage offices, and run businesses, and they are active in the governing of the state and in political affairs. It is incumbent upon us to (literally) feed them (i.e., teach) and encourage them, as far as possible.

Admittedly, he is not talking of rabbinic appointments, but he is aware of the variety of authoritative positions they hold.

6 POSTSCRIPT

MOST RECENTLY MY GOOD FRIEND AND COLLEAGUE, Prof. Aryeh A. Frimer, gave a lecture entitled "The View of Rav Joseph B. Soloveitchik *zt"l* on the Ordination of Women" (27/6/10). The *Rav* never discussed this issue openly, but Prof. Frimer found pieces of solid evidence that he opposed women serving as Synagogue Rabbis, receiving *Semicha* and being presidents of Synagogue boards. The *Rav* based himself primarily on the Rambam's position discussed above that women could not have *serarah* – authority of the community, and those positions which would give them such authority were, in his opinion, closed before them. We have discussed the Rambam's position, and reached a different conclusion. Paradoxically, Rav Soloveitchik permitted women *Mashgihot Kashrut* (*kashrut* supervisors), though we have argued they too have authority. He did not permit women slaughterers, but we have shown elsewhere that many communities appointed women slaughterers.[1]

He ends his balanced discussion with the following statement:

> This [the above] in no way contravenes the fact that a large cadre of leading *poskim* have disagreed to varying extents with the *Rav*'s sole reliance on the Rambam, his analysis of *serara*, and his distinction between *serara* and *minui kahal*. Furthermore,

1. See *Minhagei Yisrael* 4, Jerusalem, 1995, pp. 9–12; vol. 6, Jerusalem, 1998, pp. 260–263; vol. 7, Jerusalem, 2003, pp. 401–402; vol. 8, Jerusalem, 2007, p. 268.

> many *poskim* accept the efficacy of democratic elections (*kiblu aleihem*) as a means of circumventing *serara* considerations in other communal leadership positions (such as Synagogue presidency and elected political positions, and they may well feel the same about Rabbinic positions. . . .) As a result of all these considerations, it will not be a simple matter to come to a final ruling on the issue of women's ordination. . . .

While I agree that the matter is not simple, I also think it needs to be confronted, and hence I penned the above deliberation.[2]

I was also treated to Rabbi Nethaniel Helfgot's fine discussion on the subject (18.2.10). He believes that "the major issue here is (not) ultimately halachic. It rather touches more on very emotional, sociological and political self-definitions relating to what have been perceived for 30–40 years as 'bounding' issues between Orthodox and non-Orthodox movements within Judaism." However, he further states that "taking into account the practical sociological communal realities, a move perceived as ordaining women at the present moment is premature." While I have the deepest respect for Rabbi Helfgot and his reasoning, I could still venture to reply: ?אם לא עכשיו, אימתי "If not now, when?"

Finally, I also had occasion to read carefully the very sensitive study by Prof. Michael Broyde and R. Shlomo Brody on

2. In fact, I wonder how the *Rav* would have ruled had he been with us now. This, taking into account what he wrote in one of his letters, namely that one must distinguish between "pure halakhic formalism which . . . places the problem on an ahistorical conceptual level . . . [and] applied Halakhah which transposes abstractions into central realities, theories into facts . . . Under this aspect I gave thought not only to halakhic speculation, but also to [the] concrete situation" (*Community, Covenant, and Commitment, Selected Letters and Communications*, ed. N. Helfgot, Jersey City, 2005, p. 25; cited by G. Blidstein, in "Rabbi Joseph B. Soloveitchik's Letters on Public Affairs," *The Torah u-Madda Journal* 15, 2008–2009, p. 7).

See, for instance, R. Lichtenstein's statement, below in my Concluding Remarks. And he was R. Soloveitchik's most respected disciple.

"Orthodox Women Rabbis: Tentative Thoughts that Distinguish Between the Timely and the Timeless" (*Hakirah* 11, 2011, pp. 25–58). Their conclusions are very similar to that of R. Helfgot, namely that:

> A reasonable call could be put forward that there is no technical obstacle to women being ordained as rabbis. . . .

However, they feel that:

> all communities need to take small steps towards their goals, and not giant steps that rip us apart as a broad community of people who observe halacha. . . .

I can only respond that I believe such "small steps" have already been taken, as they themselves point out, in the form of "the recently-developed positions of *yoatzot halacha* and *toanot rabbaniyot*," and we may add: interns, *rosh kahal*, director of education, halachic mediator, etc.[3]

---

3. See also Hadad, ibid., pp. 88–115, for his discussion on women judges (*dayanot*), who is, however, doubtful that women will in the near future be given positions as such in the official bodies, such as the Israeli Rabbinate, but they may find a niche as advisors within such establishment institutions.

We may further note that the Brody/Broyde article changed somewhat between the earlier version entitled "Tentative Thoughts" and the later published version, which latter has a concluding paragraph which reads thus:

> Given that there does not appear a panel of Torah giants to endorse the immediate and far-reaching change of giving *semikhah* to women, those who support increasing women's leadership roles should return to the path of incremental development on which Orthodoxy has been traveling until recently. Women should sit and study for increasingly long periods of time, write serious scholarship in Torah, develop as inspiring spiritual personas, and lead torah institutions, in function if not in form. In short, they should build the Orthodox community brick by brick, and see what happens over time. The passage of time, as Rabbi Lamm observes, solves many problems. We endorse this approach.

To this we might respond that this is clearly happening: women are spending long periods of time studying halachah intensively, and recently there have been serious halachic studies published by women.

Indeed, in their 2011 article, Brody/Brodye wrote (p. 50):

> Of course, the most important practical change needed to even consider the possibility of women rabbis is the creation of women's seminaries that focus intensely on providing a top-flight multi-year Talmud and halakhah curriculum. Most rabbis in training learn in yeshiva for the better part of a decade nearly full-time before *semikhah*, and there is no program like that for women anywhere in the world now.

However, that is not the case now, for there are a number of such programs both in Israel and the U.S.A.

7 REACTIONS OF RABBINIC ESTABLISHMENT ORGANIZATIONS TO SARA HURWITZ'S SEMICHAH

HERE, WE SHOULD LIKE TO CITE IN FULL THE STATEMENTS of Agudat Israel and the Rabbinical Council of America on the issue of women rabbis.

Statement of the Moetzes Gedolei Ha-Torah of America (10 Adar 5770) [February 25, 2010] See http://torahmusings.com/2010/02/moetzes-condemns-ordination-of-women/:

Rabbi Avi Weiss has conferred "semikha" upon a woman, has made her an Assistant Rabbi at the Hebrew Institute of Riverdale where she carries out certain traditional rabbinical functions, and has now given her the title of "Rabbah" (formerly "Maharat"). He has stated that the change in title is designed to "make it clear that Sara Hurwitz is a full member of our rabbinic staff, a rabbi with the additional quality of a distinct woman's voice."

These developments represent a radical and dangerous departure from Jewish tradition and the mesoras haTorah, and must be condemned in the strongest terms. Any congregation with a woman in a rabbinical position of any sort cannot be considered Orthodox.

Moetzes Gedolei HaTorah of America
Rabbi Simcha Bunim Ehrenfeld
Rabbi Yitzchok Feigelstock
Rabbi Dovid Feinstein
Rabbi Aharon Feldman
Rabbi Yosef Harari-Raful
Rabbi Shmuel Kamenetsky
Rabbi Aryeh Malkiel Kotler
Rabbi Avrohom Chaim Levin
Rabbi Yaakov Perlow
Rabbi Aaron Schechter

March 9, 2010, 23 Adar, 5770: Upon consultation with its rabbinic leadership, Agudat Israel of America issued the following statement today: See https://www.5tjt.com/international-news/6388-a-statement-from-agutath-yisrael-of-america:

The leadership of the Rabbinical Council of America and Rabbi Avi Weiss have apparently reached agreement that Rabbi Weiss would no longer confer the title of "Rabba" upon graduates of his women's seminary, but rather the title "Maharat."

This superficial move does not in any way change the position of the Moetzes Gedolei HaTorah that placing women in traditional rabbinic positions departs from the Jewish mesorah, and that any congregation with a woman in such a position cannot call itself Orthodox.

That the leadership of a respected rabbinical organization seems to have capitulated to Rabbi Weiss' enterprise is deeply dismaying. We trust that this capitulation does not represent the perspective of the principled majority of the organization's member rabbis.

Upon consultation with its rabbinic leadership, Agudat Israel of America issued the following statement today: [March 11, 2010], See http://www.cross-crurents.com/archives/2010/03/11/agudath-israel-commends-rca-leaders/#ixzz1Axuo

Hamodia reports that Rabbi Shmuel Goldin, First Vice-President of the Rabbinical Council of America, has clarified that the RCA "in no way endorses the title '*maharat*' or the '*maharat*' program under the direction of Rabbi Avi Weiss."

Rabbi Goldin further quotes RCA President Rabbi Moshe Kletenik as having stated that ordination of women "is a breach of our *Mesorah* and is unacceptable practice in Orthodoxy," and that "it is also unacceptable for an Orthodox synagogue to have a woman on its rabbinical staff."

Agudat Israel warmly welcomes the clarification and commends the RCA leaders for their forthright and principled words.

May we all continue to stand guard to protect the integrity of our *Mesorah*.

Resolution on Women's Communal Roles in Orthodox Jewish Life Adopted Without Dissent by the 51st Convention of The Rabbinical Council of America [April 27, 2010], See http://www.rabbis.org/news/article.cfm?id=105551:

(1) The flowering of Torah study and teaching by God-fearing Orthodox women in recent decades stands as a significant achievement. The Rabbinical Council of America is gratified that our chaverim have played a prominent role in facilitating these accomplishments.

(2) We members of the Rabbinical Council of America see as our sacred and joyful duty the practice and transmission of Judaism in all of its extraordinary, multifaceted depth and richness – halakhah, hashkafah, tradition and historical memory.

(3) In light of the opportunity created by advanced women's learning, the Rabbinical Council of America encourages a diversity of halakhically and communally appropriate professional opportunities for learned, committed women, in the service of our collective mission to preserve and transmit our heritage. Due to our aforesaid commitment to sacred continuity, however, we cannot accept either the ordination of women or the recognition of women as members of the Orthodox rabbinate, regardless of the title.

(4) Young Orthodox women are now being reared, educated, and inspired by mothers, teachers and mentors who are themselves beneficiaries of advanced women's Torah education. As members of the new generation rise to positions of influence and stature, we pray that they will contribute to an ever-broadening and ever-deepening wellspring of Talmud Torah, *yir'at Shamayim*, and *dikduk be-mitzvot.*

8 WOMEN RABBIS?

By Hershel Schachter[1]

R. Hershel Schachter wrote an article on this subject which appeared in *Hakirah* 11, Spring 2011, pp. 15–23:

> (a) In the printed notes of Rav Soloveitchik's *shiurim* on *Schulchan Aruch, Yoreh De'ah,* the Rav is quoted as having said that a woman may not serve as a rabbi. The Tanna'im understood the *pasuk* in Chumash as implying that women may not be appointed to the position of King. The Talmud points out that the repetition of the verb in the *pasuk "som tasim alecha melech"* implies that this principle applies not only to the position of King, but to all positions of *serarah* and authority. Hence it would follow that a woman may not be appointed president of a synagogue or as rabbi, since these are also positions of *serarah*. . . .
>
> (b) The Rama quotes the practice of not appointing a woman as the town *shochet*. The Beis Yosef quotes the Kol Bo who

1. I had intended to republish the whole article as it appeared in *Hakirah*. However, when I requested permission to do so, the editors of *Hakirah* informed me that it is their policy to receive permission from the author for any such republications, but that they were unable to receive such permission. Consequently, I have only reprinted those select passages on which his major arguments are based. I have also not included his footnote references, all of which may be found in the original *Hakirah* version.

seems to say that although a woman may *shecht* privately, she may not be appointed as the town *shochet*. If indeed this was the intention of the Kol Bo it could be understood that this appointment would constitute a form of *serarah*.

(c) The idea behind this halachah is the principle of *tznius*. Women are always encouraged to avoid compromising on their privacy. When *tznius* is lost, sometimes this might lead to utter *churban*. . . .

(d) Usually we have a rule that one who is disqualified to serve as an *eid* [witness] in a *din Torah* is likewise disqualified to serve as a *dayan* [judge]. The Mishnah has established that women are disqualified to serve as witnesses in a *din Torah*. The combination of these two principles has led the majority of the Baalei HaTosafos to believe that women are disqualified from serving as *dayanim*. Tosafos record a minority position that a woman may serve as a *dayan*. . . .

Biblically, to qualify as a *dayan*, one must have *semichah*. Obviously this minority opinion of Tosafos feels that a woman may have *semichah*. However, this opinion has been outvoted centuries ago, and the accepted view in *Shulchan Aruch* (*Hoshen Mishpat*, Chapter 7, no. 4) is that a woman may not function as a *dayan*. . . .

(e) About fifteen hundred years ago, the Biblical institution of *semichah* was discontinued. The *Shulchan Aruch* states that today's *semichah* is not really the biblical ordination spoken of by the halachah, but merely an "imitation *semichah*" in fulfillment of the rabbinic law instituted by the later rabbis that no one should *paskin* any *halachos* unless authorized to do so by his *rebbe*. It is for this reason that in Europe many referred to today's *semichah* as "*heter hora'ah*" (permission to *paskin*). . . .

Rabbi Shaul Lieberman expressed his extreme disapproval. He quoted *Rishonim* that the modern "imitation *semichah*" is, in a certain sense, a carryover from the *semichah* of old, and since the accepted view is that women may not serve as dayanim, and the *semichah* of old was for the purpose of enabling one to function as a *dayan*, it would follow that the real biblical *semichah* was never conferred on women. And likewise, the modern imitation *semichah*, being a carryover from the *semichah* of old, cannot be conferred on women. . . .

(f) Based on the interpretation of the *Torah she'Be'al Peh*, the *pesukim* tell us that we may not appoint a *ger* [convert] to serve as King or in any capacity of *serarah*, as, for example, to serve as a rabbi of a community, or (as mentioned by the Talmud) as president of a labor union. A *ger* may not serve as a *dayan* in a *din Torah* involving a Yisrael, but may serve as a *dayan* in a *din Torah* involving other *geirim*. Obviously it is possible to confer *semichah* on a *ger*, otherwise he would not even be able to serve as a *dayan* for a case involving other *geirim*. Although a *ger* may not serve as a rabbi in a *kehillah* of Yisraelim, we still allow *geirim* to join the *semichah* program in the Yeshiva and to receive *semichah* upon successful completion of their studies, because years ago real *semichah* was sometimes conferred on *geirim*. Women, however, never received real *semichah*. Therefore, according to the *Rishonim* quoted by Rabbi Lieberman, today's "imitation *semichah*," being a carryover from the biblical *semichah* of old, ought not to be granted to women. . . .

9 RESPONSE TO RABBI SCHACHTER

We may summarize R. Hershel Schachter's arguments as follows:

(a) The Tannaim understood the biblical verse as implying that women may not be appointed to the positions of kingship, and all positions of *serarah*, authority. Hence, they may not be appointed as presidents of a synagogue or as a rabbi.

To this we respond that we have shown that if they be elected by a community to a position of authority this is permitted, and the biblical verse does not apply to such a situation.

(b) He further states that a woman may not be appointed as "the town *schochet*," and though this is not altogether germane to our discussion, we will nonetheless point out that in effect women did serve as official *shochtot*. See the material I assembled in *Minhagei Yisrael* 4, Jerusalem, 1995, pp. 9–12; ibid., 7, Jerusalem, 2003, pp. 201–202; ibid. 8, Jerusalem, 2007, p. 268. To which one may add: The *Hida*, *Birkei Yosef*, *Yoreh Deah* 1:4; R. Yosef Shaul Nathanson, Responsa *Shoel u-Meishiv*, fourth ed., vol. 2, sect. 41, who, citing his father R. Arieh Leibush on the ruling of *Hilchot Eretz Yisrael* which disallows women from slaughtering, points to the verse in I *Samuel* 28:24, "And the woman had a fat calf in the house; and she has fed, and slaughtered it (*va-tizhe-heihu*) . . . ," from which verse we may learn that women may do *shechitah*. See what Brody and Broyde wrote on this, ibid., p. 43. And see further Avraham Yitzhak Bromberg, *Ha-Gaon Rabbi Yosef Shaul Nathanson zt"l mi-Levov*, Jerusalem, 1960, p. 72; and the additional material on women *shochtot* in *Sefer Eshet Hayyil*, by Y.Y. Stern, vol. 2, Jerusalem, 2014, p. 366.

(c) He argues that this would not be modest (*tzanua*), "Women are always encouraged to avoid compromising their privacy . . . It is always best to strive for *tznius*" (p. 21). However, we have shown that there is no loss of *tznius* or modesty when acting in the public domain for the public good. (See also R. Yehuda Henkin, *Understanding Tzniut: Modern Controversies in the Jewish Community*, Jerusalem and New York, 2008, pp. 71–72.)

(d) As to the question of women being disqualified from acting as witnesses, and therefore can also not serve as judges, we showed above that women can, in fact, serve as witnesses in many categories of testimony, and moreover, if accepted by the plaintiffs, may also serve as judges.

(e) The fact that the biblical institution of *semichah* was discontinued long ago is irrelevant to our discussion, as contemporary *semichah* for men too does not have the status of biblical *semichah*, as we pointed out above.

(f) His final argument is somewhat self-contradictory. For if biblical law forbids a *ger* (convert) to act as a King, a rabbi, or a *dayan*, and nonetheless "we still allow *geirim* to join the *semichah* program in the Yeshivah and to receive a real *semichah* upon successful completion of their studies" (ibid., p. 23), women should also, by that same argument, be permitted to receive "a real *semichah* upon completion of their studies." The fact that this may not have happened in the past is an incidence of social history, and cannot serve as a halachic proof of a prohibition. See further on this subject the discussion of Zev Farber in his article "The Ger as a Judge and Public Figure," *Kerem* 1, 5773 (2013), pp. 133–245; as well as Michael J. Broyde's *A Concise Code of Jewish Law for Converts*, Jerusalem and New York, 2017, pp. 79–80.

*

And finally, the statements of the various establishment rabbinic organizations, that women's *semichah* "represent a radical and dangerous departure from Jewish tradition and *mesoras ha-Torah*," and we must "continue to stand guard to protect the integrity of our *Mesorah*," are, in fact, reformulations of the Hatam Sofer's "*Hadash assur min ha-Torah*," which we discussed extensively above, arguing that the "*masorah*" is truly a tradition of constant innovations, and cannot survive if stultified or ossified.

We may further add that it is a well-known rabbinic ruling that we do not add additional constrictions (*gezerot*) beyond those mentioned in the Talmud (*ein gozrin gezerah li-gezerah*). See the very rich collection of sources assembled by R. Ovadiah Yosef, in his *Yabia Omer*, vol. 1, second ed., Jerusalem, 1986, *Orah Hayyim* 16:1–3, p. 58, and in his *Yehaveh Daat*, vol. 5, Jerusalem, 1983, sect. 28, pp.134–135 in an extensive note, where he discusses the parameters of this principle. We must be cautious when taking a stringent position not to add new strictures, for, as R. Ovadiah wrote in *Yabia Omer*, vol. 7, Jerusalem, 1993, *Orah Hayyim*, sect. 38:3, p. 113:

> And in truth the multitude of *humrot* leads to easing (i.e., transgressing) real *mitzvot* (*gufei Torah*), as has been stated by our Rabbis the *Aharonim*.

And again there, *Orah Hayyim*, sect. 37, p. 106, we are warned not to forbid the permitted.

Now I am fully aware that I am taking to task a great *Talmid Hacham*, one who is of a different order of stature than myself, and that I am as an acolyte before his mentor (*talmid bi-fnei rabo*). Nonetheless, I have permitted myself to argue and even contradict his conclusions, following the directives of R. Hayyim of Volozin (Responsa *Hut ha-Meshulash*, by R. Hayyim Berlin, Vilna 1862, no. 9):

> Even though I served my master and rabbis, the Cohen Gadol, and I am obligated to respect him like I respect Heaven, I keep in mind what the Sages said (*B. Baba Kama* 130b), that when a halachic ruling comes before you and you see in it an [area of] refutation, do not learn from it [i.e., accept it], for the judge has only what *his* eyes see. [My emphasis, D.S.] And I have already been warned by my master, the holy one of Israel, the Gaon R. Eliyahu of Vilna *zt"l*, never to favor [anyone] in judgement.

And in his *Ruah Hayyim*, Vilna, 1859, to *Avot* 1:4, he wrote:

> And it is forbidden for a student to accept the words of his teacher if he has questions [to raise] against them, for at times the truth may be with the student, just as a little tree can light up a big one. And this is what we learned (*Avot*, ibid.), "Let your house be a meeting-place for scholars, and sit among the dust of their feet." "Sit among the dust" – *mitabek*, from the root '*va-yeavek ish imo*,' "and a person wrestled with him" (*Genesis* 32:25), which means wrestling in conflict, which is a conflict of *mitzvah* (*milhemet mitzvah*). So too we may [act] against our holy teachers who are in the country, and their souls are in the lofty heavens, those famous authors with their writings. But, behold, through their writings which are in our houses, the houses of assembly – i.e., the *Batei Midrash*. We have been cautioned and given the right to wrestle and struggle with them in learning, and to favor no man, and only to love truth.

So too R. Hayyim Palache, in his responsa *Hikekei Lev*, Saloniki, 1800–1809, *Yoreh Deah*, sect. 42, wrote that a *talmid hacham* may not "suppress his prophecy," i.e., his opinion, and must reveal his view even if it conflicts with that of the earlier authorities, and has been written in books, for one may not seek favor in these matters. And similarly in his *Kol ha-Hayyim*, Izmir, 1874, 18c; and in his *Hayyei ve-Hamra*, Jerusalem, 2002, p. 43b.

R. Ovadiah Yosef, in his *Anaf Etz Avot*, Jerusalem 2001, p.18, cites additional sources, but also calls our attention to *Shut ha-Rid* (R. Yishayah di-Trani the Elder), ed. A.Y. Wertheimer, Jerusalem, 1967, sect. 62, col. 301, who wrote in response to his questioner:

> First of all, let me reply to you concerning what you wrote to me that I should not disagree with the great rabbi, R. Yitzhak *zt"l*; God forbid that I should behave in this manner and it never occurred to me to disagree with him, for I am like a flea compared to him . . . However, this is my way, that anything that does not appear to me to be correct in my eyes, even if Yehoshua bin Nun said it, I would not hearken to him (cf. *B. Hulin* 124a). And I would not abstain from saying to him what appears to me [to be correct] in accordance with my limited understanding. And in this I follow the biblical verse, "I will speak of thy testimonies also before [i.e., against – *neged*] kings, and I will not be ashamed" (*Psalms* 119:41).[1]

Similarly, in his *Mishnat Yosef*, Jerusalem, 2005, p. 178, he explains the *gemarah* in *B. Berachot* 4a, how Kilav would disagree with Mefiboshet, though he was much younger than him, and King David his father had been Mefiboshet's student, precisely because "one must not seek favor in *halachah*," but one should feel free to express what one believes to be the truth. It is for his reason I have the temerity, as it were, with all due respect to take

1. See further on the "dwarf on the shoulders of the giant" in my shortly to be published book entitled *The Importance of the Community Rabbi*, where I discussed this.

on a major Torah scholar, and see this as a directive to all who seriously engage in genuine halachic discourse.

We may also remind ourselves what R. Arieh Lebi Tzintz wrote in his *Shut Meshivat Nefesh*, vol. 1, Warsaw, 1849, sect. 16, that:

> Though Rav Ashi said, "If the *Rishonim* were like people [we are like asses], and nonetheless we rule according to the later authorities (*hilchata ke-batrai*): from which we learn that the greatness of a person is not proof [of his correctness] so that we must [always] rule according to his opinion.

Of course, I am always willing, and even eager, to hear any critique of my suggestions, any errors I may have made, and certainly no one should hesitate to express themselves in this way, should they have good reason to do so. For none should be hesitant to learn the truth and to teach it. See the wonderful passage of R. Hayyim Palache, in his *Tochahat Hayyim, Seder Tazria*, Bnei Brak, 1999, vol. 2, pp. 79–80, which should constitute an ethical directive to every posek, where he writes as follows:

> And here I would like to give a major notice of biblical status and expressing myself that anyone who brings forth against me any argument to refute my opinion, whether it be in legal adjudication or merely oral learning, be it in written adjudication or published learning, let him argue with me or raise doubts [as to my rulings], if his intention is worthy [*la-shamayim*] to clarify the truth; let him not be shameful or ashamed, for this is my wish and desire, and most especially with regard to my disciples – may the Lord be with them, Amen; let them not take any account of my honor (i.e., let them not think they are shaming me), for that would anger me. On the contrary, this *is* my honor. And I always stated in my youth that I am extremely happy when others demonstrate that I erred, clarifying the truth in accordance with the Torah to bring satisfaction and content to our Creator, let them gain credit – not I. And I have no pride

> in my rulings. . . , for I can only thank them profusively for saving me from error. . . For they are obligated by the Torah to reveal their viewpoint and state their opinion. . . And this is the case not only in my lifetime, but even moreso after my demise, for thus will I be worthy of "the word of truth" (*alma de-kshot*). . . For real honor is in the establishment of the laws of the Torah in full truthfulness, and that is the fundamental basis for preserving the existence of the world, as it is stated in *Avot* 4 [6] that there is no honor but the Torah – a paraphrase of the *Avot* statement – as is said [in Proverbs 3:35] "The wise shall inherit glory: but shame shall be the promotion of fools." For the true honor is [reaching] the law of Torah in real truth. And I will rejoice in them [i.e., my "opponents"] and their Torah, and bless them with the blessing of heaven in that they save me from error and misleading others. And this is the way to cause light to dwell in the light of life.
>
> So I heard when I was a youth from the holy mouth of our great rabbi, may his memory be blessed [presumably he is referring to his maternal grandfather, R. Yosef Rafael Hazzan, author of *Hikkrei Lev*], who would say that he is not offended or angered by anyone who reads his books and disagrees with him, as I wrote in my small book *Hikekei Lev* (vol. 1, Salonika, 1800, *Yoreh Deah* sect. 40, 53c, see ibid).

Finally, I should add that I suspect that my responses will be unpersuasive to those who disagree with my arguments. Furthermore, normally I do not engage in polemic argumentation. For as the Hazon Ish wrote (in his *Igrot ha-Hazon Ish*, part 1, p. 28):

> It is not my way to engage in argumentations. For there are many prior factors of long lineage for differences of opinion. And any evidentiary proof will not change [the opposing opinion], for all "proofs" can be interpreted in numerous ways. And consequently, my rule is not to respond.

And much the same position was already voiced by the Ramban in his introduction to his *Milhamot ha-Shem* to *Berachot* (against *R. Zerachia ha-Levi*'s *Sefer ha-Maor*), except that there he does most vigorously respond:

> And you who look into my book, do not say in your heart that all my responses to R. Zerachiah *zt"l*, are all, in my opinion, absolute victories (i.e., rebuttles) which force you to admit [i.e., accept my arguments] despite your stubbornness . . . , and do not trouble yourself to stuff through the eye of a needle [counter-arguments] to refute the necessity of [accepting] my proofs. The matter is not so, for everyone who learns our Talmud knows that there are no absolute proofs [to establish the correctness of one view over another] in a conflict of opinion, neither [can one do so] through a plethora of decisive questions, for this is not an area of wisdom in which there are absolute certainties, unlike mathematics and astronomy. . . .

Nonetheless, as stated above, he does continue to state that he feels he must respond in accordance with his own truth, and he does so in his *Sefer Milhamot ha-Shem*, "the Book of the battles of the Lord." And so the jousting will continue, and hopefully enrich halachic discourse.[2]

2. See what I wrote at length in my *The Importance of the Community Rabbi*, section entitled "An Independent Stance," and ibid., Appendix 4.

10 CONCLUDING REMARKS

FINALLY, RETURNING TO THE CENTRAL THEME OF THIS study, I would like to recall Rav Lichtenstein *zt"l*'s somewhat cryptic comments in his conversation with R. Chaim Sabato (*Mevakshei Panecha*, Tel-Aviv, 2011, p. 177):

> I do not know what the leading adjudicators (*poskei ha-dor*) will rule in thirty years time on the question of the authority of women, and such like. I do not care to foretell the future. I am not altogether convinced, as are many women . . . to what extent women will be granted formal authority. The view of the Rambam, based on the Sifrei, on the issue of women's formal appointments, is well-known. But there are *poskim* who were not put off by it – what will be in the future I do not know. But what I do know is that nowadays it is important that the daughters of Israel learn Torah, and cleave unto the Torah.[1] Concerning all

1. This is, of course, in direct antithesis to R. Mordechai Willig's recent statement in his *shiur* to *Parshat Ekev*, August 2015. There he writes, inter alia,

> . . . although there are ample reliable sources that encourage individual women who have proper *yiras Shamayim* and whose motives [are] to further their Torah study, the inclusion of Talmud in curricula for all women in modern orthodox schools needs to be reevaluated. . . .

(See the full *shiur*.) His position, as expressed in this *shiur*, ignited considerable criticism, but also led to a lively discussion revealing different attitudes to women's Torah education, a subject of controversy over the last two thousand

> the rest I do not know. "What is your place in the secrets of the all-Merciful One" (*be-hanei kavshei de-Rachmana*)!

This is a highly ambivalent statement. On the one hand he admits the possibility of women's positions of authority, despite the Rambam's ruling. On the other hand, he is hesitant as to *the extent* of such areas of authority. His nuanced view reflects his caution in foretelling future developments, while not negating their possibility or even their legitimacy. Indeed, whether in thirty years hence, or even in a decade hence, *poskei ha-dor* will endorse women's positions of authority is indeed uncertain. But, without being a futurist, I for my part am certain that there will be such women, and that they will play an ever increasing role in shaping the future of modern orthodoxy.

Most recently, on October 30, 2015, RCA publicized a Resolution on "Policy Concerning Women Rabbis." In this resolution we read the following:

> And whereas on May 7, 2013, the RCA announced in the light of the recent announcement that Yeshivat Maharat will celebrate the "ordination as clergy" of its first three graduates, and in response to the institution's claims that it "is changing the communal landscape by actualizing the potential of Orthodox women as rabbinic leaders," the Rabbinical Council of America reasserts its position as articulated in its resolution of April 27, 2010 . . . The RCA views this event as a violation of our *mesorah* (tradition) and regrets that the leadership of the school has chosen a path that contradicts the norms of our community.

---

years, which merits a careful study in its own right. See, e.g., E.G. Ellinson, *Ha Ishah ve-ha Mitzvot: Yalkut Horaot Hachameinu u-Piskei Halachah*, vol. 1, second edition, Jerusalem, 1977, pp. 143–170; Nathan Drazin, *History of Jewish Education from 515 B.C.E. to 220 C.E.*, Baltimore, 1940, pp. 119–133; and see throughout the five volumes of Shmuel Glick's revised edition of Simchah Assaf's *Mekorot le-Toldot ha-Hinuch be-Yisrael*, New York and Jerusalem, 2012, indices svv. *Ishah*, p. 433b; *Banot*, p. 435a.

> Therefore, the Rabbinical Council of America resolves to educate and inform our community that RCA members with positions in Orthodox institutions may not
> 1. Ordain women into the Orthodox rabbinate, regardless of the title used; or
> 2. Hire or ratify the hiring of a woman into a rabbinic position at an Orthodox institution; or
> 3. Allow a title implying rabbinic ordination to be used by a teacher of *Limudei Kodesh* in an Orthodox institution . . . etc.

This far more radical statement was proclaimed by representatives of the Orthodox community in America. Clearly this latter statement grossly misrepresents the position of what they term "Open Orthodoxy," For the conference of "rabbinic ordination . . . to their graduates" can hardly be termed a rejection of "the basic tenets of our faith, particularly the authority of the Torah and its Sages."

We have tried to show throughout this study that this conference of rabbinic ordination is indeed sanctioned by our sources, and by a number of prominent rabbinic authorities, and in no way does it run counter to any "basic tenets of our faith." It is true that it does not have recognition of those who have declared themselves as the "Gedolei Hatorah of America," but they certainly do not have a monopoly on the exclusive interpretation of those "basic tenets of our faith."

As to the RCA's statement, it has little real halachic substance. There is no real definition of "the norms of our community," neither as to "the norms" nor as to what constitute "our community." Within the RCA itself there was considerable disagreement as to the statement; it was considered inappropriate by its President, R. Shalom Baum (personal communication, April 2010). Indeed the vote was closely contested.

However, one issue should again be discussed and confronted, and that is the recurring use of the argument on *mesorah* (tradition). This suggests that one may not innovate or change existing practices or update and accommodate changing norms, thus creating a new contemporary *mesorah*. To this I should like to reply as follows:

In the past I have written extensively seeking to demonstrate that what nowadays appears to be mandatory practice (*din*) is actually custom (*minhag*)[2] resulting out of a number of different causes, such as a cautionary phrase in Talmudic literature, a questionable statement in the Rambam,[3] as well as a particular formulation in our liturgy, etc. These practices of a negative nature – *not* to permit women to have *aliyot* to the Torah, *disallowing* women to have positions of halachic authority, not having *birkat Kohanim* every day[4] and so forth – are, in many cases having serious deleterious effects, alienating significant sectors of the community from Orthodox Judaism, or detracting from the spiritual experience in the synagogue. Consequently, I suggested that certain changes should be initiated, changes that would benefit the community and can be legitimated in terms of main-stream normative *halachah*.

The standard critical response to such an argument is that any such changes would constitute a breach of tradition, and not just tradition, but "time-hallowed" tradition. Thus any such act would erode the ramparts of our legal system (*homat ha-dat*).

I should like to counter this particular criticism by quoting extensively (with my own annotations) an illuminating passage in R. Ovadiah Yosef's *Hazon Ovadiah*: *Sukkot*, Jerusalem, 2005, pp. 384–385. And although it deals primarily with a question of liturgical change, its implications are of a much broader nature.

He begins by relating that R. Hayyim Palache, in his response *Lev Hayyim*, Salonica-Izmir, 1823 (sect. 9, fol. 6b) tells us a story how in 1801 R. Raphael Yitzhak Mayo, author of *Shorshei ha-*

2. See my discussion in my study in *Women and Men in Communal Prayer: Halakhic Perspectives*, ed. C. Trachtman, Jersey City, N.J., 2010, pp. 39–52.

3. See my essay in *Meorot* 8, 2010, pp. 1–12, entitled "On Women in Rabbinic Leadership Positions."

4. See *Conversations* 20, 2014, pp. 150–155.

Yam (Salonica, 1806–1815), on the first day of *Sukkot* came to the synagogue and asked all his congregants if they would agree to a certain change he wished to institute in the order of service. For hitherto the *hakafot* on *Sukkot* had been after *musaf*, and now as he wished to have them after *hallel*. See *Hazon Ovadiah*, ibid., p. 384.

His request, he argued, was in accordance with the custom in Jerusalem, as recorded in R. Moshe Galanti's *Korban Hagigah*, Venice, 1706 (sect. 86, fol. 46a).[5] All the congregants agreed, stating that "that which our master requests we will do," that is to say all except for one individual, a rich (*gvir*) and wise gentleman, Mr. Yaakov Davidi, who stood up before the Rabbi and would not allow him to change the custom. He made the case that "this was the custom of our forefathers of old, who obviously did so with good reason, even if now we do not know that reasoning and justification." When R. Mayo saw that there was a single person who objected, he recanted from his earlier suggestion, and to this day the custom remains to have these *hakafot* after *musaf*. Rabbi Palache continues that several years later he found a source supporting this practice of *hakafot* on Sukkot after *Hallel* in two versions found in the *Zohar*, as he wrote in his *Ruah Hayyim* (Izmir, 1877–1881, sect. 660), and more extensively in his response *Lev Hayyim*, vol. 2, Salonica-Ismir, 1823–1869, *Orah Hayyim*, sect. 127, fol. 93b; and *Hikekei Lev* (Salonica, 1840–1849, *Orah Hayyim*, sect. 6; and, furthermore that this was the custom in Salonica, as we know from a responsum in *Beit David* (by R. Yosef Filosof, Salonica, 1700–1707, sect. 459).

This then is what R. Hayyim Palache related. And at this point R. Ovadiah [in square brackets] remarks as follows:

> In my opinion, that rich individual acted in an unacceptable manner in opposing the Rabbi of the community, R. Rephael

---

5. See on this subject in great detail, A. Yaari, *Toldot Hag Simhat Torah*, Jerusalem, 1964, pp. 276–287.

> Yitzhak Mayo, who was renowned throughout for his greatness in Torah. Furthermore, he had opposed the will of the whole community. Such behavior is inadmissable. For already Maharicash (that is R. Yaakov Castro), in his *Oholei Yaakov* (*Yoreh Deah*, Livorno, 1783, sect. 242), wrote that if the *Hacham* wishes to institute a change in a certain custom, there is in this no slight upon the earlier authorities (*pegam la-rishonim*) for a space was left for him to exercise his own judgement (*le-hitgader bo, B. Hulin* 7a). Furthermore, I have already shown in my *Yabia Omer*, fol.10, Jerusalem, 2004, *Orah Hayyim*, sect. 21:8 et seq., pp. 32–33), that a number of Torah giants (*Gedolim*) made changes in their communities in the order of the service and also in a number of other customs, instituting practices that were, in their opinion, more correct, and no one raised any objection.

R. Ovadiah continues:

> And so too wrote R. Yosef Ergas [1685–1730], in his *Divrei Yosef*, Livorno, 1742, sect. 5 ad fin, that "any custom that does not appear to be right in the eyes of the decisors, (*poskim*), should be abolished, and a more fitting custom should be established to replace it. And one should not lean one's support on the broken cane of those who say that one may not change a custom, even if it is not fine and suitable, for such an argument has not substance, and we have not found a single authority who claims that one may not alter the prayer customs, for so wrote the Maharashdam [that is R. Shemuel di Medinah, Salonica, 1594],[6] cautioning that we should do so without triggering a

6. See response no. 34, to *Orah Hayyim*, eds. D. Avidan and S. Deutsch, Jerusalem, 2010, pp. 47–49. On the Maharashdam, see now Y.S. Spiegel's excellent introduction and historical survey on this great authority, in the last volume of *Shut Maharashdam la-Hadashot*, Jerusalem, 2015, pp. 1–80.

On p. 21, Spiegel writes as follows:

> One should bear in mind that *Maharashdam* functioned shortly after the expulsion from Spain. As a result of that expulsion there were formed

conflict." [The above is a paraphrase of Ergas' statement. D.S.] And also R. Shalom Shulal, in his *Neveh Shalom* [Livorno, 1804, sect. 582, fol. 53b], was amazed at those who said one may not change a custom, for who was greater than R. Hai Gaon who changed the custom of the *haftarah* on *Simhat Torah* and instituted to read the beginning of the Book of *Joshuah*. . . .[7]

---

complex congregations of locals and "expellees," resulting in arguments as to which customs are mandated for those congregations, those of the locals, or those of the Spanish "expellees." Consequently we find in his responsa discussions of questions touching up the status of *minhag*-custom, such as which version of the liturgy is obligatory . . . , and other questions dependent on variations in *minhag*. Note that R. Yosef Even Ezra, *Maharshadam*'s disciple, was the first to write a comprehensive work on the subject of customs, that is *Masa Melech*, Salonica, 1601. And it could appear that he wrote it precisely because it was in that generation that these issues arose.

Concerning changes in the variant of the liturgy, he refers us to that responsum in *Orah Hayyim* no. 34 [47a] which he noted above.

On his sensitivity to the needs and troubles of individuals and the community, see Spiegel, ibid., pp. 43–44.

On the situation of the "mixed congregations in the post-expulsion period, see Y.D. Gilat, on "*Lo titgodedu*," in *Bar-Ilan* 18–19, 1981, pp. 79–98, and what I wrote in *Minhagei Yisrael*, vol. 3, Jerusalem, 1994, pp. 108–112.

A somewhat similar situation may be found in early Kairawan, where Italian immigrants brought liturgical practices, which clashed with the local ones. See Menahem Ben-Sasson, *The Emergence of the Local Jewish Community in the Muslim World: Qayrawan 800–1057*, Jerusalem, 1997, p. 174 [Hebrew]. Many additional examples could be cited, but this is beyond the scope of this study.

7. The *Gemara* in *B. Megillah* 31a states that the *haftarah* should be from *1 Kings* 8. But *Tosafot* ad loc. stated that there are places where their *haftarah* is from *Joshuah* 1, and they attribute this tradition to R. Hai Gaon, but they do not know why he changed it from the Talmudic *haftarah*. *Sefer ha-Eshkol*, by R. Yitzhak Av Beit Din of Narbonne, ed. B.H. Auerbach, Halberstadt ,1867, part 2, p. 65, brought both customs, adding that the Joshua custom is based on the *Yerushalmi* (a source unknown to us, see editor's note 9), explaining that this is a natural continuation after Moses' death. Similarly the *Rosh* (*Megillah* ad fin.) in the name of the *Yerushalmi*. Likewise, the *Raviah*, R. Eliezer be R. Yoel ha-Levi (1140–1215) *Sukkah*, vol. 2, ed. A. Aptowitzer, 2nd edition, Jerusalem, 1964, sect. 595, p. 329, in the name of the *Yerushalmi* (and see editor's note 4), and *Baal Halachot Gedolot: Aspania*, ed. J. Hildesheimer, Berlin, 1888, p. 620. See B.M. Lewin, *Otzar ha-Gaonim* to *Megillah*, vol. 5,

> So too the Rivash, R. Yitzhak ben Sheshet [1326–1407] in his responsum, Constantinople, 1547, sect. 37,[8] wrote that he changed the custom in Saragossa to pray the silent prayer and its repetition in the *musaf* of Rosh ha-Shanah [even though apparently it was difficult for some members of his community, D.S.]. And so too, the author of *Knesset ha-Gedollah* [R. Hayyim Benveneshte, Livorno, 1648 (*Orah Hayyim*) sect. 282] and his *Shiyarei Knesset ha-Gedolah* (sect. 284 and 566), etc. And he too found support in the words of R. Ergas ibid. See further, R. Hayyim Palache's *Moed le-Chol Hai* [Izmir, 1861, sect. 25, no. 36]. Furthermore, Ergas' *Divrei Yosef* [sect 4 ad fin] cited R. Yosef Halevy who, though he gave great importance to the status of *minhagim*, nonetheless wrote that one may change them, and that there is no reason to fear controversy when the majority of the congregation is agreeable to the change; and in changing customs we do not pay attention to the minority (*lo haishinan le-miuta*), as is clear from the responsum of the Maharshdam.

R. Ovadiah summarizes as follows:

> In view of the above it is clear that Rabbi Mayo could have changed the custom, since the majority of the community were agreeable and were fully in consent, and stated explicitly that "everything that our master says we will do." Consequently, he

---

Jerusalem, 1933, p. 63. See further, *Sefer ha-Rokeah*, by R. Eleazar of Wermaiza (Worms, c.1140–1225), ed. S. Schneursohn, Jerusalem, 1967, sect. 224, p. 127; *Mahzor Vitri,* by R. Simhah of Vitri (12 cent.), ed. S. Halevi Horowitz, Berlin, 1888–1895, sect. 418, p. 458 [ed. A. Goldschmidt, vol. 3, Jerusalem, 2009, p. 945 (see editor's note 11, with numerous references)]; *Siddur Rashi,* eds. S. Buber and Freimann, Berlin, 1911, sect. 308, p. 149, citing R. Yehudai Gaon from *Halachot Gedolot: Seder Rav Amram Gaon*, ed. A.V. Frumkin, Jerusalem, 1912, vol. 2, p. 385. All of the above are cited by R. Ovadiah Yosef, ibid., p. 471, to which may be added the references cited by Goldsmidt, ibid. See further, A. Yaari, ibid., pp. 21, 55–56.

8. Ed. David Metzger, vol. 1, Jerusalem, 1993, pp. 41–42.

> had no reason to pay attention to the objection of the *gvir* . . . , but presumably he did so because of his extreme humbleness deciding to be passive and let things be as they were.

Now, I am well aware that this is by no means a simple issue, and there has been a great deal of literature on the subject. There is obviously an inherent psychological block against change in general, and against alterations in custom in particular. And this is understandably fortified and buttressed by a variety of arguments, such as fear of breaching the *homat ha-dat* (the ramparts of our religion), "the slippery slope," the care not to slight our forbearers (referred to above),[9] etc. Hence, inertia and passivity – *shev ve-al taaseh* – is seen as a preferable position. The result is that great care is strenuously taken to prevent any kind of change in our "time-hallowed" traditional practices. This position has been extensively discussed in numerous publications, as mentioned above.[10] In point of fact, customs are always changing, as is so clearly demonstrated by R. Yaakov Hayyim Sofer himself, in *Menuhat Shalom* sect. 2, pp. 26–31, where he brings a wealth of examples from numerous communities, such as Jerusalem, Safed, Hevron, Constantinople, Izmir, Egypt, Salonica, and so forth; and to this list may be added numerous others.

R. Ovadiah (in *Yabia Omer*, vol. 8, *Yoreh Deah* 28:2, p. 341), basing himself on Ergas ibid. sects. 1 and 5 summarizes his position on this issue as follows:

---

9. See Eliav Schochetman's excellent article on this subject in *Bar-Ilan* 18/19, 1985, pp.170–195.

10. And just to give the merest sampling I would call attention to the studies of the contemporary R. Yaakov Hayyim Sofer, in his *Sefer Menuhat Shalom* 7–8, Jerusalem, 2002, pass., and his *Maamar Yaakov* (on R. Avraham Palache's *Padeh et Avraham*, Izmir, 1899), Jerusalem, 2002. Prof. Eliav Schochetman, "*Aliyot Nashim la-Torah*", apud *Kovetz ha-Rambam*, ed. Yosef Eliyahu Movshovitz, Jerusalem, 2005, pp. 324–338, etc. See further the numerous discussions of R. Ovadiah Yosef in his volumes of *Yabia Omer*. See index volume (vol. 11) p. 330 s.v. *shinui minhag*.

> To change a custom in order to make a better one is permitted.[11]

So I suppose, when all is said and done, the ultimate question is what constitutes "improvement" in *minhagim*, and what are the

---

11. Of course, the legitimate right of a rabbinic authority to change or even annul earlier rulings, and even long-standing ordinances is mentioned frequently in early rabbinic sources. See, for instance, *B. Shabbat* 46b and *B. Hulin* 66b on Josiah's destruction of the brazen serpent dating to the time of Moses, and the justificatory phrase: "space was left to us by our forefathers giving us a measure of freedom (*le-hitga[n]der bo*)." And R. Yehudah ha-Nasi annulled a number of earlier ordinances; see, e.g., *Y. Rosh ha-Shanah* 2:1 cf. *Mishnah*, ibid., 4:2; *Y. Demai* 2:1; he even wished to abolish *Tisha be-Av*, but was unsuccessful in this matter, see *B. Megillah* 5b. And see also *Y. Sheviit* 1:1, for R. Gamliel's annulment of the additional two periods of *Sheviit*. (This was R. Gamliel's son of R. Yehudah ha-Nasi). There are numerous additional examples, which go beyond the scope of this study. See on this subject Y. Schepanski, *Ha-Takkanot be-Yisrael*, vol. 1, Jerusalem and New York, 1991, introduction, chapter 5, pp. 74–87, and pp. 378–380, 382–390, 413–414; M. Alon, *Ha-Mishpat ha-Ivri: Toldotav, Mekorotav, Ekronotav*, Jerusalem, 1973, pp. 419–421, 442–446, 527, 538 et seq., 544 et seq., 546, 552, 554, 562, 567, 594, 596–597, 616–619, 622–624, 634, 649, 651, etc. There is a very considerable body of literature on this subject. Here we have merely given points of departure for further study.

See further Rambam, *Hilchot Mumrim* 2:5, who, when discussing the principle found in *M. Megillah* 2a et alia, that a *beit din* cannot annul the rulings of an earlier *beit din* unless they are greater than them "in wisdom and number," circumscribes this statement as follows:

> If they ruled, assuming that their ruling was accepted by all Israel, and their ruling continued to be accepted for many years, and after a long period of time another *beit din* examined the situation and found that that ruling now was not accepted by all Israel, that *beit din* has the right to annul it, and even if they are of lesser status than the earlier one in wisdom and number.

The Rambam's limitation of the Talmudic principle was widely accepted by later authorities, and in practice many earlier *takkanot* and *haramot* were later annulled. See, in detail, R. Ovadiah Yosef, in *Yabia Omer*, vol. 7, Jerusalem, 1993, *Yoreh Deah* 14:3, pp. 233–234 (and also cf. ibid., vol. 3, Jerusalem, 1986, *Hoshen Mishpat* 7:4, p. 346). If this be the case for *takkanot* and *gezerot*, how much more so for *minhagim*.

Incidentally, the reason I quote R. Ovadiah so often, and less other *Aharonim*, is simply because his encyclopaedic responses cover almost all the relevant literature, both early and contemporary.

criteria for such "improvement." Does each community decide for itself in consultation with its rabbinical leadership, and follow the consensus, as would appear from the above sources? And if so, what are the parameters, the constrictions and the "fail-safes" to prevent the slide into the treacherous "slippery slope"? Undoubtedly wise counsel is required in all such determinations.[12] But what remain clears is that there exists the possibility of legitimate areas of change and evolution, to accommodate changing situations, and there is no clear monopolistic establishment that can halt the march of halachic progress.

12. See, for example, what I wrote in *JOFA Journal* IV/4, 2007, pp. 7–9, in an article entitled "The Human Element in the Commandments: The Effect of Changing Community Norms or Halachic Decisions." There, I discussed how the Talmudic prohibition of a man's walking behind a woman was gradually annulled in view of changing notions of *tzeniut* – modesty. See R. Yehuda Henkin's important book, *Understanding Tzniut: Modern Controversies in the Jewish Community*, Jerusalem and New York, 2008, especially pp. 73 et seq. But here again, the examples that one could bring are legion.

Introduction to the Afterword

This book, which deals with certain aspects of the halachic status of women, has been written by a male, and with all its sympathy for women's issues, it still reflects a male-oriented perspective. It is, therefore, much to my satisfaction, and, indeed, gratitude, that Rabbanit Dr. Michal Tikochinsky very generously agreed to write an "Afterword," which will give a feminine viewpoint vis-à-vis halachah. Through close analysis of some representative case studies, she seeks, and indeed demonstrates, how to turn our attention to the ways in which a woman decisor might approach these halachic issues. In her summarizing conclusions, she makes a clear plea to the rabbinic world that the female voice be heard. Her essay is, therefore, a most suitable addition to this study, supplementing it with yet another level direction of halachic inquiry, and thus broadening the horizon of our rabbinic endeavor.

Daniel Sperber

AFTERWORD: WOMEN IN POSITIONS OF HALACHIC LEADERSHIP

by Rabbanit Dr. Michal Tikochinsky

Translated by Rabbi Shalom Z. Berger, Ed.D.

In recent years, there has been an increase in high-level programs teaching Jewish law to women, both in Israel and throughout the world. As these programs are held under the auspices of different institutions, there are differences to be found among them. Some of these programs have relatively modest requirements, while in others, the requirements are quite expansive. In some, the syllabus encompasses a wide range of halachic disciplines, while others limit themselves to specific areas of study. Some of the programs conclude with a *semichah* ordination, while others conclude by granting alternative certificates or degrees. In terms of curriculum of study, the focus is usually on materials that parallel topics generally covered in the men's *Rabbanut Semichah* ordination.

But if we ignore for a moment the unique features and different declared goals of these programs, a common denominator among them emerges: All of the programs only prepare a woman for *Hora'ah Behalachah* – to rule on questions of Jewish law. The various *Batei Midrashot* have already produced quite a few graduates, and, in practice, those graduates all serve as *Morot Halachah* – as decisors of Jewish law.[1] They serve as an address

1. *Morot Halachah* was the title granted to the graduates of the program

for questions of *halachah*, either in a formal framework such as in a position within the community or a *beit midrash*, or, alternatively, as someone who is recognized by those around her as a learned woman who is knowledgeable and can respond to such questions. The public has also begun to recognize these women as trailblazers in these religious and spiritual realms, and they continually receive questions on a wide variety of topics in these areas. The need for this type of leadership is clear. One question that remains is whether the change that has ushered women into leadership roles is, ultimately, something beyond the simple rectification of a historical injustice. Is this merely a **quantitative change** (i.e., there are more women responding to halachic questions then there were before) or does it also indicate a **qualitative change** (the response model has changed)?

Of course, the answer to this question will only emerge in the future when a historical retrospective will be possible, but already today we can observe a fresh, new spirit that has entered into the halachic conversation. In this essay, I will try to illustrate where and how the new spirit of critical contributions of women Torah learners to the world of halachah is expressed – or how it has created a desire for such expression.

Broadening the Range of Halachic Considerations

As a result of the entry of women into the halachic discussion, we can observe a change in the range and variety of considerations taken into account in making halachic decisions. The way we analyze and view halachah completely changes on a conceptual level in light of the new perspective that women bring to the discussion. In a visionary article, Tamar Ross writes:

---

at Beit Morasha. Later on, this title was also used by Matan Ra'anana for its graduates. In this essay I am not using it as a title, but as a simple description of the accomplishments and activities of these women.

> It is likely that women entering into the halakhic discussion will contribute their unique perspective, impacting on any given topic. Taking into consideration different concerns can bring about different conclusions regarding the law.
>
> Even in situations where there is prior awareness of these concerns, women may very well make use of different principles in the assessment of the relative weight of different factors, based on a different hierarchy of values.
>
> To the extent that there is a "feminine way of thinking" in relation to the overall value system, this too can sometimes lead to a change in conclusions.[2]

In my opinion, Ross' words have been found to be accurate, and we can already see the first fruits of this paradigm. I would like to demonstrate these "new directions" by means of examples in two topics in halachah. One example is a change in the "discussion pathways" that are used in making decisions, and the other involves possible changes in the approaches and the types of factors that might be taken into account when such decisions are made.

1. *Mechitzah* in the Synagogue

One of the topics that might be affected by a fresh halachic conversation is how to define the height and width of the *mechitzah* that separates the men's and women's sections of the synagogue. The *Ezrat Nashim* (women's section) is first mentioned as one of the areas on the Temple Mount.[3] The mishnah in Tractate Kelim explains that the holiness of the *Ezrat Nashim* is less than that of the *Ezrat Yisrael*, implying that there are people who are ritually impure who may not enter the *Ezrat Yisrael*, but who

---

2. T. Ross, *Expanding the Palace of Torah: Orthodoxy and Feminism* (Tel Aviv, 2007), p. 407.

3. Mishnah Middot 2:5.

are allowed to enter the *Ezrat Nashim*.[4] The *Ezrat Nashim* is not meant to specifically serve women, just as the *Ezrat Yisrael* is not meant to specifically serve men. Women were permitted to enter into the *Ezrat Yisrael* if they purified themselves properly.[5] In *Sefer Yehezkel* this part of the Temple is called the *Hatzer Hahitzonah* – the "external courtyard" (see, for example, Ezekiel 40:7, 42:1) – and the name *Ezrat Nashim* is not even mentioned.

The separation between men and women in the Temple was primarily relevant during the *regalim* (the three annual pilgrimage holidays), at the time of the rejoicing of the masses where there was a concern for *kalut rosh* (frivolous behavior). It is likely that the name *Ezrat Nashim* was given to this area only in a later time period, in light of the use of the area to serve the women for a temporary period during the holidays.[6] Between the external courtyard and the inner courtyard there was a separation of 15 steps. In time, this separation was viewed as being insufficient, as is described in the Mishnah in *Tractate Sukkah*: "On the night after Yom Tov of the first night of the holiday, the people went down to the *Ezrat Nashim*, and they decreed a *tikun gadol* (a 'great rectification')."[7] The implication being that the decree of *Ezrat Nashim* was put in place in honor of *Hol HaMoed*.

The commentators disagree as to the nature of the "rectification." Some suggest that a raised balcony was added above the *Ezrat Nashim* since the courtyard itself served the men who were engaged in a *Simhat Beit HaShoeva* celebration. The balcony allowed the women to observe the celebration without intermingling with the men.[8] It would appear that throughout the year,

4. Tractate Kelim 1:8.

5. See *Tosafot Kiddushin* 32b, *s.v.*, *Ve-shevah*, Rambam, *Hilchot Bi'at Mikdash*. Rashi disagreed and thought that women could not come to the *Ezrat Yisrael*; see Rashi *Kiddushin*, ibid.

6. It is also possible that the main activities of women were in this courtyard so they did not enter the *Ezrat Yisrael* at all or entered only for certain purposes, as will be explained below.

7. *Mishnah Sukkah* 5:2.

8. See *Tiferet Yisrael*, Ibid.

there was no separation and no *mechitzah*. Some say there was an elevated area for the women all year long, and that it was reinforced for the holidays.[9] The *baraita* in the Talmud phrases the matter of the rectification differently. While in the mishnah it appears that they would reassemble the balcony every year afresh in honor of the holiday, in the *baraita* the implication is that the meaning of the "rectification" was a *Takanat Hachachamim* (i.e., a decree of the Sages):

> The Sages taught: Initially, women would stand on the inside of the Women's Courtyard and the men were on the outside in the courtyard and on the rampart. And they would come to conduct themselves with inappropriate levity. Therefore, the Sages instituted that the women should sit on the outside and the men on the inside, and still they would come to conduct themselves with inappropriate levity. Therefore, they instituted in the interest of complete separation that the women would sit above and the men below.[10]

From the Temple, the idea of a separate *Ezrat Nashim* was transplanted to the *Beit Knesset* (synagogue), which is called a *Mikdash Me'at* – or "Mini Temple." However, in the transition from the description of the Temple to the laws of the synagogue, in the discussion about the height of the *mechitzah* in the *Beit Knesset* – its width, thickness, and the measure of its opacity – the differences between the alternative rationales given for the rectification in the Temple are sharpened. These alternative rationales come into play when we examine the underlying purposes suggested for the *mechitzah*.[11] According to the Talmud in *Tractate Sukkah*, the problem was that before the building of the balcony in the Temple, the people would come to *kalut rosh*.

9. Rambam, *Commentary to the Mishnah, Sukkah* 5b.
10. *Sukkah* 51b.
11. *Mishnah Sukkah*, 5b; *Mishnah Midot* 2:5; *Babylonian T. Sukkah* 51b.

In his *Commentary to the Mishnah* the Rambam suggests that the purpose of erecting the balcony was so "the men would not look at the women," while in his *Mishneh Torah* the Rambam rules that the purpose of the addition was "so that they would not intermingle with each other."[12]

These opinions already appear in the *Rishonim* and coalesced into three central halachic positions. The following question was posed to the *Tzitz Eliezer*: "What amount of visibility is permitted in the *mechitzah* of the synagogue, and how high should the *mechitzah* be?" He answered as follows: "From the above-mentioned sources we learn that the appropriate opaqueness of the *mechitzah* that needs to be established, must be built thick enough that the men will not be able to gaze upon the women standing in the *Ezrat Nashim* . . . and in terms of the height of the *mechitzah*, it appears that it needs to be about as tall as a man, that is, a height of about three and a half *amot*."[13] In other words, the *Tzitz Eliezer* bases himself on the words of the Rambam in his *Commentary to the Mishnah* that we must limit the ability of men to gaze upon the women.

Therefore, the conclusion is that the *mechitzah* needs to be fully opaque and 1.75 meters (a little less than 6 feet) in height, for otherwise it would not accomplish the halachic purpose that the *Ezrat Nashim* is meant to achieve. Like the *Tzitz Eliezer*, the Satmar Rebbe and the Hungarian Rabbis held that one should create a completely opaque *mechitzah* which does not leave any place or possibility to see the women on the other side.[14]

In contrast, Rav Yechiel Yaakov Weinberg, the author of the responsa *Seridei Esh*, writes: "In the Laws of Lulav he (the Rambam) writes 'so that they would not intermingle with each other' and the truth is it was said in *Tractate Middot*, 'so that they will

---

12. *Bavli Sukkah* 51b; The Rambam's *Commentary to the Mishnah*, *Sukkah*, 5:2; Rambam, Laws of Hallel, Shofar and Lulav, Ch. 8, Halakhah 12.
13. *Shu't Tzitzit Eliezer*, 20:7
14. *Shu't Seridei Esh* 1:14.

not be mixed with each other.' For this reason, in the lands of Poland and Lithuania, we are not so stringent, for the individual stands and prays with a *siddur* and doesn't raise his eyes above. . . ."[15] Rav Weinberg also places the ruling in the context of the society and culture, arguing that we can be lenient regarding the height of the *mechitzah* and the concealment it provides, because, in his opinion, today there is no concern for "sinful thoughts" from seeing women at the time of prayer. Therefore, Rav Weinberg only stresses the factor of separation: "So they will not intermingle." At the moment that prayer is not taking place in an intermingled manner, the *mechitzah* has achieved its purpose. Logically, if we take this position into account, it should be sufficient to put up a *mechitzah* that separates the women's and men's sections in synagogues, and there is no need for the *mechitzah* to be tall or thick and opaque.

Rav Moshe Feinstein in *Shu't Igrot Moshe* takes a middle path. He writes that the central purpose of the *mechitzah* is to prevent the possibility of conversation between men and women, and not just intermingling. Therefore, it is sufficient to place a *mechitzah* at shoulder height, which is approximately 18 *tefahim*.[16] It appears to me that those who follow Rav Feinstein's ruling should be able to find architectural solutions that will prevent the possibility of conversation without unnecessarily tall or opaque separations, by establishing distance between the different areas of the synagogue or by other means.

This brief overview of the halachic rulings on this matter makes clear that generally speaking the discussions about the need for *mechitzah* are presented from the male perspective. The concerns center on questions related to gazing upon and thinking about women, and the question is what will lead to *kalut rosh* in the synagogue. At no point is the question asked: "How do we ensure that women feel like they are a part of the prayer service,

15. See the summary of the *Shu't Seridei Esh*, 2:1.
16. *Shu't Igrot Moshe*, *Orach Chaim* 1:39.

and what type of *mechitzah* will best achieve this need?" This is the case despite the fact that the Mishnah in *Tractate Midot* points out regarding the *azarah* (Temple courtyard): "The Wall around the Women's Courtyard was originally smooth (with no protrusions from it) but later a balcony was built around it, so that women could **see** from above . . ."[17] It is true that the Mishnah also mentions the problem of intermingling, but it appears that if the balance appearing in the words of the Mishnah were echoed in the rulings of the *poskim*, we would have found a more balanced approach in the discussion of the way to place a *mechitzah* in the synagogue.

The consideration that goes unmentioned in the discussion is when and in which situations should women be able to see what is taking place in the synagogue. Even worse, the most fundamental question is not asked. Are women considered to be part of the *tzibbur* (congregation)? What obligations derive from this, related, for example, to the architectural structure of the synagogue?[18] Is it important to arrange that the women can see the *Aron Kodesh* when it is opened? The *Sefer Torah* when it is read or when it is raised up?

The question of whether women are part of the *tzibbur* brings with it additional ramifications regarding the laws of prayer and the synagogue, and for this reason this discussion is particularly critical. Notwithstanding, it has not taken place to date. The only discussion relates to how women are excluded, i.e., that women are not counted as part of a *minyan* (prayer quorum).

---

17. *Mishnah Midot* 2:5.

18. I have broached the fundamental question regarding the defining of women as part of the *tzibbur* in an article that has not yet been published. See my article: "Women Within the Congregation," in press.

2. Immersion of Women for Conversion in the Presence of a *Beit Din*

Another example that should be discussed is the topic of the immersion of women undergoing conversion before a *beit din* (a rabbinical court). The accepted halachah is that converts, as a part of the conversion process, must immerse in a *mikvah* before members of the *beit din* to complete the process of conversion. This immersion is an essential part of the conversion process for both men and women who seek to convert.[19]

Historically, objections have been raised in many places to having male rabbinic court judges enter into the area of the *mikvah* while women immerse. These objections appeared mainly because the *mikvah* was situated in a public bathhouse that was used by both Jews and Gentiles, and it was impossible to remove all other women from the bathhouse. This led to the recognition that nonideal solutions had to be found. Thus, Rav Ben-Zion Meir Hai Uziel wrote, when he was asked about such a situation that took place in Salonika:

> And when we walk into a bathhouse where there are other women who bathe, or are even getting dressed, this matter cannot be avoided without intention. This has led to a situation that it is impossible to arrange for a female convert to immerse in the *mikvah* in the presence of the members of the *beit din*.[20]

Rav Shmuel Salant was asked about a similar situation and wrote that when men are unable to enter into the bathhouses, "the rabbis should wait on the outside and women should enter inside . . . ."[21] Rav Ovadia Yosef encountered the opposite situation.

---

19. See for example Rambam, *Hilchot Issurei Bi'ah* 13:6.

20. *Shu't Mishpetei Uziel*, Y.D. Part 1, Siman 13.

21. Sefer Torat Rabbeinu Shmuel Salant, published by Rabbi Nissan Aharon Tikochinsky, Jerusalem, 5758, vol. 1, *Orach Chaim*, *Yoreh De'ah*, Section 29, p. 175.

When he came to Egypt, he discovered that the rabbinical court judges were not accustomed to enter to see the immersion of the female converts, following the ruling of his predecessor, the author of *Nehar Mitzrayim*. Rav Ovadia tried to effect a change and ruled that judges must view the immersion. As part of the considerations for his ruling he wrote:

> Behold, although there were some modern men who believed themselves to be wise, who objected to this in a forceful manner, arguing that it is not appropriate for members of *beit din* to enter into the women's bathhouse at all at a time when a woman is in the *mikvah*. Only a shameless doctor would be permitted to examine women while they are naked, in the event that they are suffering from pain or the like, and modest Torah scholars may not do so. This is the Torah of the moderns, which is the opposite of our holy Torah which distinguishes in the law of *yihud* in an opposite fashion, between *kesherim* (upright men) and *perutzim* (promiscuous men). . . .[22]

After Rav Ovadia argued that the halachah does not concede to modern thinking and the belief (in his opinion, misguided) that only doctors are permitted to see unclothed women and that it is forbidden for Torah scholars to do so, he added another factor to solidify his position that rabbinic court judges must be present at the convert's immersion:

> And all the more so today, since our generation has diminished and most of the women coming to convert do not come with pure intentions, but only for the sake of marriage . . . But to add on more lenient rulings, like immersing when not in the presence of *beit din* so that we should not close the door before converts?! God-forbid to say such a thing! On the contrary – let the door be closed before them!!

---

22. *Shu't Yabia Omer*, Helek Aleph, *Yoreh De'ah* 19.

This additional factor posits that there may be an advantage if women refuse to convert because of the halachah that restricts them – the advantage limiting the number of converts, who may not all be truly acting with pure intentions and may not truly be accepting upon themselves the "complete yoke of mitzvot." In a very explicit and direct manner, Rav Ovadia refused to pay attention to the feminine perspective, denying its existence entirely. In contrast to these two perspectives – that of Rav Ovadia's rejection and that of Rav Uziel's acceptance, based on reasons of respect for a *beit din*, and for lack of choice – the feminine perspective was brought to the front line of the discussion in an article that I wrote more than a decade ago:

> The modesty of women who desire to become part of the Jewish nation is a very important matter which we should not discount, even when it stands in contrast with other values connected with this matter. These poor women who stand in line and wait with bated breath to be accepted into the Jewish nation – who will defend them? Who will hear their voices? We must be very careful to avoid trampling on the honor of a woman whose only desire is to be a daughter of the Jewish people and to join them under the wings of the Divine Presence.[23]

Until the current generation, a feminine perspective had never been brought into the discussion of the laws of conversion. Such a perspective requires further examination of the sources and new thought as to the question of whether weight should be given to this factor in halachic rulings. In my article, I pointed out that this perspective could find support in earlier sources. One example is the source that appears in *Tractate Gerim* that establishes that a

23. See M. Tikochinsky, "And the Woman Immerses a Woman – Towards the Question of the Immersion of Women for Conversion before *Beit Din*" [Hebrew], *Akdamot* 21 (2008), pp. 65–82. For more information, see ibid.

"woman immerses the woman, but not the man."[24] Also noted are the words of the *baraita*, which distinguishes between the immersion of a man and the immersion of a woman: "And as for a woman; women place her in water until her neck, while two Torah-scholars stand outside. . . ."[25]

At the time, my article was groundbreaking and the first to raise a new interpretive possibility that relied on these and additional primary sources, bringing about a new discussion on this topic from a contemporary perspective in which the feminist stance is presented in a straightforward, well-grounded manner. The article inspired a broad, public discussion of the halachah, and to this day it is found on the tables of policymakers. It is important to note that the halachic discussion takes place using accepted mechanics of halachah, in the same manner that primary sources have been analyzed throughout the generations. The article does not attempt to erase sources or object to their existence; rather, it aims to conduct the discussion within the framework of the sources, as has been done from generation to generation when a need has arisen for a new halachic direction. In this sense, all that was necessary was the emergence of a woman with the ability to express the practical needs of women in our time, making use of traditional halachic tools.[26]

Highlighting the Problem of Inconsistency in *Psak* Regarding Women's Issues

The entry of women into the world of halachic rulings offers an additional contribution, as a result of which perhaps *a priori*

24. *Tractate Gerim* 1:4.

25. *Bavli Yevamot* 47b.

26. For a reading of additional references on the subject, see: S. Dikovsky, "Conversion of a *giyoret* before the *beit din*" [Hebrew], *Tchumin* 35 (2017), p. 199; D. Bass, "The obligation of the immersion before a *bet din* of a convert," *Drishah* 3 (2018); pp. 79–108; Rabbi Jeffrey S. Fox: https://www.yeshivatmaharat.org/teshuvot-text2

positions underlying rulings of some *poskim* will be corrected. These positions have led to inconsistencies in the application of the various considerations in halachic rulings regarding women. It appears that at times, different standards are applied when a given ruling relates to women, standards that do not appear to be required by the standards of halachah. Application of a feminine perspective has the ability to restore the crown of Torah to its former glory and to clarify the halachah.

Two examples will be brought here to illustrate the matter.

An issue that recently appeared in the Israeli media and ultimately was decided by the Israeli Supreme Court was the demand of women to immerse themselves without the supervision of a *balanit* (a female *mikvah* attendant). Women demanded autonomy and protection of their rights to privacy and the Supreme Court upheld this right, after the Chief Rabbinate had ruled otherwise, proclaiming that a woman who immerses on her own without the supervision of a *balanit* is not considered to have immersed.[27] To express the severity of their disagreement, in their response, the Rabbinate equated someone who immersed in a *mikvah* without the supervision of a *balanit* to someone who goes for a dip in a swimming pool. An examination of the matter reveals that in official *mikva'ot* the prevalent practice is that the *balanit* is responsible for the *mikvah* and its operation, and that her role includes standing above the woman who immerses in order to confirm that the immersion was done properly. Many women report that they encounter difficulties due to the presence of a *balanit* during immersion. The desire to immerse oneself in privacy may be due to several factors. These are intimate and personal moments; some women express a sense of contradiction between their spiritual understanding of the immersion and a

27. https://www.srugim.co.il/151974-%D7%94%D7%A8%D7%91%D7%A0%D7%95%D7%AA/ Also see Joshua Van Dyke, "The presence of a woman supervisor at the time of the immersion of a woman from her *niddah*" [Hebrew], *Tchumin* 37 (2017), pp. 202–208.

formal ritual that feels foreign to them. More than a few women are uncomfortable due to past traumas, vulnerabilities and the distress that some suffer from low body image and sensitivity to any external gazing upon them.[28]

A fundamental principle in the laws of *niddah* is the rule that is derived from the verse: And she shall count for her (Leviticus 15:28) - "for her – for herself."[29] This rabbinic interpretation also serves as a stepping stone for the principle of the women's *ne'emanut* (halachic trustworthiness) relating to other areas of prohibition.[30] According to some, this is the basis for the general rule that "one witness is trustworthy regarding matters of prohibitions."[31] By all accounts, a woman is considered trustworthy regarding the laws of *niddah* in a broad and comprehensive manner. This means that the responsibility for purity rests on her shoulders, and she does not need any outside supervision in the process of purification or for the granting of validity to it. Thus, the Rashba wrote regarding menstrual stains:

> A woman who found a stain on a cloth but then misplaced it, who then testified: "it was similar in color to this shade of green or white – I saw it but then I lost it," will be trusted . . . for the

---

28. For more information on this issue, see also M. Tikochinsky, "The Waters of Life: The Question of Immersion of Women with Disabilities" [Hebrew], *Responsa* 4 (Av 5774). The Israel Democracy Institute (2014), available on the Israel Democracy Institute website.

29. *Bavli Ketubot* 72a.

30. With regard to the expansion of the woman's trustworthiness to other spheres, see *Ketubot* 30a–b, and *Tosafot Gittin* 2b s.v. *Ed Echad*. In principle, the Ritva rules that women were considered trustworthy only regarding *niddah*. R. David rules that women are as trustworthy as men. *Tosafot* rule that women are trustworthy in matters in which they have the ability to change the status, as in the laws of *niddah*. In the opinion of the *Shitah Mekubetzet*, she is believed in routine matters.

31. See my article, M. Tikochinsky, "One witness is trusted regarding prohibitions" [Hebrew], *Granot* 3 (2002), pp. 41–57.

> Torah establishes her trustworthiness, as is written, "And she shall count."[32]

A woman's trustworthiness is only undermined when her testimony and her words are contradictory. This can be deduced from the Talmud's puzzlement in *Tractate Ketubot* on the Mishnah that teaches that a woman who engages in sexual relations with her husband when she is a *niddah,* transgresses *dat Moshe* (lit., the precepts of Moshe, i.e., the traditions of Israel) and is divorced without receiving her *ketubah*. The Gemara asks: "If he knows that she is a menstruating woman, he should abstain. And if he does not know, then he should rely on her." The Gemara assumes that the basic trustworthiness of a woman negates the possibility of suspicion that she is engaging in sexual relations when she is a *niddah*.[33] Her trustworthiness is undermined here only when she makes her actions dependent on a sage by saying: "This sage purified the blood for me."[34] In such a case, if in a clear inquiry with the sage it was revealed that her claim was a lie, her words are determined to be contradictory and unreliable.[35]

Another case in which the woman is not trusted is when her testimony contradicts our factual findings, as found in the Rashba who rules, "With one who errs with comparisons we also do not rely upon her." The Rashba is discussing a case in the Gemara

---

32. *Torat haBayit haArokh*, Bayit 7:1.

33. *Bavli Ketubot* 72a.

34. On the other hand, if her husband sees blood on her clothes and the woman says, "I passed through the butcher's market," she is believed. Hence there is evidence that not every *reyuta* (questionable fact) detracts from her trustworthiness, but only a *reyuta* that arises precisely because she is trustworthy, and because she is trustworthy there is contradiction in her words. Or, if it is clear that she is lying, then she cannot be trusted. See Rosh, *Ketubot* 87: 9. Similarly, *Taz, Yoreh De'ah* 185:3, s.v. *haHakham ne'eman*. He believes that when the words of the sage contradict the woman's words, the woman is believed unless she makes her words dependent on the sage. See also *Torat haShelamim*, 185:7; *Shulhan Aruch Harav Yoreh De'ah*, 185:8.

35. *Bavli Ketubot* 72b.

where the woman reports that in the past a sage purified a stain of blood similar to the questionable stain that she brought now. In the words of the Rashba:

> Whenever there is a *hazakah* (presumption) of blood before us, there is no place to accept her trustworthiness, for we can see that she is mistaken with her comparisons. Even regarding something which is doubtful we do not rely upon her words, as perhaps, just as it is not clear to us, and we cannot determine its status, she may also not be certain and simply made a statement thinking it was so. . . ."[36]

In a few cases of proven incapacity, external assistance is required from women to supervise the process of purification:

Regarding a deaf woman, a *shotah*, a blind woman, or a woman whose cognition has been impaired, if they have able-minded women to care for them, they prepare them [i.e., help them check themselves and immerse for purity].[37]

Even this supervision is limited in halachah to the minimum required. Therefore, it is explained regarding the blind woman that she checks for herself and shows her friend. In other words, only at the point where there is a proven inability should we make use of community support and only to the extent required. Even in the case of a blind person we trust that the examination is done properly. It is only because she cannot determine the nature of the stain and identify it properly that it requires assistance, and only in this matter alone.[38]

It follows that when we are certain that a woman is unable to purify herself, or when the woman herself is unsure about her purity, or when her trustworthiness is placed in doubt because she is found to be lying, or when she is clearly mistaken according to

36. *Torat haBayit*, ibid, and see *Tur Yoreh De'ah* 188.
37. *Mishnah Niddah* 2:1.
38. *Bavli Niddah* 13b, Rosh Niddah 2b, among other places.

the facts in a given case – only in such cases is her trustworthiness questioned, requiring observation by an outsider and a halakhic ruling regarding her status.

Hence, any determination that requires women to have a test from "an external eye" contradicts the fundamental principle of a woman's reliability and her exclusive responsibility for the process of purification. Needless to say, immersion without a *balanit* does not place any doubt on the validity of the immersion, and therefore claims that halachah requires external involvement and supervision over immersion must be proven. Here it should be noted that women report that it is rare for the *balanit* to request that one or more of the three (or more) immersions be repeated because the woman's body was not fully immersed in the water. It happens only once or twice throughout many years of marriage. Women report that in these rare cases at most one of the immersions was insufficient, but the rest of the immersions were adequate, and there is no woman who only immerses once to purify herself. In most of these cases, the woman herself was aware that there was a problem with the immersion because she touched the walls of the *mikvah* and so forth.[39] Thus, there should not be concern in these cases. The woman is to be believed if she immersed on her own.

Up until now, we have reviewed only the difference between the trustworthiness of a woman as it appears according to the primary sources, and the way in which various rabbis presented the status of the *balanit* during immersion. I would now like to show that not only is the ruling of the Chief Rabbinate far

---

39. For comparison, consideration can be given to the rule of *mi'ut hamatzuy* – a minority that is readily found – in the laws of forbidden foods. According to this rule, the obligation to check food does not apply when there is no real likelihood of finding something forbidden mixed in the food. This is despite the fact that there is a small possibility of ingesting serious prohibitions, like that of *sheretz* (creeping insects or animals) and the like. See Rashba's *responsa*, part II, section 274, and see G. Goldman, "Insect Testing in the Food Industry (cauliflower)" [Hebrew], *Tchumin* 19 (1999), pp. 300–302.

removed from halachah, but that it suffers from a lack of consistency regarding the way these rulings are applied to men and to women. To illustrate this, we will examine the sources regarding the obligation to immerse.

In Temple times when the laws of ritual impurity and purity were practiced, the requirement for immersion existed at the same level of halachic severity for men and women. Men and women immersed for a variety of reasons: Priests who desired to partake of tithes – food which was permitted only to the priest – were subject to the severe punishment of *karet* (excision) if they ate while ritually unclean. There were those who purified themselves from their status as a *zav* (having experienced seminal emissions), to bring sacrifices to the Temple, or to be allowed entrance to the camp of Levites.[40]

In addition to these, there were *metzoraim* who suffered from biblical leprosy, those who touched an impure creature, and so forth. In many of these cases of impurity, the halachic intensity of the impurity is identical to that of *niddah*, and the halachic importance of the required immersion is identical, as well. The source that teaches that immersion removes ritual impurity is derived from a single source and relates to women and men alike.

Moreover, the Torah does not specifically mention the obligation of immersion for women who wish to purify themselves from the ritual impurity of their menstrual status; regarding the *zavah* (a woman who experienced an emission related to venereal disease), it states in general "and afterwards she will be purified."[41]

The source from which we derive the obligation of a woman's immersion is one that relates to the impurity of both men and women: "They shall both bathe themselves in water, and be unclean until the evening" (Leviticus 15:18). This verse deals with

40. Or simply to purify themselves from their state of ritual impurity, about which there are various opinions whether such a requirement exists. One element of this issue involves the question of whether immersion by a woman at her time (appropriate to her cycle) is a requirement.

41. See Leviticus 15:19–28.

the case of impurity caused by an emission of semen after sexual intercourse, causing both the man and the woman to become ritually impure.[42] From this we learn that the act of immersing in the *mikvah* is identical for both man and woman and that a woman immerses the same way as a man.[43] This is what is stated in the *Sifra:*

> *They shall both bathe themselves in water, and be unclean until the evening.* Her bathing is juxtaposed with his bathing. Just as his bathing is with cleanliness, also her bathing is with cleanliness. Just as his bathing requires 40 *se'ah* (of water), so too, her bathing requires 40 *se'ah*. . . .[44]

---

42. In other words, regarding a woman, we are speaking of an impurity which does not come from her body, so her impurity is secondary to that of the man. At the same time, a woman who expels semen is defined as "seeing" rather than "touching." The *Rishonim* disagree whether this concerns only the question of ritual purity or the prohibition of a wife to her husband. See *Bavli, Niddah* 32b; *Hiddushei Ha-Ramban*, s.v. *ha d'ba'a minei*; Rosh, *Niddah* 84a; *Torat haBayit haArukh*, house 7, gate 5; *Beit Yosef, Yoreh De'ah*, section 176, subsection 11.

43. The comparisons and connections between the immersions are correct not only for the specific matters mentioned in the Midrash. Whenever a decree is enacted or a regulation established relating to immersion, it is applied to both men and women. Thus, for example, the *Shem Yosef* comments about the decree of the bathhouse: "And in the words of our Master, it appears that we are concerned with fear [that may cause the person immersing to do it improperly] only regarding a woman, but not for a man. . . . Perhaps it can be said that there is no problem, because Rava made mention of the case that was more commonplace because it is more common for women to immerse in our times, which is not the case for men. This also helps explain the opinions of the *Ra'avad* and the *Rashba*, who rule that the decree of the bathhouse is as our Master wrote on this law. Still, Rava's reference to a woman specifically makes sense because in our times we do not have rules of ritual purity in our day-to-day lives, so he chose to refer to women rather than to men. See *Shem Yosef Hilchot Mikva'ot* 1:11.

44. *Sifra Metzora, Zavim* 3:9. It should be noted that the source for immersion in 40 *se'ah* is taught in relation to a man and it is derived from there to apply to a woman. This is true regarding the law of *hatzitzah*, as well. The only rule whose origin is found relating to women and then is applied to men

This exegesis compares the immersion of a woman to that of a man. The main point of the exegesis is to explain that the details of the laws connected to the purification of a man and the purification of a woman are identical, and therefore the requirements of immersion are the same for both. Therefore, the prohibition of having a *hatzitzah* (an obstruction that negates the immersion) is identical for both of them, and so are the required dimensions of the *mikvah* and its laws. The *Aruch HaShulhan* writes:

> A great principle of the Torah teaches that no ritual impurity passes without immersion, and this is true even for minor impurities. This applies to "evening impurities," like contact with *sheratzim* of which it is written in the Torah portion *Shemini*: . . . *shall be dipped in water, and it shall remain unclean until evening; then it shall be clean* (Leviticus 11:32).
>
> And so too by the "evening impurities" such as nocturnal emissions, as it is written in the Torah portion *Metzora*: . . . *they shall bathe in water and remain unclean until evening* (Leviticus 15:18).[45]

The words of the *Aruch HaShulhan* emphasize the fact that the Torah does not specifically mention that the *niddah* and the *zavah* must immerse to be purified. The obligation to bathe is mentioned in connection with the less serious ritual impurity of a nocturnal emission and turns it into a broad and essential principle in the laws of ritual impurity and purity. From *a fortiori* logic it can be learned from this less serious impurity about other impurities: If the only manner of purification for lesser ritual impurities is immersion, *a fortiori* that for more serious impurities, purification must require immersion.

The *Aruch HaShulhan* continues:

---

is that of *beit hasetarim* (whether the water must reach even hidden places on the body).

45. *Aruch HaShulhan*, section 183:4.

> And all the more so the uncleanness of seven [days of impurity] of *niddah*, *zavvah* and a woman who gave birth. This is why the Torah was not detailed regarding the *niddah*, as there is *a fortiori* logic from the "evening impurity." And so it is written regarding the *zavvah* without details: *and count for her seven days and then she would be purified* (Leviticus 15:28). The purification is by means of immersion in water as indicated by the verse referred to previously.

An exception is the *zav,* which the Torah also explicitly mentions as requiring immersion, because of the unique, severe law requiring the *zav* to immerse in *mayim hayyim* – fresh spring water – rather than in the waters of the *mikvah*.

> And only regarding this is Scripture explicit: *When a zav becomes clean of his discharge . . . and bathes his body in fresh water; then he shall be clean.* (Leviticus 15:13).
>
> A *zav* requires *mayim hayyim*, while for the *niddah* and the *zavvah* and the mother of a newborn a *mikvah* is sufficient. And therefore it is explained only regarding the *zav*. This is the way of the Torah to rely on the Oral Torah in all *mitzvot*.[46]

The Rosh cites a number of other sources for the immersion of the *niddah*, the first of which is from a midrash that is based on the verse: *The woman who has her monthly period* (Leviticus 15:33).

> It was taught in a *baraita*: *The woman who has her monthly period.* The early sages taught: It shall be in the *niddah* period, that you will not apply cosmetics or rouge until you come in water. Until Rabbi Akiva came and taught that were it so, she would become distasteful to her husband and her husband would divorce her. But how will I fulfill the verse: *The woman*

46. *Aruch HaShulhan*, Ibid.

> *who has her monthly period?* She will remain in her *niddah* status until she comes in the water.[47]

From here, they derived the immersion of the *niddah* from the Torah. Still, while the derivation here refers directly to the verse concerning the impurity of *niddah,* it appears to rely on the well-known immersion law of the *niddah* by means of an inference in the verse referring to her impure status.

Another source is brought by the Rosh in the name of Rav Yehudai Ga'on:

> Rav Yehudai Ga'on of blessed memory wrote in a *responsum*: Immersion of the *niddah* is from the Torah, from an *a fortiori* argument from touching. Just as the person who touches the bedding where a *niddah* lay down is obligated to immerse in water, all the more so when touching her. And certainly the *niddah* herself, when she is in her impurity, until she immerses.

According to Rav Yehudai Ga'on, just as someone who comes into contact with the bedding where a *niddah* lay down is obligated to immerse, so the *niddah* herself is obligated to immerse.

Again, our source for the requirement to immerse is derived from another case of an obligation to immerse, and we make a comparison between the various immersions.

Another position presented by the Rosh is Rabbeinu Tam's position:

> And Rabbeinu Tam says, the immersion of the *niddah* is learned from the verse: *They must be cleansed with* mei niddah – *waters of niddah* (Numbers 31:23).[48]

---

47. *Sifra Metzora, Zavim,* 9:12.

48. Numbers 31:23. The verses relate to the purification of the spoils of Midian.

> And we expounded: In the water that the *niddah* immerses in.[49]

In contrast with what we have seen before, here it appears that the waters that purify a *niddah* are the source of the derivation of the law regarding other immersions, to the extent that the purifying waters of the *mikvah* are referred to as "the waters of *niddah*." According to this, the laws requiring the immersion of a woman who is a *niddah* are used as a model and a source of derivation for others who are ritually impure.

One general statement that can be made is that whether the source of immersion is derived from the verses relating to minor ritual impurities, whether there is a common source for all, or whether *niddah* is the source for other immersions, it is clear to anyone studying the sections of the Torah on ritual impurities that immersion is a general law that applies to all cases, and that its rules and details are identical for men and women and do not change from one type of ritual impurity to another.[50]

The one exception is the immersion of the *zav*, which is unique. The Rosh summarizes:

> "And it is established that the *niddah* and the *zavah* do not require *mayim hayyim*. As was taught in the *baraita*: There is no difference between the (male) *zav* and the (female) *zavva* except that the *zav* requires *mayim hayyim*, and the *zavvah* does not require *mayim hayyim*, but only the water of the *mikvah* where the entire body is immersed in it. And how much water is required? A cubit by cubit to the height of three cubits. And

49. Babylonian T., Avodah Zarah 78b.

50. See the summary of the Rambam, *Laws of Mikva'ot* 1:2. And see *Tosafot, Niddah* 67a, s.v. *Pat'ha Eine'ah* (the second on the page), and there *Tosafot* bring a disagreement among the early authorities as to whether the immersion of the *niddah* for her husband is as severe as her immersion to eat those things that require ritual purity. Some suggest that this immersion is less severe.

> the sages established that the water required for a *mikvah* was 40 *se'ah*."[51]

It turns out then, that the concept of immersion is a uniform concept, and that its sources, principles, and the details of its laws are identical for men and women. Therefore, when discussing the obligation to immerse oneself before a *balanit*, it should be noted that the imposition of such a requirement should be identical to the requirement imposed on men. It follows that if a woman is required to have a *balanit* for her immersion, then a man would also require the presence of a *mikvah* attendant for his immersion. This should certainly be required when it comes to immersion for the purpose of going up to the Temple Mount, which is an immersion that purifies a person from being liable for *karet*, since entering the Temple Mount even today cannot be done unless one is in a state of ritual purity. It is therefore necessary to examine and understand whether the presence of a *balanit* in a woman's immersion is a halachic necessity or a regulation whose sole purpose is to eliminate the fear lest the woman's hair will poke out of the water which will nullify the immersion (a concern that does not apply to most men because their hair is short).

If we are talking about a practice which was instituted for a particular reason and which is not an independent law, we cannot require the presence of a *balanit* if there are other ways to accomplish that goal. If the general rule of trustworthiness removes the need for an independent observer in the case of a man's immersion, it must apply to the same extent regarding the immersion of a woman.[52]

---

51. *Bavli Eruvin* 4b; Rosh *Tractate Niddah* 10:8.

52. At the time I submitted a response to *Tchumin* in the form of an article on this topic. In the end, however, the article was not published, as the policy of the journal is not to publicize articles written solely by women. The full article has now been published: "*Ve-Safra Lah* – On immersion without a *mikvah* attendant" [Hebrew] Akdamot 31, pp. 143–154.

This analysis reveals that there are times when, unintentionally, there is a ruling that is inconsistent in terms of its approach, and it appears that there is no one willing to point this out. The case of immersion in the presence of a *balanit* highlights the various criteria applied to issues of halachah that apply to women. The growing number of women who are knowledgeable in halachah gives women the tools to point to this problem, and thus illuminate many issues from a new perspective. This approach does not suggest making radical changes or ignoring existing sources. On the contrary, this suggests a reading that is free from biases.[53]

* * *

We cannot conclude our discussion on this topic without mentioning the ruling of Rav Moshe Feinstein in the matter of women who wear wigs as a means of covering their hair. This question was addressed when a man turned to Rav Feinstein because of his opposition to his wife wearing a wig. He claimed that he objected because it was *maarit ayin*, i.e., it gave the appearance that she was sinning because it looked as if she was not covering her head at all. Rav Moshe Feinstein rejected the concern for *maarit ayin* with many arguments, among them that it was recognized and known and understood that we are dealing with a wig and not an uncovered head.

> As most of the time it is apparent that the hair is a wig, and even if it is not apparent to men who are not accustomed to gaze upon women, nonetheless, the vast majority of women, and perhaps all of them, recognize the difference. Therefore, it is not forbidden just because of the infrequent occurrence that a wig is not recognized as such.

---

53. It is also worth mentioning the doctoral dissertation of Ronit Irshai who examined the issue of contraception through this perspective. See Ronit Irshai, *Fertility, Gender and Halakhah: Gender Aspects in Contemporary Halachic Literature*, [Hebrew] Ramat Gan, 2006.

As he notes, women know how to distinguish between a wig and natural hair, and men are not supposed to look and cannot distinguish between these differences. At this point, Rabbi Feinstein adds an extraordinary ruling comparing men who shave and women who wear a wig:

> As something of a proof to the fact that there is no *maarit ayin* regarding wigs, is the fact that it is permissible to shave the beard with scissors even though the result looks like that of a razor. Yet they (the sages) did not forbid that due to *maarit ayin,* even though it is forbidden by a negative commandment and there are also five negative commandments that appear to be violated. This shows us that they did not apply this rule in all cases.
>
> And perhaps this is also because the great majority of the times it is clear to those accustomed to shave that he has not shaved with a razor, they do not forbid it on the basis of the rare times that the manner of shaving would not be recognized, and even though they are also found among people who do not shave and who would not recognize the difference so much. Since those who shave do recognize the difference, it is already clear and well known, since friends have friends, and everyone must know that this person must shave with scissors or depilatory cream or the like, and not with a razor.[54]

In an insightful manner, Rav Feinstein compares the concern of the husband regarding his wife's *maarit ayin* and the lack of concern about the *maarit ayin* of the husband himself in the case of shaving, even though shaving also has the appearance of violating a prohibition.[55] Needless to say, the prohibition against shaving with a razor is more severe than that of a woman revealing her hair. The comparison between the two situations

54. *Igrot Moshe Even ha-Ezer*, part 2, section 12.

55. My thanks to Rabbanit Pnina Neuwirth, who brought this responsum to my attention.

and occurrences raises the idea that the sages did not always use identical considerations in case law for women and men, and similar concepts were not interpreted in similar ways for both genders.[56] In this case, we see that it was not necessary to have a female voice express the puzzlement created by "double standard" interpretations that are adapted to the identity of the questioner and yield to a hidden distinction between men and women.

A Reexamination of Halachic Practices and Clarification of Fundamental Questions

As women have begun to join the ranks of Torah study and have started to delve into the "sea of halachah," there is a need to review certain issues of Jewish law that became formalized in past years, when women were not yet partners with men on these areas of inquiry.[57] First and foremost, the question arose of whether women can serve as rabbis and community leaders. As part of the discussion, the sources dealing with the possibility of women serving in roles of power became prominent.[58] The great questions of the place of women serving in roles as judges or in the rabbinate have been debated throughout the generations, and these discussions have intensified in our generation as well. At the same time, other new questions have arisen: Can a

---

56. It is hardly necessary to cite all of the halachic authorities who forbid wearing a wig, because of *maarit ayin*. Another example of this is the use of the concept of *lifney iver* ("do not place a stumbling block before the blind") in relation to women's modesty: Rav Ovadia Yosef makes use of this prohibition when he discusses women who are dressed immodestly. Of course, the use of this term in the context of the laws of modesty does not meet the accepted criteria in other settings, for example the idea that *lifney iver* does not apply when offering a forbidden cup of wine to a *nazir* if he could otherwise obtain it easily.

57. *Even ha-Ezer*, section 1, subsection 1.

58. *Shulhan Aruch, Even ha-Ezer*, Siman 15, Seif 14:9.

woman recite the *Sheva Brachot* blessings?[59] Can a woman be in charge at a Jewish marriage ceremony? Can a woman read the *ketubah* at a wedding? These are just some examples of new questions. Common to them is a sincere attempt to clarify the meaning of primary sources in an attempt to understand what is truly obligatory according to Jewish law and what is custom that became established for historical, sociological reasons. The entry of women into this discourse and the halachic discussions of these issues does not indicate that we are engaging with a field that has not been dealt with until now. But there is certainly much room for the female voice to be heard in these questions. Among other things, the central issue these questions raise is the degree of connection to the traditions that span the generations and the question of how to best preserve the stability of Jewish law.[60]

It is very important for women to let their voices be heard on these fundamental issues, and not only in the limited arena of specific deliberations, since the fundamental questions are always lurking behind the scenes in the discussions of individual halachic matters. These are areas where women must be accepted as participants in the discussion and where their voices must be considered in a serious manner. The position taken by Rav Yaakov Medan, writing about whether women can be included in the *zimun* invitation to *birkat hamazon* (Grace After Meals) in a family setting, serves as a good example of a case in which fundamental questions arise as an aside to the specific discussion:

> The author is certainly correct in arguing that the exclusion of women from the *zimun* would show *halachah* as disconnected from the reality of our lives.
>
> We should consider very seriously the argument that he makes against my argument and we must ask: Which risk is preferable – breaking with the customs of our forefathers on

59. See Y.Y. Fuchs, *Halachot Bat Yisrael*, Jerusalem, 1984.
60. *Taz*, *Even ha-Ezer*, section 15, par. 14.

> the issue of modesty, or having *halachah* disconnected from contemporary reality in this matter?
>
> I have no clear answer to this question . . . *and deliverance is in a multitude of counsellors* (Proverbs 11:14)[61]. . . .

Rav Medan relates to the difficulty inherent in the application of halachah in the modern world. Are we prepared to give up the ethos and values with which we have grown up? How will we make sure not to overstep the boundaries? He adds and emphasizes his specific concerns:

> Will this not lead to the "*Shira Hadasha* synagogue syndrome"? Might it not lead to having synagogues where men and women sit together?[62]

In the same context, and with regard to the issue of women joining the *zimun*, these important meta-halachic questions were raised. An alternative formulation of these difficulties from a feminine perspective was offered in my words as follows:

> The prevailing wisdom seems to be that there is nothing to lose by hewing to a conservative position. Indeed, in some respects, to repeat yesterday's mantra is the most convenient way of doing things and has considerable benefits.
>
> Sharp changes in halachic rulings that appear to be a radical break with the past can greatly harm the communal sense of trust and confidence in the halachic system. This system is maintained by the slow development of halachah over generations through minor changes. This sense of security is not only a psychological or a religious belief. It is rooted in the fact that halachah is not

---

61. Y. Medan, "Must cultural change bring about change in Halachah: A response to the question of women joining a *zimun* in a family setting" [Hebrew], *Akdamot* 26, pp. 25–27.

62. Ibid.

> only shaped by the realities of its time, but that it plays a role in shaping that reality . . .
>
> At the same time, conservatism also exacts a very high price – religious practice that remains frozen in place loses its existential significance. That religious practice become a tradition with no cultural context and no contemporary meaning.
>
> Simply copying traditions from one generation to the next without thought and analysis of their spiritual sources ultimately leads to halachic formalism and the use of analogies derived from logical fallacies.
>
> All of this is done instead of examining contemporary life and reality in an attempt to apply the spirit of halachah and its values in the new conditions of today's world. The result is the suppression of the vitality of the halachah to the periphery of our lives.[63]

This is the greatest question faced by women in their entry into all spheres of contemporary Jewish life: Conservatism or change? How are we to balance between these two urgent needs of halachah? This discussion cannot be limited to a debate between male rabbis; it is a discussion that must include women's voices. Women's voices must be heard because halachah is important to us, and because the concept and image of halachah is even more important than updating specific details. As women we must be partners in navigating the "halachic ship" and not only maintaining the limited place that we have been granted on it.

Filling in the Lacuna

One of the most striking phenomena in rabbinic literature throughout the ages is that the authors did not view women as

63. See also what I have written in my article, M. Tikochinsky, "The Fabricated Identity of Jewish Women in our Generation" [Hebrew], *Akdamot* 30 (5775/2015), pp. 61–71.

the primary address of halachah.[64] To illustrate this argument, it is sufficient to open the *Even ha-Ezer* volume of *Shulhan Aruch*, where the first paragraph of the first section reads:

> "A person must marry a woman in order to be fruitful and multiply."[65]

The expression "person" in this section is directed at men, whereas a woman here is the object of halachah and not the one to whom the halachah is directed. This, of course, is just an example. The interested reader who continues to learn the section until its end will not find an answer in the *Shulhan Aruch* to the question of whether a woman must marry a man or not. Only in subsection 13, the *Shulhan Aruch* writes that a woman is exempt from being fruitful and multiplying. Perhaps we can conclude that in his opinion a woman is not obligated to marry, even though this is not stated explicitly. Only in the Rema's gloss do we find a reference to this most basic question when he writes: "Some rule that she should marry, lest there be suspicion."

Throughout the section there are few references to laws pertaining to women, and many details of halachah relating to women on this subject are not mentioned at all. The second

---

64. Clearly there are quite a few topics in the *Shulhan Aruch* that deal directly with issues relating to women, such as the sections that discuss marriage of a woman to a man with deformed or missing genitals, a *katlanit* (a woman whose husbands die) and so forth. Still, there are many cases where women desire answers to their questions, yet they are not found in traditional halachic literature, as I will illustrate. I will add that I was recently asked whether the mother of a newborn could recite one of the blessings at the circumcision ceremony. The section in the volume of *Shulhan Aruch Yoreh De'ah* that deals with circumcision does not relate to this question at all, and we must attempt to answer the question based on our own speculation, considering questions like: Is it a blessing of praise or a blessing associated with a commandment? Does the fact that circumcision is mentioned in the blessing disqualify a woman - who is not commanded in this *mitzvah* – from reciting it? I raise this example in addition to the others that appear in the body of this essay.

65. *Shulhan Aruch*, *Even ha-Ezer*, section 1, subsection 1.

section, which deals with the question of genealogy, is addressed to a man, recommending that he choose a wife with good lineage. Should women choose their spouses? What should their criteria be? What guidelines are recommended to them? None of these questions are discussed anywhere in this section. It should be noted that at least part of the issue is that there are almost no discussions relating to these matters in rabbinic literature, and certainly not from a woman's perspective.

Nevertheless, if we turn back to the Bible, there is at least some discussion of the subject, where, regarding the daughters of Zelophehad we are told: They may marry anyone they wish (Numbers 36:6). Rebecca, too, was asked: Will you go with this man? (Genesis 24:58). It turns out that there are primary sources that deal with these questions, but somehow they have disappeared in the process of time.

Throughout *Even ha-Ezer,* the woman is the object in question: she might be a *katlanit* (a woman whose husbands die), she might be the wet nurse of another man, she might be pregnant, and so forth. In section 14, the question is asked whether a man is permitted to marry when he is mourning, but there is no discussion of the parallel question regarding a woman. In section 15, we find a list of those with whom a man may not engage in relations because it would be considered an incestuous relationship, but there is no account of those who are forbidden to a woman. At first glance, it appears that the reason for this is because there is symmetry, and whenever a woman is forbidden to a man – he would be forbidden to her. This symmetry is not always precise, however.

For example, if a woman was the great-granddaughter (the daughter of the daughter of the daughter) of a certain man, then the man is the father of her mother's mother. It is not clear that a "downward relationship" and an "upward relationship" is the same in halachah, and it is possible that there are differences between the number of generations that concern us when looking at "upwards generations" vs. those in "lower generations."

Indeed, we find this discussion in the *Taz*:

> There is a question on the Rambam, who rules leniently that there is conclusion (i.e., that those specified cases alone are forbidden, but other generations above and below are not forbidden). What is the difference between the case of an "upward relationship" with his mother, and with his mother's mother, and with his father's wife, where everyone agrees that there is no conclusion, yet in the case of a "downward relationship" regarding her daughter and her daughter's daughter we say that there is conclusion?
>
> Seemingly we can suggest that there is a greater level of closeness in an "upward relationship" than there is in a "downward relationship" . . . .
>
> But it is impossible to say this, for if he permitted him to marry her in this case because of conclusion in the "downward relationship," nonetheless regarding the woman who he marries, the relationship is an "upward relationship."

After the *Taz* presents the problem of the asymmetry and therefore the difficulty of distinguishing between closeness in an "upward relationship" vs. that of a "downward relationship," he quotes the words of the Drisha that we are only concerned with the relationship as far as the man is concerned and that the woman does not violate the prohibition of incest at all:

> And the Drisha writes that this can be explained, since we always follow the man who marries, since he is the one whose actions cause the marriage to take effect.
>
> But the woman is not explicitly warned in the Torah not to "be taken" [in a prohibited relationship]. It is therefore possible that she does not transgress at all.

The *Taz* then argues with the Drisha, protesting his statement, and even questioning whether the Drisha could have been the source of these words.

> Begging the pardon of his great honor, he wrote here things that – God forbid – distinguish between the woman and the man. For were she to marry in a situation where there was a negative prohibition or the punishment of *karet*, she would be liable for the same punishment as her husband.
>
> This is a clearly stated biblical verse: *All who do any of those abhorrent things—such persons shall be cut off from their people* (Leviticus 18:29), meaning that both the man and the woman are held liable.
>
> Surely it was a mistaken student who wrote these words, and, in an attempt to support himself, hung it on a great tree (i.e., made it appear that it was written by a great man).[66]

Such important and significant issues, dealing with the question of whether or not women are subject to the prohibitions of incest, are not found as the main focus anywhere in the main codes of Jewish law, and only those willing to plumb the depths of the marginal remarks of the commentaries will discover that they are raised for discussion. The fact is that in *Even ha-Ezer*, the volume of the *Shulhan Aruch* that deals with marriage and with building a family, women do not appear. These laws encompass the institution where man and woman partner. It is where they build their home together and where they are commanded to uphold the purity of their joint household, to choose a worthy partner, and so forth. Nonetheless, women's voices are silent. This reality demands explanation.

We can move from *Even ha-Ezer* to *Orach Chaim* and to continue to examine these issues in the context of the day-to-day service of God.

For example, in subsection 3 of section 13 of *Orach Chaim* it is possible, yet again, to see that the main focus is to topics relating to men. Throughout the laws of *tzitzit*, there is no discussion of the exemption of women from this commandment, and women

66. *Taz*, *Even ha-Ezer*, section 15, par. 14.

are only mentioned in the context of a discussion as to whether the *tzitzit* that a woman made is kosher. I do not believe this to be a matter of discrimination, nor of deliberate disregard of their status in Jewish law. Rather, it is simply the normative way of halachic thinking.

Today, a woman who wants to study the laws that apply to her must make an effort to read all the fine print and commentaries. Sometimes she will find an answer to her question and sometimes she will get lost in the thicket of sources. Alternatively, she can choose to open a book written for beginners, like *Halichot Bat Yisrael,* to study the laws. This, of course, is not an ideal way to study, given that the book is not at all comprehensive, and it deals almost exclusively with the classic women's questions – modesty, *yihud*, education, separating *hallah*, prayer, blessings, mourning, and so forth – and all this from a perspective that was appropriate at the time of the book's publication more than a generation ago.[67]

Here, perhaps, lies a great and important project that has yet to be begun. We need to have scholars who will sit and write an updated *Shulhan Aruch* for women. Included in it will be commentaries, disagreements and disputes. But the task has not been started yet, and a generation of women is standing by and waiting. This mission can only be accomplished by women. It will not be a response to the *Shulhan Aruch* as it was written, nor will it examine the religious activity of men and ask whether women should be included, as is the current situation in matters of the synagogue and so forth. Examination of these issues must begin from a feminine point of view on halachah, from its foundations. It also requires developing an image of the Jewish woman – not as an antithesis of the Jewish man, and not as a mirror image of the already written laws, but rather in the simplicity of learning and renewal.[68]

67. See Y.Y. Fuchs, *Halachot Bat Yisrael*, Jerusalem, 1984.
68. See my article, M. Tikochinsky, The Fabricated Identity of Jewish

Conclusion

The processes of integrating women into rabbinic leadership in our generation should serve to respond to expectations that go beyond establishing the place of women as legitimate Torah personalities. The female voice waited for many years in hiding and there is a world that waits for that clear voice to be heard. To accomplish this, women in these positions need to take pen and paper and begin to execute the great challenge that stands before us. The road is long, and it is difficult. It is difficult because in many cases the sources are silent. It is difficult because this is a heavy responsibility that rests on the shoulders of all who are willing to bear this burden. It is difficult because every new, modern thought shakes the world of halachah.

It would be appropriate for each of us to inculcate in ourselves the demanding words that Mordechai spoke to Esther: *And who knows, perhaps you have attained to royal position for just such a crisis* (Esther 4:14).

Women in our Generation" [Hebrew]. *Akdamot* 30 (5775/2015), pp. 61–71.

APPENDIX I

I STARTED WRITING ON THIS SUBJECT SEVERAL YEARS AGO,[1] when the issue of women's rabbinic ordination first sparked off a range of reactions, some enthusiastic and many often highly critical. I then responded to the main areas of criticism as cited above, and there followed a period of relative dormancy. However, most recently the controversy was reignited with the statement of the OU, which was not only severely disapproving of the growing phenomenon of ordained women, but which even went so far as to forbid its membership synagogues to employ such women. So in order to bring this study up-to-date I decided to include the OU statement and some select responses to it. No doubt there are many others, but these are the ones that have come to my attention, and represent different reactions to the OU statement.

Now I can well imagine that some readers will argue, "How can such 'lesser luminaries' have the arrogance to challenge the authority of the OU 'Gedolim'?" I have already countered such a position above, arguing that it is the right, and indeed the duty, of every learned individual to express their own opinion, even when it contravenes the statements of earlier and greater authorities. There is in doing so no mark of arrogance, as stated so clearly in the Shach's introduction to his *Nekudot ha-Kesef*, where he justifies his point of controversy with the *Taz*. And the *Taz*

1. See, e.g., my essay "On Women in Rabbinic Leadership Position," in *Meorot* 8, 2010, pp. 1–12, etc.

himself, in his introduction to the *Shulhan Aruch* also expresses himself most overtly, stating that "when it comes to halachic adjudication, and the decisor's eyes are opened and he sees that there is a refutation of a *Aharon*, that *Aharon* will certainly forgo his honor, and actually will feel a sense of satisfaction, for there [in this] is no envy nor any competitiveness, only the search after the truth from whosoever expresses it."

And here we may add what R. Aharon Azriel wrote in his *Ozen Aharon*, Jerusalem 1886 (*Musar Av*, sect.1):

> And receive the truth from whosoever stated it, and if he is smaller [i.e., lesser] than you do not think that by doing so you will be down-graded in his eyes. On the contrary, he will respect you all the more for this is a mark of merit for a person.

Such a position was held by the greatest of rabbis throughout all generations, from the time of the Talmud[2] right up to our modern times. Thus, for example, the Rashba (R. Shlomoh ben Aderet, c. 1235–1310), in his responsa (vol. 1, no. 253, ed. Machon Yerushalayim 1997, p. 108a), after stating that one follows Alfasi and the Rambam, adds:

> However, if there is a certain scholar, who is worthy of adjudicating (*ra'ui le-horaah*) and he sees a proof to forbid that which they permitted, he should act as though it is forbidden, for they are not really his mentor. And if there is a scholar who is worthy of adjudication, and he sees a reason to be lenient, he may act according to that leniency. . . .[3]

---

2. See, e.g., *B. Hagigah* 3b, and Rashi ad loc.

3. This responsum is a source of a controversial discussion between R. Yaakov Hayyim Sofer, in his article in *Zechor le-Avraham* 1993, pp. 204–236 (and cf. idem, ibid. 1994–1995, pp. 27–47, and R. Yitzhak Yosef, in his *Yalkut Yosef* to *Orah Hayyim* sects. 1–7, Jerusalem 2004, pp. 25–26, also ibid. pp.13–14; and again in his *Ein Yitzhak* vol. 3, Jerusalem 2009, pp.100–101. However, that controversy bears no relevance to our discussion. Nonetheless

Similarly, see the Rosh, in his Responsa (*Klal Hamishim ve-Hamesh* 9, ed. Y.S. Yudlov, Jerusalem 1994, p. 237a:

> . . . and he is not suited to adjudicate unless he has the following two characteristics: the one, that he has straight and correct thinking (*baal sevarah nechonah*), and secondly, that he knows Arabic reasonably. And when he is truly competent in these two requirements, he may rely upon his rulings and act in accordance with them. And even if Rav Ashi were to come and disagree with him, we would not listen to him, for he who has these two requirements, he with regard to this law is the master-craftsman and he has in his hands his [necessary] implements.

And so too we read in the Responsa of R. Yishaiya de-Trani ha-Zaken, sect. 62, ed. A.Y. Wertheimer, Jerusalem 1967:

> However, this is my position: anything that does not appear to be right in my eyes, even if Joshua bin Nun said it, I would not listen to him (see *B. Hulin* 124a), and I do not fear to say unto him what appears right to me, in accordance with my own limited understanding. And in this I fulfil what the verse says, "And I will speak of Thy testimonies before [i.e. even against] Kings, and will not be ashamed" (*Psalms* 119:46), "and as a faithful witness in heaven, Selah" (*Psalms* 89:38).

The references are too numerous to bring here;[4] but the above should suffice for our purposes.

*

R. Yosef attempts to refute R. Sofer's assertions are both forced and contrary to the plain reading of the Rashba's responsum.

4. See e.g. *Piskei Maharai* (Isserlein) sect. 238; *Ritba* to *Pesahim* 48b, *Hatam Sofer* vol. 2, *Even ha-Ezer* 102; see further the copious reference cited by R. Yitzhak Yosef in *Yalkut Yosef* ibid., pp.46-55, also referring to the many discussions of this subject in the writings of his father R. Ovadiah Yosef.

The OU issued a statement in 2017 barring women from such a leadership position in its membership communities. We present here the OU Statements and two rabbinic responses. They are being reprinted exactly as originally publicized, with the exception of Rabbi Herzl Hefter's response which was later updated by the author.

ORIGINAL ORTHODOX UNION STATEMENTS ON FEMALE CLERGY (FEBRUARY 2017)

This two-part statement can be found online at: https://www.ou.org/assets/OU-Statement.pdf and https://www.ou.org/assets/Responses-of-Rabbinic-Panel.pdf

Within mainstream Orthodoxy, more women than at any prior time in Jewish history are learning and teaching Torah, with passionate commitment and at unprecedented levels of scholarship and professional achievement. Motivated by yirat shamayim and ahavat Hashem, they seek not only to learn, but to teach and inspire others. Similarly, highly qualified and dedicated women are increasingly assuming leading roles in Orthodox communal life, both as professionals and within the laity. These positive developments have transformed the face of synagogues and the Orthodox community.

As women have assumed an expanding array of roles, including leadership positions of all sorts, often closed to them in the past, it becomes our challenge – and responsibility – to help define the contours of professional synagogue roles that may be played by women that are permissible within the bounds of halacha and our mesorah – and that conform to the norms of traditional halachic process.

Accompanying this memorandum are the Responses of the Rabbinic Panel to two questions posed to it by the Orthodox Union, in reference to professional synagogue roles:

1. Is it halachically acceptable for a synagogue to employ a woman in a clergy function?
2. What is the broadest spectrum of professional roles within a synagogue that women can perform within the bounds of halacha?

The Need to Address These Issues

The Orthodox Union presented these issues to our Rabbinic Panel for several significant and interrelated reasons. First, many Orthodox Union synagogue Rabbis, and their lay leadership, have requested the Orthodox Union to serve as a conduit for definitive guidance in this complex arena.

Second, the Orthodox Union concluded that the community would benefit greatly by receiving comprehensive, fully elucidated responses regarding women's professional roles that would inform and educate our increasingly sophisticated community membership. This was an instance in which brief and narrow responses – a simple "yes" or "no" – would be insufficient.

Third, over the past several years, certain synagogues have chosen to have women assume rabbinic roles and responsibilities, or rabbinic-like titles, never before practiced within Orthodox Judaism. As a lay body it was our impression that the issues presented were perceived, certainly by segments of our community, as aspects of Orthodox communal practice not necessarily governed by halacha. Other segments of our community believed that such practices were halachically impermissible. The need for halachic and hashkafic guidance was clear. And, as an Orthodox lay organization, the Orthodox Union felt it was of critical importance that we respond to these contemporary religious issues in the manner undertaken by our community for millennia – by presenting questions to our leading Rabbinic authorities, from whom we and our community's Rabbis have regularly sought guidance on critical and sensitive matters of halacha and hashkafa.

The Process We Followed

The Orthodox Union recognized that matters of religious practice cannot be decided by lay bodies. It was our view that such determinations should be made – in the time honored tradition of Orthodox communities throughout the millennia – by a group of leading rabbinic scholars. To that end, we identified rabbis each enjoying an exceptional national reputation for scholarship and integrity, each a significant, recognized talmid chacham; individuals to whom large segments of our communities' rabbis routinely turn for psak on issues of significance and who have, as a consequence, dealt with national issues in communities both large and small, and both homogeneous and heterogeneous in hashkafa. We also sought to include several panel members who are, or were, themselves pulpit rabbis.

With these criteria in mind, we approached the following distinguished poskim (listed in alphabetical order), who each agreed to serve on the Rabbinic Panel:

- **Rav Daniel Feldman** – Rosh Yeshiva, Rabbi Isaac Elchanan Theological Seminary, Yeshiva University
- Rabbi of Ohr Saadya of Teaneck, NJ
- **Rav Yaakov Neuburger** – Rosh Yeshiva, Rabbi Isaac Elchanan Theological Seminary, Yeshiva University; Rabbi of Congregation Beth Abraham of Bergenfield, NJ
- **Rav Michael Rosensweig** – Rosh Yeshiva, Rabbi Isaac Elchanan Theological Seminary, Yeshiva University
- **Rav Hershel Schachter** – Rosh Yeshiva and Rosh Kollel, Rabbi Isaac Elchanan Theological Seminary, Yeshiva University
- **Rav Ezra Schwartz** – Rosh Yeshiva, Rabbi Isaac Elchanan Theological Seminary, Yeshiva University; Rabbi of Mount Sinai Jewish Center in Washington Heights, NY
- **Rav Gedalia D. Schwartz** – Av Beis Din of both Beth Din of America and Chicago Rabbinical Council
- **Rav Binyamin Yudin** – Rabbinic Faculty, Yeshiva University; Rabbi of Congregation Shomrei Torah of Fair Lawn, NJ

Over a period of many months, the Rabbinic Panel met frequently, both in person and by phone.

The Orthodox Union is enormously grateful to each of these individuals for their past and ongoing commitment to the community, but in particular for the countless hours, and profound seriousness and thoughtfulness, with which they assumed this responsibility.

As part of our process, we also convened a series of forums to enable members of the Rabbinic Panel to hear from a broad and diverse group of women and men regarding their perspectives on the issues being addressed. Forum participants included pulpit rabbis, educators, yoatzot halacha, communal professionals and lay leaders. In addition to meeting in small groups with members of the Rabbinic Panel, forum participants, as well as other community members, submitted brief statements outlining a variety of perspectives; each of these written statements was provided to the Rabbinic Panel.

Some Observations on the Responses of The Rabbinic Panel

We note, at the outset, that the American culture of personal autonomy and the egalitarian ethos inexorably clashes with the Torah values of placing normative halachic conduct above individual choice and halachic dictates above individual freedom. This clash is particularly pronounced in the area of gender equality in religious practice. Many have raised, and pondered, the following question: if women serve as CEOs or senior executives of major corporations – as they surely do – if they can head government agencies, and perform at the highest levels of professional achievement – as they surely do – how can we fail to provide them with identical opportunities within the institution seemingly most significant to us outside of our families – the synagogue.

As Orthodox Jews, we believe in the deference to rabbinic authority, accepting the authority of gedolim and poskim, who in each generation translate Hashem's will into practical policy and specific application for the Torah community. Reared in the modern world, we believe in self-actualization and the ability to choose our own paths; yet as Torah Jews, we subordinate the Western emphasis on autonomy to our willing and unabashed embrace of deference to the values and principles conveyed by the Torah, as interpreted by our leading Torah scholars and halachic authorities. Halacha and halachic advocacy do not belong to the purview of circulated petitions, op-ed pieces or Facebook posts. Religious practice must, rather, be the product of a halachic *weltanschauung*, as elucidated by our mesorah and the careful, systematic explication of Torah and Torah values by renowned halachic authorities, applying time honored methods of halachic analysis developed over the millennia, and accepted over the millennia. The exploration of halacha must reflect the aspiration of uncovering G-d's will, even when uncomfortable or difficult to comprehend.

Second, we recognize that too often, the centerpiece of our communal discourse has been on what women cannot do within our synagogue structure, rather than how they contribute to, enhance and advance synagogue life. That emphasis is, in our view, both misplaced and fundamentally counterproductive to advancing our communal needs and maximizing the contributions that can be made by the totality of our community, both men and women.

Accordingly, we note that just as the Rabbinic Panel has made clear that women serving in clergy roles or holding clergy titles is at odds with halacha and our mesorah, the Panel has also proclaimed – and celebrated – the important, and fundamentally successful roles that women can and must play within our communal and synagogue structures, including as educators and scholars. Women must be encouraged to share their Torah knowledge, and their enthusiasm and wisdom, with the broader community.

We therefore urge all segments of our community to recognize and focus upon what unites us.

As articulated by the Rabbinic Panel, women can and should teach Torah, including at advanced and sophisticated levels; give shiurim and divrei torah; assume communally significant roles in pastoral counseling, in bikkur cholim, in community outreach to the affiliated and unaffiliated, in youth and teen programming; and in advising on issues of taharas hamishpacha, in conjunction with local rabbinic authority, when found by a community's local rabbinic and lay leadership to be appropriate. Let us focus our energy and communal creativity on increasing and enhancing the contributions that women make to our shuls and communities, rather than being consumed with limitations.

Third, we feel it important to comment on Yoatzot Halacha. The Rabbinic Panel recognized that Yoatzot Halacha have strengthened religious observance in many segments of our community. In these communities, the introduction of Yoatzot Halacha trained and certified by Nishmat, has resulted in a substantial increase in the number of hilchot nidda and related sheelot posed by women, who are asking far more sheelot than ever before, and receiving responses from a cadre of dedicated, knowledgeable and committed women. While the Rabbinic Panel did not unanimously encourage the institution of yoatzot, they concluded that a Yoetzet Halacha may be employed with the approval of the community's rabbinic and lay leadership, and, where employed, should continue to work in close consultation with the community rabbi(s). We believe that the recommendation of the Rabbinic Panel that the utilization of Yoatzot Halacha continue to be evaluated by poskim and communities alike, is a useful one that will foster greater exposure to and awareness of the importance of this institution, and recognition of the significant role of yoatzot in many of our communities.

Fourth, in Kohelet, Shlomo Hamelech taught that: "Divrei hakhamim b'nachat nishmain."

The words of the wise are most likely to be heard when communicated pleasantly. Efforts must be made to create an atmosphere of education and persuasion, rather than fulmination and coercion. In that spirit, the Orthodox Union has striven, and will continue to strive to encourage achdut and mutual respect. Ultimately, our community will be far better served by convening and promoting substantive dialogue and sophisticated discourse on issues that are, often, complex and nuanced. Such dialogue should bring together our eminent poskim and roshei yeshiva, our pulpit rabbis, and our laity, both men and women. Likewise, community leadership should endeavor, within the bounds of normative halachic conduct, to reach out and be inclusive, and resist pushing away any individuals who are committed to the observance of halacha and who seek to remain within the Orthodox camp.

The Broader Communal Agenda

Quite apart from the specific questions posed to the Rabbinic Panel, it is clear that numerous issues regarding the role of women within the Orthodox community remain unresolved, and require serious communal attention. Many of these challenges are not new, but have been highlighted to the Orthodox Union by comments of both men and women in the course of the series of forums that were convened by the Orthodox Union for the benefit of the Rabbinic Panel, and in the attendant written submissions we received.

We, therefore, underscore that the responses of the Rabbinic Panel that we transmit today are but the beginning of a process and not its end. We envision a continuing process of dialogue and exploration to begin to address these – and other – critical issues in a deliberate manner.

Many forum participants noted that our community would benefit greatly, and the synagogue experience would be enhanced by, an even greater presence of women functioning as educated, knowledgeable and halachically committed role models, teachers, and pastoral counselors, modelling the joy and fulfillment of Torah learning, of teaching, leadership, spiritual growth and emotional support in time of need. The failure to fully embrace the talents of women and encourage women to assume greater lay and professional roles is a tragic forfeiture of communal talent. We should focus on creating and institutionalizing roles for women that address the needs of Orthodox Jews today, by removing barriers that impede women from further contributing to our community, in halachically appropriate ways. We should fully utilize their talents and commitment, thereby fostering shmirat hamitzvot, enhancing limmud torah and expanding the richness and vibrancy of Jewish life.

Further, we must ensure that the community does not inappropriately disparage the sincere quest of many women for growth in limmud Torah, or in communal participation, as being improperly motivated. When applied, this blanket attitude not only alienates growth-oriented Torah Jews, but also diminishes the next generation's access to talented and passionate teachers of Torah, and role models.

This subject likewise merits the thoughtful consideration and attention of our community.

Other issues likewise require careful review, exploration and communal consideration. For example, consideration should be given, within acceptable halachic parameters, to developing appropriate titles for women of significant accomplishment, holding professional positions within the synagogue and communal structure, thereby acknowledging their achievement and status. Though such titles could not – and should not – connote ordination or rabbinic function, the Rabbinic Panel has made clear that words – and titles – matter. In short, the dignity accorded such positions must be commensurate with the importance we place on them. As a result, we urge our community, with sensitivity, creativity and full regard for halachic and hashkafic norms, to constructively consider whether and, if so, how to design both appropriate job descriptions and titles for the critically important roles described above. Such titles would make manifest the degree of skill, training, and preparation necessary for such roles, and the significant status and respect to be accorded to them. We further urge consideration of the related issues of tenure, compensation (including pay equity) and benefits accorded such roles. We resolve to utilize our organizational resources to foster such communal dialogue.

Finally, certain forum participants emphasized the need for greater communal attentiveness to, and rabbinic focus on, the spiritual engagement of women in synagogue services, particularly within certain community segments, and at certain critical life stages. For example, while many within the community, both women and men, feel an inadequate sense of "connection", some women, upon completing their Jewish studies in high school and beyond, may not find the same sense of religious engagement in shul attendance as may be enjoyed by certain of their male counterparts. Whether, and, if so, to what extent, such feelings are widespread require careful communal attention and consideration and, if found to be significant, must be addressed in deliberate and concrete ways.

We recognize that the issues raised above are hardly the only ones that must be considered.

We, as a community, should strive to identify others that must be placed on the communal agenda, and that require both meaningful attention and deliberation, and creative solutions.

The Way Forward

We offer the following observations:

(1) The unity and health of our community will be impacted by the degree to which approaches are identified to substantively encourage, support and expand women's engagement in synagogue communal roles, within the bounds of halacha as explicated by the Rabbinic Panel. It is essential that the voices of individuals who are yirei shamayim and committed to Torah values, both men and women, are heard in communal discussion and leader-

ship. Accordingly, the Orthodox Union commits to explore and identify approaches by which the concerns identified herein, and other challenges and opportunities, can be discussed and studied.

(2) The OU undertakes, and will continue to strive, to live by the principles enunciated in this Statement. On the professional side of the organization, the OU's recruitment, training, mentoring and promotion of talented women within our professional ranks has been a key organizational priority for the past several years. We have significantly enhanced our maternity/parental leave policy, as well as our part-time and telecommuting work options, to create a more family-friendly work environment. We established the OU Women's Affinity Group as a forum for professional women within our organization, where women can gather on a regular basis for seminars, networking and brainstorming on issues of common concern. We instituted a new compensation system whereby each program position within the OU is assigned a grade and corresponding salary range, thereby ensuring pay equity across the board. And while there remains much work ahead, our management ranks are now beginning to reflect the totality of the talent pool within our community, both male and female.

On the lay leadership side, following consultation with our Poskim, the 2015 OU elections included six talented women elected as national officers. Women populate our commissions and committees, bringing their skill and expertise to bear for the benefit of Klal Yisroel.

But there is much more that the OU can – and should – seek to achieve. The OU is, therefore, in the process of forming a new Department of Women's Initiatives. This Department will be led by a senior professional, and will allow us to coordinate all of our programming for women, whether serving our community's schools, shuls or individuals directly. The objective of this initiative is to advance the spiritual, religious and communal engagement of women at all stages of life, in all segments of the Orthodox community, in areas of personal and professional growth, including Torah study and community leadership.

(3) We adopt as a statement of OU policy the Responses of the Rabbinic panel transmitted herewith and anticipate that Orthodox Union member synagogues will act in accordance with these Responses. The OU, through its Synagogue Standards Commission, will enter into a dialogue with synagogues to encourage and facilitate implementation of the Responses. In addition, the OU will explore various ways in which all shul members, women and men, can enhance their synagogue experience and realize greater spiritual enrichment.

Further, the OU will work with member synagogues, at the request of their respective Rabbinic and lay leadership and with their cooperation and guidance, to encourage women's involvement in all appropriate areas of leadership and participation within such member synagogues.

Moishe Bane, **President**
Howard Tzvi Friedman, **Chairman of the Board**
Allen I. Fagin, **Executive Vice President / Chief Professional Officer**

TO THE ESTEEMED MEMBERS OF THE ORTHODOX UNION'S EXECUTIVE COMMITTEE AND BOARD OF DIRECTORS, IN RESPONSE TO YOUR QUESTIONS:

(1) Is it halakhically acceptable for a synagogue to employ a woman in a clergy function?
(2) What is the broadest spectrum of professional roles within a synagogue that may be performed by a woman?[1]

These inquires must be answered in a way that goes beyond a simple yes or no, permitted or prohibited. The issue of female clergy is complex, and touches upon not only the dictates of *halakhah*, but also upon fundamental issues in our *hashkafat olam*. Indeed, the questions relate to the philosophy of the halakhic process itself. Furthermore, we recognize that this issue is emotionally charged; some perceive limitations on women's roles and titles as barriers to full involvement in the Orthodox community, while others view the lifting of traditional gender distinctions in ritual as representing a rejection of the *mesorah*. This tension pits egalitarianism, a central value of modernity, against a time-honored tradition that clearly speaks of equally valued, yet different, roles for men and women.

In contemporary discourse, rabbinic discussion of these issues often appear to focus primarily on what functions performed by men are inappropriate for women. By contrast, our intention is

1. At the request of the OU, we have presented our response in a style that differs somewhat from a classic *teshuva*. While traditional responsa are penned in Hebrew and include extensive sourcing and elaboration of arguments, we present here a position paper that summarizes our extensive deliberations, yet reflects the certainty of our conclusions. In addition, please note that if asked individually, each one of us would, no doubt, have written a response in our own styles, emphasizing the particular approaches that we each found most compelling. This paper represents elements of the thought of each of its seven writers.

to define halakhic parameters with the goal of clarifying practical roles that women can and, depending on the particular *kehillah*, indeed should, play in our community institutions.

The following represents our collective opinion. For the reasons noted above, we will begin with an outline of halakhic methodology.

Halakhic Methodology

There are three primary factors that may be considered by a halakhic decisor when developing a ruling: legal sources, precedent, and a relevant halakhic ethos.

Legal sources, which may include both textual and oral rulings, are sometimes dispositive, but often require interpretation or the application of principles. Particularly when navigating multiple sources and competing considerations, years of sophisticated mentoring and significant experience in *psak* are required for a reliable conclusion to be reached. Self-contained, commonplace *sheilot*, such as those relating to basic *hilkhot berakhot* and *kashrut*, can often be resolved by reference to explicit legal sources alone. Issues with wider implications and multiple spheres of impact, however, demand consideration of factors that transcend strictly legal sources and require a broader approach.

Second, the Torah community's historical and widespread observance of a particular practice establishes a default position for halakhic decision-making. The Talmud resolves halakhic questions by examining the prevailing normative practice, instructing younger students, "*puk chazi mai amma de-var*" – "go out and observe the common practice" (*Eruvin* 14b). Time-honored traditions of the Torah community are revered, and *Chazal* have attributed a level of Divine sanction to those who sustain its practice: "*Im einam nevi'im – b'nei nevi'im heim*" – "if they are not [actually] prophets, they are sons of prophets" (*Pesachim* 66a).[2]

2. See, also, *Arukh Hashulchan* (OC 345:18) with regard to the common

This is not to say that an established practice can never be altered; it must be assumed, however, that normative practice reflects a baseline truth that must be grappled with when innovations are suggested.[3] Great caution must be employed before altering *mesorat Yisrael*. This deep respect for established communal norms can be found throughout the works of the *Ba'alei HaTosafot* whose writings often invoke the validity of communal practice even in the face of apparently conflicting Talmudic texts.[4] This is true regarding *minhagim* (customs),[5] and all the more so regarding matters that are dependent on the application of Jewish law. In fact, many practices that currently find expression in textual sources, and are thus understood to be textually based, were actually resolved based on the authority of precedential practice.[6]

---

practice to rely upon the fact that, in a place with less than 600,000 people, the prohibition to carry is only *miderabbanan*. The *Arukh Hashulchan* raises a multitude of difficulties with this opinion, but concludes:

אבל על כל פנים מה מועיל האריכות אחרי שהעירובין נתפשטו ברוב ערי ישראל הרבה מאות שנים מקודם – ורק על סמך היתר זה. וכאלו בת קול יצא – "הלכה - כשיטה זו".

Furthermore, *siyata dishmaya* is assumed to guide halakhic decisions themselves – so long as they are made in a proper manner. See *Sotah* 4b and *Ketubot* 60b.

3. See *Yerushalmi Yevamot* (12:12):

אם יבוא אליהו ויאמר שחולצין במנעל - שומעין לו. שאין חולצין בסנדל - אין שומעין לו - שהרי הרבים נהגו לחלוץ בסנדל. והמנהג מבטל את ההלכה.

See further, in the responsa of the Rosh (45). Dr. Haym Soloveitchik has written extensively on the strength of "*minhag*" – common practice – as a determining factor in halakhic inquiry. See, for example, H. Soloveitchik, *Ha-Yayin bi-Yemei ha-Beinayim: Yayin Nesekh – Perek be-Toledot ha-Halakhah;* and "*Minhag Ashkenaz ha-Kadmon*: An Assessment," printed in the second volume of the *Collected Essays* of Dr. Soloveitchik.

4. See, for example, *Tosafot Berachot* 2a, *Berachot* 18a, and *Avodah Zarah* 2a.

5. The *Talmud Yerushalmi* (*Bava Metzia* 7:1) rules that "*minhag mevatel halakhah*." While this idea is not meant literally, and this rule is applied only with regard to monetary practices where Torah law is not explicit, this provocative phrase speaks to the extent to which *halakhah* considers normative practice to be a significant factor in determining legal reality.

6. Such examples include the prevalent practice to be lenient regarding the eating of *chadash* in areas outside and not bordering *Eretz Yisrael* (see the first

Not only is there enormous significance in the Torah community's manner of observing a particular custom or behavior; equally significant is the community's failure or refusal to practice a certain custom or adopt a particular behavior. Although the *Mishnah* (*Eduyot* 2:2) states that "*lo ra'inu – aino raya*" (the fact that something has not been observed cannot be brought as a proof to one side of a legitimate halakhic dispute rooted in *pesukim* or *sevara*), the nonperformance of a particular practice does constitute a *minhag*, and such a *minhag* attains binding status. In addressing the implication of a community practice, the Maharik (quoted by the Shakh at the beginning of *Yoreh Deah*) rules that, by inference, the community's failure to adopt a particular practice can be understood to reflect an objection to that practice.[7]

Finally, it is essential for a halakhic decisor to be aware of, and keenly sensitive to, the broader context of Torah values. Such values originate from, but frequently extend beyond, specific legal dictates. *Halakhah* itself, if examined closely, reflects underlying themes, and sources from *mikra, aggadah*, and *kabbalah* complement the halakhic rulings to express values that direct our *avodat Hashem*. These core values, derived from these multiple sources, form a "Halakhic Ethos," and throughout our history,

---

page of *Kuntres Shem Chadash* from the author of *Magen ha-Elef*, Aryeh Leib ben Moshe Zuenz (c. 1768–1833)) and the universally accepted Ashkenazic practice that *kohanim* only recite *birkat Kohanim* on *Yom Tov* in the Diaspora.. See *Beit Ephraim* #6 and *Arukh Hashulchan* (*Orach Chaim* 128:64). See the relevant remarks of Dr. Soloveitchik, ibid, on the issue of *birkat kohanim*, in the article quoted in footnote 3.

7. An example: A question arose in New Orleans in 5620 regarding an *andarta*, a bust, in memory of a communal leader. The question was sent to the *rabbanim* of Europe, who issued a prohibitive ruling. Rav Shimshon Rafael Hirsch based his response on the fact that, in practice, Jews had no history of commemorating through human statues. Rav Hirsch quotes the aforementioned opinion of the Shakh that in the area of *minhag*, "*lo ra'inu*" is, in fact, a valid argument. Rav Nathan Marcus HaKohen Adler, the Chief Rabbi of Great Britain, offered a similar explanation. See "*Be-din Tzurat Adam ba-Olam ha-Chadash*," by Yitzchak Ehrenberg and Zev Eleff, in *Beit Yitzchak*, vol. 44 (5773), pp. 394–398.

these values have been integrated into the technical, practical resolution of complex halakhic issues. This important idea will be further explained in the coming section.

The Halakhic Ethos

A *weltanschauung* emerges from the totality of the vast sea of *halakhah* and Torah thought, and this collective world view serves as the basis of our *avodat Hashem*. These overriding principles are mined through the examination of *mikra*, *halakhah*, and precedent.

Mikra: While most legal sections of the Torah are comprised of specific commands, many general injunctions can be found as well. Examples of such general directives include "*kedoshim tihiyu*" (*Vayikra* 19:2), "*shabbaton*" (*Vayikra* 23:24) and "*v'asita hayashar v'hatov*" (*Devarim* 6:18). The Ramban's commentary to these *pesukim*, as elaborated below, highlights the manner by which these general exhortations significantly shape normative practice.

Halakhah: A comprehensive study of the details of specific *halakhot* reveals fundamental principles which provide guidance for the development of a deeper and more expansive understanding of the details themselves. As our Rebbe, Rav Yosef Dov Soloveitchik, *zt"l*, wrote, "Out of the sources of *halakhah*, a new world view awaits formulation."[8] For the Rav, the appreciation that Torah values could be derived through the examination of the Torah's legal sources was fundamental to an understanding of Torah and the halakhic decision making process. These fundamental principles represent an important part of what we call the *mesorah*.

Precedent: The Torah worldview is also shaped by precedent. While, as discussed earlier, long-established practice assumes presumptive validity that is due enormous respect and deference, historical practice also serves as a source of more general

8. *The Halakhic Mind*, p. 102.

guidance. Precedent in one area of *halakhah* is assumed to reflect fundamental truths and principles that help shape the halakhic ethos, and which thereby influence the resolution of *sheilot* in related areas. In particular, the halakhic ethos plays a critical role in providing guidance in addressing the original halakhic challenges of each generation.

Torah literature is permeated by the impact of the Torah ethos on halakhic practice. The Ramban comments that the *pasuk's* phrase "*v'asita hayashar vehatov*" (*Devarim* 6:18), conveys much more than an exhortation to carefully follow the explicitly referenced laws. The Ramban teaches that "[T]he intent of this statement is that . . . He has said that you should observe the laws and statutes which He had commanded you. Now, He says that with respect to what He had not commanded, you should likewise take heed to do the good and the right in His eyes, for He loves the good and the right. And this is a great principle, for it is impossible to mention in the Torah all aspects of man's conduct with his neighbors and friends and all of his various transactions and the ordinances of all societies and countries." Through this *pasuk*, *Hashem* has provided an overarching value to be used as a yardstick to measure situations not actually addressed directly by the text.[9] [10] Similarly, the Talmud applies the *pasuk* and concept

9. A similar idea can be found in the Ramban's understanding of the mitzvah of "*shabbaton*" (*Vayikra* 23:24) on Yom Tov (and Shabbat) as extending beyond the *melakhot*. "Thus we are not to be engaged the whole day in wearisome tasks, measuring out crops of the field, weighing fruits and gifts, filling the barrels with wine and clearing them away by themselves, and moving stones from house to house and place to place" despite the fact that none of these activities entail *melakhot*. Similarly, if not for the value of *shabbaton* that extends beyond the technicalities of Yom Tov violation, "The marketplace would be full for all business transactions, the shops standing open and the shopkeepers giving credit . . . and the workers would rise early to go their work and hire themselves out for such works just as on weekdays!" (Translation by Rabbi Dr. Charles B. Chavel.) The Ramban's famous exposition of "*kedoshim tihiyu*" (*Vayikra* 19:2) likewise extends a halakhic ethos to determine practice in areas not explicitly covered by the letter of the law.

10. Other examples include the Talmud's proscription against inflicting pain

of "*Derakheha darkhei noam vekhol netivoteha shalom*" (*Mishlei* 3:17) to determine halakhic issues not at all referenced by the *pasuk*.[11]

The ethos of *halakhah* also plays a critical role in directing communal practice. For example, the *Chofetz Chaim*'s decision to champion women's Torah study,[12] as well as the Rav's expansion of this endorsement, was compelled primarily by extra-legal considerations.

Notably, the Rav turned to the halakhic ethos in explaining the prohibition of praying in a synagogue with mixed gender seating.[13] While the Rav briefly mentioned (but did not elaborate upon) possible legal concerns, his arguments relate primarily to the precedent of separate areas for men and women in the *Beit HaMikdash*, as well as various aspects of the "Jewish spirit of prayer." The Rav's global understanding of the Torah system led him to vehemently oppose the structural changes being suggested in the Orthodox synagogue of his time.[14]

The same is true of the Rav's nuanced embrace of secular

---

on animals which, despite the absence of a technical legal source, is predicated on Torah values and is considered binding (see *Minchat Asher Bereishit* 21:4 based on Radvaz).

11. See *Yevamot* 87b and *Sukkah* 32a.

12. *Likkutei Halakhot, Sotah* 20b: "It seems that all of this [prohibition against women learning Torah] applies only to times past when all daughters lived in their fathers' home and tradition was very strong, assuring that children would pursue their parents' path, as it says, 'Ask your father and he shall tell you.' On that basis we could claim that a daughter needn't learn Torah but merely rely on proper parental guidance. But today, in our iniquity, as parental tradition has been seriously weakened and women, moreover, regularly study secular subjects, it is certainly a great *mitzvah* to teach them *Chumash*, Prophets and Writings, and rabbinic ethics, such as *Pirkei Avot*, *Menorat HaMaor*, and the like, so as to validate our sacred belief; otherwise they may stray totally from God's path and transgress the basic tenets of religion, God forbid."

13. "On Seating and Sanctification," in Litvin, Baruch, *The Sanctity of the Synagogue*, third edition, pp. 114–118.

14. Similarly, the Rav's approach to the question of interfaith dialogue was primarily guided by Torah values. See "Confrontation" in *Tradition*, 1964, vol. 6 #2 and *Community, Covenant and Commitment*, pp. 259–265.

knowledge and modern civilization. Based on his Torah *welt-anschauung*, Rav Soloveitchik developed Avraham's words to Ephron in *Parashat Chayei Sarah*, "*Ger v'toshav anokhi imakhem*" (*Bereishit* 23:4), "I am a stranger and an inhabitant with you," into a sophisticated, practical philosophy for engaging the world.[15]

Moreover, embracing the inner logic of *halakhah* as a source of values is the *sine qua non* for navigating this engagement with society in a manner that is in consonance with the Torah. Our community's mandate to understand both the world *Hashem* created, as well as the society in which we live, must never blind us from recognizing that there are frequently societal trends which run counter to the ethos of the Torah.

Mesorah: Tradition and a Cumulative Approach

These principles, conveyed by the Torah ethos, underlie the oft-referenced concept of "*mesorah*."

The idea of *mesorah* is often mistaken as a mere historical record of Jewish practice. That misunderstanding, combined with both the absence of historical uniformity of normative practice, and the gradual evolution of *halakhah*, can be misconstrued as compromising the authenticity of *mesorah*. Authentic *mesorah* is rather an appreciation for, and application of, tradition as the guide by which new ideas, challenges and circumstances are navigated.

Our precious *mesorah* has thereby been the cornerstone of not only the preservation, but also the development of our religious and spiritual heritage. *Mesorah* is the bridge between our past and our future. When studying a proposed innovation, in addition to considering its immediate implications and whether it is consistent with Torah principles, attention must be paid to the potential impact of such changes on generations through the dis-

15. Rabbi Joseph B. Soloveitchik, *The Rav Speaks*, pp. 70–80.

tant future. Each and every generation confronts an ever-changing social, cultural and technical environment. Halakhic leadership must, therefore, continually probe whether proposed changes and accommodations will enable the community to advance the objectives of an authentic Torah ethos, or simply accommodate prevailing values and expectations, often in opposition to the Torah worldview.

No doubt, a commitment to follow the ethos of the Torah, in addition to the letter of the law, requires faith, commitment, and a willingness to embrace timeless principles – even when counter-cultural and incompatible with prevailing societal values. In the words of the Rav, "It is very important [that] we must not feel . . . an inferiority complex, and because of that complex yield to the . . . transient, passing charm of modern political or ideological *sevaros* . . . There is no need for apology; we should have pride in our *mesorah*, in our heritage."[16]

Halakhic Perspectives on Women Clergy

By application of halakhic methodology, we will now examine the specific questions addressed to us. Reference will be made

16. Conveyed in a 1975 speech to the Rabbinic Alumni of the Rabbi Isaac Elchanan Theological Seminary. The full relevant text reads as follows: "Second, we must not yield – I mean emotionally, it is very important – we must not feel inferior, I mean develop or experience an inferiority complex, and because of that complex yield to the charm – usually it is a transient, passing charm – of modern political and ideological *sevaros* (logic). I say not only not to compromise – certainly not to compromise – but even not to yield emotionally, not to feel inferior, not to experience an inferiority complex. And it should never appear to me that it is important to cooperate just a little bit with the modern trend or with the secular, modern philosophy. In my opinion, [Judaism] does not have to apologize either to the modern woman or to the modern representatives of religious subjectivism. There is no need for apology – we should have pride in our *mesorah*, in our heritage. And of course, certainly it goes without saying, one must not try to compromise with these cultural trends, and one must not try to gear the halakhic norm to the transient ways of a neurotic society, [which] is what our society is."

to each of the three aforementioned factors used to arrive at a halakhic decision: legal sources, historical precedent, and the halakhic ethos. While each factor will be addressed independently, the factors inherently overlap, as emphasized earlier.

From a legal standpoint, there are multiple challenges to the ordination of women and the appointment of women to formal clergy positions:

The *Sifri* (#157, to *Devarim* 17:15) states that a woman may not be appointed king. The Rambam (*Hilchot Melachim* 1:5), based on the Talmud (*Yevamot* 45b), extends this prohibition beyond kingship to any position of *serarah* (formal communal authority).[17] As Rabbinical positions have been traditionally understood as paradigmatic of *serarah*, they would be restricted to men in accordance with the Rambam's position.

Furthermore, the Rav assigned great significance to the ruling of the Rema (*Yoreh Deah* 1:1) barring a woman from being appointed as a community *shochet* as being representative of a general preclusion of women from *all* formal religious appointments (*minuyim*) over the community at large. The Rav explained that during the times of the Rema, appointment as the community's *shochet* required the earning of a formal "license" (*kabbalah*) from a *chakham*. When the position of *shochet* became an official religious appointment in the community, it became restricted to men.[18]

---

17. The opinion of the Rambam is accepted by the *Arukh Hashulchan* (*Hoshen Mishpat* 7:4) all well as by many other authorities; See *Amud HaYemini* (12), *Mishpetei Uziel* (*Hoshen Mishpat* 4:6). Rav Moshe Feinstein, in a set of oft-quoted responsa (*Yoreh Deah* 2:44–45) permitted a woman to serve as a *mashgichah* for *kashrut* noting that there are opinions in the *Rishonim* that *serarah* applies only to positions of royalty. However, it is clear from his responsa that Rav Moshe saw the restrictive position of Rambam as the normative ruling. Nevertheless Rav Moshe ruled that there was room to rely on the non-normative lenient position with regard to the position of *mashgichah*, which is arguably not a true position of *serarah* (and even so, Rav Feinstein suggested a way to further assure that the position would not be classified as *serarah*) and in the particular case of an impoverished widow.

18. See the opening pieces in *Sefer Shiurei HaRav al Inyanei Shechitah Melichah Basar B'Chalav veTa'arovot*, edited by Rav Elyakim Koenigsberg.

Consideration of the ordination of women also raises questions regarding the nature of *semikhah*. While contemporary *semikhah* differs from classic *semikhah* (as described in the Talmud) in many regards, it must, nevertheless, be viewed as an extension of the original institution of *semikhah*.[19] Parallels between the current and original forms of semikhah therefore, are relevant and valid.[20] Various sources indicate that the classic *semikhah* involved, and in fact may have centered on, designating individuals to serve as court judges.[21] Since the majority halakhic view[22] is that only men are eligible to be ordained as judges, even contemporary ordination would be restricted to men.[23]

Finally, the sanctity of the synagogue demands a particularly

---

The formal, communal role of the *shochet* is evidenced historically. In early American synagogues, a *shochet* was employed in an official capacity even when a rabbi was not engaged by the congregation. See *The Synagogue in America*, pg. 7.

19. See *Shulchan Arukh Yoreh Deah* 242:5-6 based on *Maharik*, 113:3 and 169. The Maharik derived two *halakhot* by assuming that what was true for classical *semikhah* is still true for modern day *semikhah*. Also see Rambam (*Hilchot Sanhedrin* 4:8) who includes the current function of *netilat reshut* in the laws of *Sanhedrin* as an extension of the original *semikhah*.

20. See *Shu"t Rema* (24) and *Aruch Hashulchan* (*Yoreh Deah* 242:30) who seem to require eligibility for original *semikhah* in order to receive contemporary *semikhah*.

21. סנהדרין יג: – "קרי ליה 'רבי' – ויהבי ליה רשותא למידן דיני קנסות". This is quoted in the Rambam (*Hilchot Sanhedrin* 4:2) with a similar language.

22. See *Tosafot* (*Bava Kama* 15a). *Tosafot* quote a minority opinion that women may serve as judges. *Shulchan Aruch* (*Hoshen Mishpat* 7:4) rules like the overwhelming majority view in the *Rishonim*. Similarly, the *Talmud Yerushalmi* (*Yoma* 6:1) explicitly restricts women from *dayanut*. The one-time phenomenon of Devorah as *shofetet* (*Sefer Shoftim*, chapters 4-5) is discussed extensively by the *Rishonim* (to *Bava Kama* 15a and elsewhere) and is not seen as paradigmatic in any way.

23. Women are excluded from positions that reflect the paradigm of *dayanut* – even when a full-fledged judge is not specifically required. For example: although a panel for *hatarat nedarim* does not share the technical requirements of a bona fide *beit din*, women are nonetheless excluded. Rabbi Akiva Eiger explains that a panelist for *hatarat nedarim* must meet the theoretical requirements for a *dayan*. See *Sefer ha-Hinuch* 406, *Shu"t* R. Akiva Eiger quoted in *Pitchei Teshuvah Yoreh Deah* 228:2, and *Arukh Hashulchan* 228:10.

enhanced level of modesty – as illustrated by the requirement of a *mechitzah*. This elevated demand for the separation of genders is incompatible with a woman presiding over a male quorum.[24]

Members of this group differ as to the relative weights accorded to each of these concerns as well as whether each factor carries definitive halakhic significance independently, or only cumulatively. It is our unanimous opinion, however, that these considerations, combined with factors discussed below, impose a legal preclusion to the appointment of women clergy.

Precedent Regarding Women's Clergy Roles

Furthermore, halakhic history evidences a precedent of precluding women from serving as clergy or receiving ordination. Even the Rema's restriction against appointing a woman to be a *shochetet*, referenced above, has always been normative.

Current women's roles in society – even in Jewish society – are undoubtedly different than in the past. While, *baruch Hashem*, advanced Torah learning opportunities for women continue to multiply, and more women today are interested in, and capable of, learning in-depth *halakhah*, it is clear from historical and halakhic literature that women's Torah scholarship is not an entirely new phenomenon. Nonetheless, women scholars in the past, while clearly acknowledged and appreciated, impacted and guided the community without the formality of rabbinic titles or ordination.

The existence of female scholars throughout the history of our nation is, in our understanding, ample proof that the notion of semikha for women was conceivable. However, a continuing mesorah existed that dictated against it. We find it implausible to say that the question of female ordination has never presented itself throughout the history of our mesorah.

24. See *Eretz Ha-Tzvi* (Rav H. Schachter) 12:11–12 for a further elaboration of this concept.

Finally, even if the absence of women rabbis throughout Jewish history is not fully dispositive, this phenomenon does establish a baseline status quo. We feel that the absence of institutionalized women's rabbinic leadership has been both deliberate and meaningful, and should continue to be preserved.

Our group believes that the combination of these two considerations, precedent and halakhic concerns, precludes female clergy. Given the status quo that we feel is meaningful and intentional, the burden of halakhic proof rests on the side of changing the established practice.

The Halakhic Ethos of Gender Roles

The Torah affirms the absolute equal value of men and women as individuals and as *ovdei Hashem*, but clearly and consistently speaks of role differentiation.

Kedushat Yisrael applies identically to both women and men; indeed, it is actually passed on to future generations specifically through Jewish women. Rav Shimshon Rafael Hirsch writes, "The concept of man created in the image of G-d embraces both sexes; together, male and female comprise the term 'human.' G-d has created them both equally close to Him and for the same active purpose according to His Will: "*zachar u'nekeivah bara otam*."[25] Similarly, expectation of, and capacity for, personal spiritual achievement does not differ between the genders,[26] and the vast majority of halakhic obligations apply equally to women and men.[27]

Differences between the roles of men and women are, however, axiomatic, and are reflected in a multitude of legal and extra-legal

25. *Collected Writings*, Vol. VIII, p. 85. Rav Hirsch spells out his views in a long essay entitled "The Jewish Woman". See, in particular, the first section of this essay – pp. 83–90 in *Collected Writings*.

26. See Rabbi Joseph B. Soloveitchik, *Family Redeemed*, p. 71.

27. *Kiddushin* 29a.

sources starting with the Torah itself[28] and continuing through the *Achronim*. Rav Soloveitchik stressed this idea in lectures and shiurim over many decades and in many contexts.[29] "Two humans were created who differ from each other metaphysically, not only physiologically, even as they both partake of Divine qualities. This contradicts the perverse notion that Judaism regards woman as being inferior to man. It also cuts away another false notion that there is no distinction between them in terms of their spiritual personalities. Two sexes were formed not only for propagative purposes, but [in addition,] they constitute existential originals. They differ in their psychical natures."[30]

Rabbi Soloveitchik arrived at his worldviews not simply through sources that would classically be considered *machshavah* or *hashkafah*, but particularly through an understanding of the intricacies of *halakhah*. The distinctions between men and women in the observance of *mitzvot aseh she-ha-zman grama* (*Kiddushin* 29a), matrilineal, as opposed to patrilineal descent (*Kiddushin* 66b), laws applying to *Kohanim* (see, for example, *Sotah* 23), court testimony (*Shevuot* 30a), appointment to the monarchy (*Sifri* 157 to *Devarim* 17:15), and in inclusion in the

28. The *Avot* and *Imahot* were equally critical for the development of and the transmission of the mesorah. However, it is undeniable that they played very different roles.

29. Many examples can be found in the essays published in *Family Redeemed*: "Adam and Eve" (1971), pp. 3-30 (especially 18-27); "Marriage" (1959), pp. 31-72 (especially 67-72); "Parenthood: Natural and Redeemed" (undated), pp. 105-125; Torah and *Shekhinah*" (1968), pp. 158–180 (especially 158-166).

30. Rabbi Avraham Besdin, *Man of Faith in the Modern World*, pp. 84-85. Elsewhere, the Rav writes, "Sexual differentiation expresses more than a physical property; it manifests an ontic contrast, a dual aspect within the essence of creation, something deeper and more fundamental than natural sexual differentiation which finds its full expression in two bi-existential experiences, in two ideas of personalism" (Rabbi Joseph B. Soloveitchik, *Family Redeemed*, p. 70). Rav Hirsch, too, stresses the distinctions between men and women throughout the essay mentioned above, and in his famous explanation of the exemption for women from time bound mitzvot (see his commentary to *Vayikra* 23:46).

composition of a minyan for communal prayer are each indicative of different roles for men and women.[31]

Gender differences have, historically, been particularly evident in the arena of public service. We believe that these distinctions are not merely a relic of times bygone; instead, they reflect a Torah ethos – a *mesorah* – of different avenues and emphases by which men and women are to achieve identical goals – the service of G-d and the perpetuation of the Jewish people.[32] It is the majority opinion of our panel that the appointment of women to clergy positions would be a contradiction to this halakhic ethos.

Role distinctions are not absolute. We celebrate the fact that many women engage in high-level *Torah* learning – despite the fact that their obligation in *talmud Torah* differs from that of men.[33] We encourage mothers and fathers to share responsibility and to pool their talents and abilities to best bring up their children – despite archetypal parenting roles in our tradition.[34] However, there is, naturally, greater room for flexibility in the informal world of one's personal *avodat Hashem* and in the nuances of one's family dynamics, than in the more formalized

---

31. The Talmud's invocation of the verse "*kol kvudah bat melech pnimah*" (*Tehillim* 45:14) as a factor in establishing a detail of *halakhah* highlights this notion (*Yevamot* 77a). This is yet another example where a Torah value impacts directly on a legal decision.

32. 32 It is not unusual for the Torah to differentiate between different categories of people, both in *halakhah*, with regard to specialization of roles and in terms of formal positions of religious leadership. For example, only a *Kohein* can perform service in the *Beit Hamikdash* and eat from certain *korbanot*. Similarly, unlike an Israelite, a *Levi* played a unique role in the *Beit Hamikdash* and was entitled to receive *ma'aser*. These distinctions reflect the idea of assigning different communal responsibilities to different categories of people, while messaging that these distinctions carry with them no implications regarding their respective spiritual value.

33. 33 Women are exempt for the overriding commandment to study Torah (*Kiddushin* 29b). However, they are obligated to study the laws relevant to the mitzvot incumbent upon them (*Yoreh Deah* 246:6).

34. 34 See, for example, Rav Soloveitchik, *Family Redeemed*, p. 118.

public arena. The formal structure of synagogue leadership should more closely reflect the halakhic ethos.

Women Clergy

For the reasons stated above we believe that a woman should not be appointed to serve in a clergy position.

This restriction applies both to the designation of a title for women that connotes the status of a clergy member, as well as to the appointment of women to perform clergy functions on a regular ongoing basis – even when not accompanied by a rabbinic-type title. The spectrum of functions appropriately considered as the role of clergy can be identified by duties generally expected from, and often reserved for, a synagogue rabbi. These common functions include, but are not limited to: the ongoing practice of ruling on a full-range of halakhic matters, officiating at religiously significant life-cycle events, (e.g. *brit milah*, baby naming, *bar mitzvah, bat mitzvah*,[35] weddings and funerals),[36] the regular practice of delivering sermons from the pulpit during services, presiding over or "leading services" at a *minyan* and formally serving as the synagogue's primary religious mentor, teacher, and spiritual guide.

While a synagogue rabbi performs myriad functions, it is these common functions most often performed by a rabbi that characterize his role as the synagogue's formal religious leader. The gamut of rabbinical responsibilities has evolved over time,

---

35. 35 Of course, at a *Bat Mitzvah* celebration attended primarily or exclusively by women, it is likely that the arrangement most in keeping with the Torah ethos of *tzniyut* will involve women playing frontal roles and not men.

36. 36 Women *speaking* at these events is common practice in our community and is not a "clergy function."

37 In responding to the questions posed by the OU, our suggestions focus on the professional contributions of women within the synagogue. Of course, we continue to support the critical role that women have played, and must continue to play, in our educational institutions. The issue of lay leadership positions is beyond the scope of this paper.

adapting to the needs of each generation and locale. Nonetheless, the designated role of spiritual synagogue leader can be identified through the prevailing rabbinic duties.

Communal Roles for Women

That being said, female role models are, of course, absolutely critical for the spiritual growth of our community. Communities depend, and have always depended, upon women's participation in a wide array of critical roles, both lay and professional, that are wholly consistent with Torah's guidelines. Women should most enthusiastically be encouraged to share their knowledge, talents, and skills – as well as their passion and devotion – to synagogues, schools and community organizations. The restriction on assuming a clergy role has not precluded, and need not preclude, women from making vital and substantial contributions to the Jewish people.

The needs and standards of communities differ significantly. As appropriate to each community and, subject to the guidance and the approval of the synagogue's lay and rabbinic leadership, we believe that it is appropriate for women to assume the following non-exhaustive list of professional roles within the synagogue setting[37] *in a non-clergy capacity* (as defined above):

1. Roles women are currently assuming:
   a. Teaching ongoing classes and *shiurim*, and delivering lectures.
   b. Serving as a visiting scholar-in-residence
   c. Serving in senior managerial and administrative positions, such as executive director, or director of programming and/or adult education.
2. Roles women are beginning to assume in some synagogue settings:
   a. Serving as a synagogue staff member in the role of community educator or institutional scholar to supplement

synagogue rabbis in enhancing the community's educational opportunities.

b. Serving as a synagogue staff member in the role of professional counselor to address the spiritual, psychological, or social needs of the community.
c. Serving as a teacher and mentor to guide females through the conversion process.

While by no means an exhaustive list, these examples are illustrative of the myriad contributions that women can provide within the synagogue structure without assuming a formal clergy role. With the guidance of their local rabbi, communities can explore the opportunities that can be best implemented to deepen and enrich the Torah learning and religious experience of men and women alike.

Halakhic Advisors

Segments of our community have engaged highly knowledgeable and dedicated women who are trained to serve as halakhic advisors ("*yoatzot halakhah*") for issues of *taharat hamishpachah*. In a number of communities these advisors have played a deeply significant role and have increased the comfort level of many women in posing halakhic questions in this most sensitive area of observance. These *yoatzot halakhah* have fielded many thousands of important questions which might not otherwise have been asked.

There may, however, be significant advantages in posing *taharat hamishpachah* queries to the same individual to whom one generally turns for *hora'ah*. This is especially true in the Diaspora where, as opposed to *Eretz Yisrael*, communities are typically organized around a synagogue rabbi and rebbetzin and *psak* is generally handled on a local level. Furthermore, answers to questions regarding *taharat hamishpachah* are often integrally connected to the dynamics of a particular family and marital relationship. Consequently, it is recommended that these questions be posed to the community rabbi who is knowledgeable in *hilkhot niddah* and also integrally involved with the couple on many levels.

We strongly encourage synagogue rabbis to take all necessary steps to ensure that their congregants are comfortable asking questions in these areas. Rabbis should collaborate with their congregants – certainly women, but men as well – to devise practices that will provide maximum comfort for those with questions. We also encourage synagogue rabbis to further increase their sophistication and training in the applicable halakhic, medical, and psychological spheres to serve as a valuable resource.

We recognize and understand, however, that some women are, and may remain, uncomfortable asking these *sheilot* to their synagogue rabbi and often cannot, or will not, avail themselves of the options presented above. Accordingly, those best positioned to assist in this area are knowledgeable and highly trained women who are passionate and committed to helping their communities, and who are imbued with *yirat shamayim*.

Significant differences exist between the clergy functions outlined above and the role of a *yoetzet*. *Yoatzot* distinguish themselves from female clergy because, as their title implies, *yoatzot* advise, rather than issue novel rulings or decisions in disputed matters, and they do not perform other rabbinic functions. They specialize in a limited area of *halakhah* – an area that is most relevant to women and where *tzniyut* is essential – and function outside the context of prayer services.

We do not have a consensus opinion with regard to all of the halakhic issues involved with the official position of *yoetzet halakhah*. We agree that *yoatzot* provide a valuable service, but some feel that, with regard to normative wide-spread community practice, halakhic and meta-halakhic concerns outweigh the benefits.

In light of all of the above-referenced considerations, the utilization of *yoatzot halakhah* should continue to be evaluated carefully by *poskim* and communities alike. Under all circumstances, a *yoetzet halakhah* should only be employed with the approval of the synagogue's or community's rabbis, and should continue to work in close consultation with the local rabbi(s).

Conclusions and Further Suggestions

Ultimately, our mission must be to enhance the commitment of the Jewish People to Torah and *mitzvot*. All of our actions must be measured against this foundational standard. There is much we can do as a community, both men and women, to further advance these lofty goals.

Our synagogues must continue to serve the needs of women and men. While the traditional synagogue experience continues to offer religious fulfillment to many women in our communities, some women – and men for that matter – feel disengaged from their shuls and uninspired in the synagogue. They yearn for a closer connection to *Hashem* and seek to intensify their *tefillah* experience.

It is axiomatic that the timeless traditions of *Chazal* provide the framework for living a Torah life; however, we are not always successful in bringing those traditions to life. We recognize that many who are looking for new avenues to increase their shul involvement are motivated by a genuine desire to strengthen their connection with *Hashem*. As such, the importance of *tefillah* for women and men (and children) must be stressed and efforts must be undertaken by communal leadership, both rabbinic and lay, to create an environment and *tefillah* experience that will engage every individual.

We encourage our communities to address these genuine aspirations in a manner compatible with *halakhah* and consistent with Torah values. For example, care should continue to be taken to construct *mechitzot* that not only follow halakhic requirements, but are also sensitive to the degree of engagement with the services that can be felt from the *Ezrat Nashim*. Similarly, women seeking greater involvement in synagogue prayer services should be encouraged to come to *shul* for weekday and *Shabbat minyanim*, and the *Ezrat Nashim* should be inviting and available for their attendance. Each synagogue should be encouraged to reach out to women – and particularly single women when applicable – to create meaningful ways to involve them in synagogue life. Women should be actively included in conversations related to *tefillah* and synagogue atmosphere.

The spiritual growth of our community is dependent upon a steady stream of talented women both serving as role models and teachers, and filling positions of influence. As a community, we need the best and brightest women – and men – to be motivated and well-trained to pursue careers in *avodat hakodesh*, whether in schools, synagogues or *chesed* organizations. Finally, steps should be taken to properly recognize women who dedicate their lives and their abilities to serving and educating our community, including the attribution of fitting titles that convey the significance of these roles.

As we broaden our perspective from the letter of the law to the values that emerge from the totality of our tradition, we encounter the opportunity to more fully understand the Divine and to walk in His ways. We seek to follow the values of the Torah, preserve them, and embrace them as our guide, which we can only do by respecting our tradition and upholding the instructions and values that emerge from within it. It is with this deep level of engagement with the Torah that we are infused with a sense of purpose and transcendence, and it is through the medium of *halakhah* and Torah ethos that we find liberty and exaltation in surrendering ourselves to the Divine will.

Rabbi Daniel Feldman
Rabbi Yaakov Neuberger
Rabbi Michael Rosensweig
Rabbi Ezra Schwartz
Rabbi Gedalia Dov Schwartz
Rabbi Hershel Schachter
Rabbi Benjamin Yudin

* * *

RABBI HERZL HEFTER'S RESPONSE

Rabbi Herzl Hefter's response was originally published in The Times of Israel on February 8, 2017 at http://blogs.timesofisrael.com/on-female-rabbis-the-ou-statement-and-slavery/.
The response being reprinted here has been updated by the author.

On Women Rabbis, the OU Statement and Slavery

Rabbi Herzl Hefter

> *Gender differences have, historically, been particularly evident in the arena of public service. We believe that these distinctions are not merely a relic of times bygone; instead, they reflect a Torah ethos – a mesorah . . .* (from the OU statement)

The OU statement was correct in framing the issue of women serving as rabbis as a meta-halakhic question. Acquiescence to halakha is obligatory for a Jew committed to his or her tradition. However, when normative directives are acknowledged by all parties as being contoured by understanding of the tradition itself, we have an obligation to look closely at the nuances of the assumptions implicit in that understanding.

In this response I will compare the OU statement to a sermon delivered in the period leading up to the American Civil War concerning slavery. This will highlight the profoundly problematic and disturbing assumptions of the OU statement. By this analogy I do not intend to draw a moral equivalent between the two instances. It is to the ***method of argumentation*** that I wish to draw attention and which I find so disturbing.

My purpose in writing is not to score debating points or ridicule the authors of the OU statement. I am writing out of fear for our *mesorah*, our tradition.

*

In January 1861, on the eve o4f the American Civil War, Rabbi Dr. M.J. Raphall of Congregation B'nai Jeshurun in New York City delivered a sermon in which he defended the institution of slavery based on the authority of the Torah. While the plight of women in our community is very far from the brutality of slavery as practiced in the antebellum South, there is room for analogy. Denying people recognition for their achievements and limiting their opportunities to serve is a form of servitude.

The similarity of the argumentation given by both Rabbi Raphall and the OU statement should give us pause.

The sermon is characterized by scorn for "new ideas," appeal to authority and a naïve ignorance of historical process. Reminiscent of the attitude toward the "Untouchables" in India, he adheres to an essentialist view concerning slaves, attributing their miserable station to Heavenly decree. It has a paternalistic tone of a defender of the faith against impiety. (The entire sermon can be accessed here http://www.jewish-history.com/civilwar/raphall.html)

*

As an uncompromisingly committed Jew, I own my tradition and it owns me. I must answer to it and it makes me what I am. Looking forward, the *hakhmei hamesorah*, those who transmit our tradition, interpret what they have received and pass it on to the next generation. We own it and we fashion it. This puts an awesome responsibility in the hands of the interpreters and framers of our tradition.

Let us begin with an excerpt from the sermon.

> *... "Is slaveholding condemned as a sin in sacred Scripture?" How this question can at all arise in the mind of any man that has received a religious education, and is acquainted with the history of the Bible, is a phenomenon I cannot explain to myself, and which fifty years ago no man dreamed of. But we live in times when we must not be surprised at anything.... and*

> *when, lastly, I remember the scorn with which sacred Scripture (Deut. xxxii. 18) speaks of "***newfangled notions***, lately sprung up, which your fathers esteemed not;" when I consider all this, I think you and I had rather continue to take our "requirements for moral instruction" from Moses and the Prophets than from the eloquent* [abolitionist – HH] *preacher of Brooklyn.....*

Rabbi Raphall heaped scorn upon an abolitionist preacher who appealed to more refined human sentiments and morality which evolved post-Scripture.

And here is the gist of the argument against women rabbis as formulated in the OU document.

> *...American culture of personal autonomy and the egalitarian ethos inexorably clashes with the Torah values of placing normative halachic conduct above individual choice and halachic dictates above individual freedom.*

We are exhorted to toss out an ethos of personal autonomy AND RESPONSIBILITY in a non-halakhic question of value, based not upon dialogue and persuasion, but upon authority. "Even when difficult to comprehend." [Read: Defies our moral sensibilities upon which we were nurtured.]

Even as the OU statement reiterates its commitment to submission to authority, it implicitly recognizes the weakness of the argument. The bottom line is that we simply do not understand God's will.

> *As Orthodox Jews, we believe in the deference to rabbinic authority, accepting the authority of gedolim and poskim, [...] Reared in the modern world, we believe in self-actualization and the ability to choose our own paths; yet as Torah Jews, we subordinate the Western emphasis on autonomy to our willing and unabashed embrace of deference to the values and principles conveyed by the Torah, as interpreted by our leading Torah*

scholars and halachic authorities . . . The exploration of halacha must reflect the aspiration of uncovering G-d's will, ***even when uncomfortable or difficult to comprehend.*** [emphasis added]

Similarly, Rabbi Raphall, after presenting his arguments for slavery, implicitly recognizes the moral weakness of *his* position. His solution is the same as that of the OU document; authority trumps morality. We must accept slavery because we do not understand the ways of our Lord.

I bid you reflect on the words of inspired Isaiah (lv. 8.), ***"My thoughts are not your thoughts, neither are your ways my ways, saith the L-rd."***

*

I find it humiliating and unconscionable that the institution of slavery should have been thus defended based upon the authority of the Torah.

I actually couldn't learn yesterday or sleep last night because of this sermon. I couldn't sleep because this sermon is connected to me whether I like it or not. I feel the desecration of God's name in the attitude of the teacher who piously warns against the adaptation of newfangled ideas (the moral condemnation of slavery) in defiance of the bible.

And the tone. The paternalistic self-confidence of one who speaks in the name of Scripture is rivalled only by the obtuseness he conveys.

How dare you, in the face of the sanction and protection afforded to slave property in the Ten Commandments – how dare you denounce slaveholding as a sin? When you remember that Abraham, Isaac, Jacob, Job – the men with whom the Almighty conversed, [. . .] that all these men were slaveholders, does it not strike you that you are guilty of something very little short of blasphemy? And if you answer me, "Oh, in their time slave-

> *holding was lawful, but now it has become a sin," I in my turn ask you, "When and by what authority you draw the line?" Tell us the precise time when slaveholding ceased to be permitted, and became sinful?"*

The ignorance of historical process is stunning.

Regarding the following section from the OU statement, which also displays a feeble understanding of historical process, I can only paraphrase Rabbi Raphall: How the following statement can at all arise in the mind of any man that has received an education, and is acquainted with history, is a phenomenon I cannot explain to myself.

From the OU statement:

> *The existence of female scholars throughout the history of our nation is, in our understanding, ample proof that the notion of semikha for women was conceivable. However, a continuing mesorah existed that dictated against it. We find it implausible to say that the question of female ordination has never presented itself throughout the history of our mesorah.*

*

How do we feel when we read the following words from the sermon in which moral abomination is enshrined in the holy Torah and attributed to God?

> *Noah did not bestow any blessing on his son Ham, but uttered a bitter curse against his descendants, and to this day it remains a fact which cannot be gainsaid that in his own native home, and generally throughout the world, the unfortunate negro is indeed the meanest of slaves. Much has been said respecting the inferiority of his intellectual powers, and that no man of his race has ever inscribed his name on the Pantheon of human excellence, either mental or moral. But this is a subject I will not discuss.* ***I do not attempt to build up a theory, not yet to defend***

> ***the moral government of Providence. I state facts;*** [emphasis added]

The miserable plight of the downtrodden "meanest of slaves" is affirmed by the biblical narrative and enshrined by divine decree. It is a "fact."

The OU statement affirms similar "facts."

> *Finally, even if the absence of women rabbis throughout Jewish history is not fully dispositive, this phenomenon does establish a baseline status quo.* ***We feel that the absence of institutionalized women's rabbinic leadership has been both deliberate and meaningful, and should continue to be preserved.*** [emphasis added]

The "baseline status quo," the OU tells us, is a "fact." A divine decree. Not a challenge, not something to struggle with, nor a curse to overcome. A fact, a divine decree to be embraced and preserved.

*

Please note, the good Rabbi was not an evil person. He had no affinity towards slavery, yet he felt a sacred responsibility as a teacher of God's Torah to present it as it is. The ways of God are beyond us and we must submit.

> *My friends, I find, and I am sorry to find, that I am delivering a pro-slavery discourse. I am no friend to slavery in the abstract, and still less friendly to the practical working of slavery.* ***But I stand here as a teacher in Israel; not to place before you my own feelings and opinions, but to propound to you the word of G-d, the Bible view of slavery. With a due sense of my responsibility, I must state to you the truth and nothing but the truth, however unpalatable or unpopular that truth may be.*** [emphasis added]

The OU rabbis are good men, men who have devoted their lives to the study and dissemination of the Torah. I believe that they are driven by authentic concern for the Jewish people and the desire to bring them closer to God and the Torah. Yet, I believe that their concern is contaminated with a fear and lack of faith both in the Jewish People and the Torah as a potent force in leading the people to God. Resorting to arguments which exhort us to deny what we deeply believe is right – which indeed as is implied from their own statement, that ***they also believe is right*** – in the name of an authoritarian essentialist view of the inherent irrevocable differences between men and women in a way which results in the unfair treatment of women is deplorable. I worry less for those women unjustly denied proper recognition and opportunity; they and we shall overcome. My heart aches for the Torah thus perceived and the Desecration of God's Holy Name which results.

This pre-Civil War sermon shows how a fundamentalist interpretation of the Torah along with a knee jerk desire to maintain the status quo can insert morally indefensible positions into our tradition. This is not the Torah which I will pass on to my children. I will not make them own such moral opacity.

The moral revulsion which decent people should feel upon reading Rabbi Raphall's sermon is that of experiencing a desecration of the Holy Name. It needs to serve as a terrifying reminder of the warning of our sages,

> Avtalyon says, "Sages, be careful with your words, lest you become obligated in an obligation of exile and are exiled to the place of evil waters, and the students who follow after you will drink, and thus the name of Heaven is profaned."

* * *

Rabbi Herzl Hefter is the founder and Rosh Beit Midrash Har'el in memory of Belda Kaufman Lindenbaum, in Jerusalem. It is a beit midrash for advanced rabbinic studies for men and women. He is a graduate of Yeshiva University where he learned under the tutelage of Rabbi Yosef Dov Soloveichik zt"l, *and received smikha from Rabbi Aharon Lichtenstein* zt"l *at Yeshivat Har Etzion where he studied for ten years. Rabbi Hefter taught Yoreh De'ah to the Kollel fellows at the Gruss Kollel of Yeshiva University and served as the head of the Bruria Scholars Program at Midreshet Lindenbaum. He also taught at Yeshivat Mekor Chaim in Moscow and served as Rosh Kollel of the first Torah MiZion Kollel in Cleveland, Ohio. He has written numerous articles related to modernity and Hasidic thought and was most recently a research fellow at the Hartman Institute in Jerusalem. His divrei Torah and online shiurim can be accessed at har-el.org.*

RABBI ETHAN TUCKER'S RESPONSE

Rabbi Ethan Tucker's response was originally published in The Times of Israel on February 9, 2017 at http://blogs.timesofisrael.com/misunderstanding-tradition/
It is being reprinted here as it originally appeared.

(Mis)understanding Tradition

The recent discussions about female clergy in Orthodoxy are flooded with the rhetoric of tradition and change. Given that Judaism, writ large, has certainly had a longstanding tradition of male leadership and full, public ritual citizenship has classically been largely male, can contemporary communities transcend this history without severing their link to that past?

In religious terms, doesn't *halakhah* – Jewish legal and normative discourse – and *mesorah*/tradition – the communal patterns of our ancestors – make the embrace of female clergy revolutionary and rebellious?

There are of course so many angles to think about here, but I just want to highlight one, which, in my view has barely been addressed but is perhaps the most important.

One can talk at length about what we have and haven't seen in the context of Jewish history in terms of leadership. This can take more descriptive forms – we haven't seen women acting as rabbis in the past – and prescriptive forms – quoting texts from authorities like the Rambam who say that women should not be in positions of authority and power. "One should not appoint a woman to any position of authority" (Laws of Kings 1:5). Indeed, recent statements opposing the ordination of female rabbis *de jure* and *de facto* cite these sorts of texts and the absence of women from female leadership in the past as support for their position today. The premise that Jewish law and history preclude female leadership having been established, the discussion predictably turns from substance to form. We stop engaging the topic and then talk exclusively about who has the power to change how much of Jewish tradition for what ends.

But I fear that the entire premise of this discussion may just be wrong. Those opposed to female clergy today on the basis of *halakhah* may make no errors in legal methodology, but they may simply have their facts wrong. Put another way: I think contemporary opponents of female clergy in Judaism quite possibly misunderstand the very tradition they rightly seek to defend. Being a traditionalist is not dispositive of the question of just what tradition you are defending and why.

Let me give a counter example, from a totally different area of law and practice. There are a series of laws designed to prevent people from feeding the market for stolen goods. When there is a reasonable presumption that the person selling you something could not have legitimately come into possession of that item, you have to assume it is stolen and not buy it from them. One text in the cluster of sources dealing with this issue says the following:

תוספתא ב"ק יא:ה

לוקחין מן הנשים כלי צמר ביהודה ואין לוקחין פירות יינות שמנים וסלתות לא מן הנשים ולא מן העבדים ולא מן הקטנים.

Tosefta Bava Kama 11:5

One may buy items made of wool from women in Judea, but one does not buy produce, wine, oil or flour neither from women, nor slaves nor minors.

This is a text that forbids buying any sort of food items from women anywhere. It is a fairly clear directive. Would anyone imagine saying that this is in force with respect to contemporary women today? Of course not. Would that be because we had to update the *halakhah* in order to make it more friendly to contemporary assumptions and values? No. It would be because the underlying values of the *halakhah* have to be properly applied to contemporary reality. A close reading of this *halakhah* reveals that the term "women" here is clearly just a placeholder for one of a set of characters who don't have economic independence. That is clear from the context – there is no reason laws about theft should have anything to do with biological sex; it is clear from the other (nonfemale) characters included here – slaves and minors – and it is clear from the other details of the law – under certain circumstances women clearly are trusted to have the items in question on legitimate authority (wool in Judea, where it is plentiful and in excess). And we could also trace how this trend of interpretation was maintained over time. It would therefore be bizarre today to imagine that this law had anything to do with biological essentialism and order traditional Jews to avoid buying produce from women except in very highly defined circumstances. In the contemporary Western economy, there is no more reason to presume theft when it comes to goods sold by a woman as opposed to a man.

Was there a tradition not to buy things from women in the Talmudic period? Yes there was. But that tradition almost perfectly overlapped the tradition not to buy things from people who were presumed to lack any meaningful financial independence. You technically could interpret these texts as only making highly circumscribed exceptions for buying from women in cases like the sale of wool in Judea, perhaps licensed for inscrutable divine reasons, and one could also argue that this *halakhah* is meant to enshrine a role for women: they ought not to be in the business of retail. I think there are few of us for whom that reading would stand up, but that is not because the word נשים/women forces us to one reading or the other. When we read a text like this, we do not reveal our hermeneutics and traditionalism as much as we reveal our assumptions around gender, sex and the value behind the law in question.

Similarly, it doesn't help much to quote texts from the past that bar women from power. Because those texts also come from a world in which women, like slaves and minors, were not generally taken seriously as principals. Yes, there were queens here and there (always unusually inheriting the throne through patriarchal systems that privileged men in descent), but as a class of people, women were inferior in terms of power and citizenship in a consistent fashion. The Sifrei captures this best when considering the fact that Moshe seems to specify אנשים/men when describing the sorts of people the Israelites should select as judges. It asks with bewilderment:

אנשים!? וכי עלתה על דעתנו נשים? מה תלמוד לומר אנשים?!
"Men?! Could we possibly have thought women? Why did Scripture say, "men?!"

The bewilderment here is not from a prooftext, not from a settled principle of Jewish law; indeed, the passage being commented on here is just Moshe's reflection on the past. The astonishment is just from life – "How could anyone think to appoint a woman as a judge?" Isn't it obvious that doing so is a deep disrespect for the institution?

Similarly, when the Sifrei elsewhere says מלכה ולא מלך – "a king and not a queen" – in defining the terms of the Jewish monarchy, this seems to reflect the notion that a female monarch is inherently less serious and stable than a male monarch, not least because, in a patriarchal society, her marriage to another sovereign might well deprive a Jewish polity of its independence and distinctiveness. And when the Talmud (Yevamot 45b and Kiddushin 76b) and then the Rambam adopt the paradigm of the monarchy for positions of leadership, we arrive at the notion that women should not serve in any serious leadership capacities in the Jewish community.

Aside from whether all agreed with the Rambam's analysis, however, it is a huge stretch to pluck his ruling from the 12th century and drop it down in the 21st. Has there been a Jewish tradition to exclude women from leadership? Yes there has. Can we distinguish this tradition from the tradition to exclude more marginal citizens from leadership? No we cannot. Some of us find that so obvious that we would approach this *halakhah* the same way virtually everyone would approach the *halakhah* from Bava Kama above. In fact, we would say that the *exclusion* of women from leadership positions is a violation of the tradition that those with full social and economic independence are meant to serve and lead barring other obvious limitations. But even for those who are not so strident, it is surely not completely obvious that the sources excluding women from leadership are about biology!

And here is where some humility is in order. I think the time has come where we cannot give a free pass to conversations that simply assume the biological/chromosomal meaning of נשים/women in all Jewish texts and then run away to questions of authority and tradition. Those discussions of authority and tradition are often masks that conceal deep-seated gender essentialist positions about a whole host of things. Those assumptions are not self-evidently the products of texts that speak about women, especially when they speak about slaves and minors as well. We will only fully confront the underlying issues here when people speak directly to the values at stake. And the conversation should not be one of greater or lesser respect for the tradition – there is only one winner in that fight – but of how to properly understand it and apply it with reverence.

Rabbi Ethan Tucker is Rosh Yeshiva at Mechon Hadar and Chair in Jewish Law. Rabbi Tucker was ordained by the Chief Rabbinate of Israel and earned a PhD in Talmud and Rabbinics from the Jewish Theological Seminary and a B.A. from Harvard College. A Wexner Graduate Fellow, he was a co-founder of Kehilat Hadar and a winner of the first Grinspoon Foundation Social Entrepreneur Fellowship. He was named one of America's Top 50 Rabbis by Newsweek in 2011, 2012, and 2013.

APPENDIX II: RABBI SOLOVEITCHIK'S POSITION ON WOMEN AS SHOHATOT AND THE DEVELOPMENT OF CUSTOMS OF ABSTENTION

Rabbi Jeffrey S. Fox

THIS ESSAY[1] ANALYZES THE OPENING SHIUR IN SHIUREI Ha-Rav (Jerusalem: Mesorah, 2005), Rabbi Eliakim Koenigsberg's book of summaries and transcriptions of Rabbi Soloveitchik's shiurim on Yoreh De'ah.[2] The shiur's analysis of women serving as shohatot, ritual slaughterers, has recently been used by the rabbinic panel of the OU to articulate the panel's opposition to women serving as Orthodox clergy. In the opening two essays on Rabbi Soloveitchik's shiur on the laws of Kashrut, the Rav offers two approaches to the following passage in the Yoreh De'ah section of Shulkhan Arukh (1:1):

1. This essay was originally published in The Lehrhaus on Feb. 23, 2017, at https://bit.ly/2xCFUpv. Excerpted with permission.

2. I would like to thank the students of Yeshivat Maharat as well as Rabbanit Devorah Zlochower for their helpful comments and insights in the formation of this article. There may very well be different versions of this shiur as the Rav was well known for revisiting material that he had taught in the past as though it was the first time he was encountering those texts. However, I can only evaluate the Rav's Torah based on what appears in writing. It was (loosely) translated by Rabbi Gil Student. In addition, Rabbis Aryeh and Dov Frimer used this shiur to argue that the Rav would certainly be against the granting of semikhah to women. I will deal with their claims below.

הכל שוחטין לכתחלה, אפילו נשים. הגה: יש אומרים שאין להניח נשים לשחוט שכבר נהגו שלא לשחוט. וכן המנהג שאין הנשים שוחטות.

Everyone is permitted to slaughter from the outset, even women. Rema: And some say that we should not permit women to slaughter because the custom has developed not to slaughter. And that is the custom, that women do not slaughter.

Rabbi Yosef Karo decided that women may, if properly trained, serve as shohatot. That ruling was in accordance with the simple understanding of the Gemara and the majority of *Rishonim* (See Tosafot Chullin 2a "Ha-kol Shohtin," Rosh Chullin 1:1(2), Mishneh Torah: Sefer Kedushah- Hilchot Shehitah 4:4, Rashba Torat ha-Bayit 1:1, 7a, Ran on Rif page 2a "v-kulan she-shahatu) The Rema, in response, claims that we should not allow women to do shehitah and that such is the minhag.

Rabbi Soloveitchik's Approach to Women as Shohatot:

It is important to state upfront that this is not a conversation of equals. The gadlut of the Rav far surpasses my learning. However, I feel that responding to a written essay is appropriate. Everyone who is writing about this sensitive issue must do so from a place of honest humility. I would like to analyze the written position of the Rav and make three basic claims:

1. This first claim will address a textual problem within the shiur. Rabbi Koenigsberg, in his transcription of the notes from the shiur, relies on a text from the Semak that does not appear in the standard printed edition.
2. Second, the Rav, based on his understanding of the exclusion of women from shehitah, read Rambam's approach to serarah in a way that leads to an internal contradiction within Rambam.
3. The creative application of a 'custom of abstention' to explain a passage from the medieval period reflects a world in which there was no reality of advanced women's learning in

the Orthodox community. In addition, the Shakh's position, which is central to the Rav's thesis, is only operational regarding matters of 'common' practice. Some later Aharonim appear to ultimately reject the Shakh.

These three claims make the article of the rabbinic panel read less like a formal pesak and more like rabbinic advice (חוות דעת). It is certainly the case that different rabbinic scholars can and should express their opinions on matters of communal policy. No one questions the gadlut be-Torah, and indeed the courage, of these rabbanim, but given the range of possible positions on this matter, it is unwise for the OU to adopt this paper as a matter of national policy.

Claim I: The text of the Semak

The Rav claims that a woman may not serve as a shohetet because it violates Rambam's understanding of serarah (coercive communal authority) or mesimah (appointment).[3] The Rav links this minhag to serarah in order to help explain a strange formulation found in the Kol Bo (n.107) and cited by the Beit Yosef (Yoreh De'ah 1). The Kol Bo quoted the Semak (Mitzvat Aseh n.197) as saying "women may only שוחטות לעצמן—slaughter for themselves." One implication of this phrase might be that women may not slaughter on behalf of others, or the community.

It is important to note that the Beit Yosef (Yoreh De'ah 1) quoted the Kol Bo's version of the Semak (Mitzvat Aseh n.197) in which the word "לעצמן—for themselves" appears. The Agur (Hilchot Shehitah, Siman 1062) cites the Semak in the same way. However, the standard printed editions of the Semak do not have this phrase. The standard printed editions simple have נשים

3. See Sifrei on Devarim, ed. Louis Finkelstein (New York: Jewish Theological Seminary of America, 1969), 209, lines 5-7. See also Mishneh Torah: Sefer Shoftim, Hilchot Melachim 1:4-5.

שוחטות without any qualification. The Orhot Hayyim (Shehitah n.3) does not have the words "for themselves." Much of the Rav's shiur is built on the distinction between "לעצמן", and for the community.

In his first comment in Yoreh De'ah, the Peri Hadash accepts the inference that לעצמן means that women may slaughter for themselves and not the community. However, he does not refer to Rambam and serarah. Instead, he claims that the job of the town-shohet requires hard work (זריזות גדול) and that women are too lazy (עצלניות) to perform the task. This is not a generous way to speak about women. However, it is clear that the Peri Hadash did not see the appointment of a woman as the town-shohet as a problem of serarah or minuy as he forbids that job for tangential reasons that I think all would agree no longer apply to women today.

To be clear, the position of Rema himself is based on the Agur (Hilchot Shehitah, Siman 1062) who simply states that women may not serve as shohatot (the Agur is, in turn, based on the unusual approach of Eldad ha-Dani, quoted in Tosafot on Chullin 2a "Ha-kol Shohtin").[4] Rema did not quote the Kol Bo's version of the Semak. Rather, he stated unequivocally that the minhag is that women may not slaughter. The Rav explains his inference from the Kol Bo's citation of the Semak that women may not serve as a shohetet for others because it is a position of communal authority. He posits that once there was an office of the "town-shohet", that appointment could not be filled by a woman.

---

4. Eldad ha-Dani was a Jewish traveler from the ninth century who wrote a small Hebrew handbook of halakhah that dealt with the laws of slaughter. He was from Africa; likely Ethiopia. Many of his traditions violate standard talmudic law.

Serarah and Converts

Before turning to the internal contradiction created within Rambam, let us understand the full extent of the Rav's position. Rambam's approach is based on a parallel between the types of serarah that women and converts may attain. In chapter one of Hilchot Melachim, Maimonides first describes the limitations of the convert (Hal. 4) and then moves on to women (Hal. 5). There is a connection between the limitations placed on female leadership and what might be available to converts. The halakhah is that a convert may serve as a shohet (Mishneh Torah, Hilchot Shehitah 4:4; Tur, Yoreh De'ah 1; Darkhei Moshe 2). If that is case, asks the Rav, how are we to distinguish between women, who may not serve as shohatot, and converts, who are permitted to serve as shohtim?

Accordingly, the Rav offered two different categories of appointments: מינוי של חשיבות ומינוי של שררה an appointment of importance and an appointment of (communal) authority. For the Rav, a convert can attain the status of an appointment of importance, חשיבות, just not one of authority. Therefore, since the shohet is only a מינוי של חשיבות (an appointment of importance) a convert may serve in that capacity. However, since a woman may not serve in any kind of מינוי—neither of importance nor of authority—she may not function even as a shohetet.

The Rav's position is very extreme. According to Rabbi Soloveitchik, the appointment of a woman to nearly any position of communal leadership would ultimately violate his understanding of serarah. For most of the Modern Orthodox community today, placing these kinds of limitations on the leadership potential of either converts or women is anathema. In theory, being hired or appointed by a synagogue to serve as a halakhic adviser (Yo'etzet Halakhah) ought to be at least a position of importance. In addition, there are women who serve in administrative positions of Modern Orthodox day schools across the country. These professional capacities would likely fall under the category of a forbidden appointment for the Rav.

Claim II: Rambam on Shehitah—Internal Contradiction

Rambam (Hilchot Shehitah 4:4) rules that women may serve as shohatot. To him, it is clear that a woman may study with an expert and be trained by a hakham in order that she too may be considered an expert (מומחה). Rav Moshe Isserles, the Rema, in his Darkhei Moshe on the Tur (Yoreh De'ah 1:3) claims that the practice and requirement of receiving formal training and a kabalah has its source in Rambam himself (Hilchot Shehitah 4:3).

The language of Rambam is significant in order to understand some basic shehitah terminology. He wrote (Hilchot Shehitah 4:4):

> היודע הלכות שחיטה ושחט בפני חכם עד שנעשה רגיל הוא הנקרא מומחה. וכל המומחין שוחטין לכתחלה בינן לבין עצמן. ואפילו נשים ועבדים אם היו מומחין הרי אלו שוחטין לכתחלה.
>
> One who knows the laws of slaughtering and slaughtered in front of a hakham until they became accustomed is called an expert. And all experts may slaughter even from the outset by themselves (בינן לבין עצמן—meaning without someone watching over their practice). And [this law applies] even to women and slaves, for if they became experts they can slaughter from the outset.

When Rambam uses the phrase "בינן לבין עצמן—by themselves," he does not mean to imply that women who are experts may only slaughter for themselves. Rather, his point is that once a person has become an expert they no longer need supervision to ensure that they are carrying out the physical behaviors according to the law. This usage is likely what the Kol Bo's version of the Semak means as well.[5]

---

5. See the Peri Toar (Yoreh De'ah 1) who explains the word לעצמן from the

What emerges from Rambam's own words is that serving as a shohet(et), which requires training and expertise, simply cannot be a violation of serarah or mesimah. The Rav argued that the implementation of training and the granting of a degree (kabalah) shifted the status of the shochet(et) from "איסור והיתר בעלמא (just a prohibited and forbidden matter)" to a "מינוי הקהל (communal appointment)." Therefore, women became ineligible.[6] However, I submit that this position cannot be maintained within the language of Rambam himself. It may be a way to explain the Kol Bo's citation of the Semak (which does not reflect the extant version of the Semak himself, and is not the most convincing read of that passage), but it does not work within Rambam.[7]

What is perhaps even more interesting is that semikhah in the twenty-first century is often categorized as "איסור והיתר בעלמא—'just' a prohibited and forbidden matter," which is not, by definition, a problem of serarah.

While the Rav's lomdus here is creative in helping to under-

Kol Bo as "לחודייהו" which is the language of the Rabbis. This is a much more convincing explanation for this strange formulation. In addition, Rabbi Eliyahu Landsaufer, in his Kanfei Yonah uses the phrase in exactly this way.

6. The formulation of the Rav's language by Rav Koeningsberg is important here. The key line reads as follows:

"ונראה דמאחר שנהגו ליטול קבלה מחכם כדי לשחוט, ממילא לא חשוב ענין השחיטה כמעשה איסור והיתר בעלמא שכל א' ראוי לו, אלא הרי הוא כמינוי הקהל".

This makes it clear that for the Rav, the receipt of a degree makes the shift from one category to the other automatically (ממילא).

7. In addition, Rambam's position on serarah is a minority voice among the *Rishonim*. The Rav's expansion to nearly all appointments, is an even greater minority position. See Rabbis Aryeh and Dov Frimer, who wrote: "the fact [is] that a large cadre of leading poskim have disagreed to varying extents with the Rav's sole reliance on the Rambam, his analysis of serara, and his distinction between serara and minui kahal. Furthermore, many poskim accept the efficacy of democratic elections (kiblu alayhu) as a means of circumventing serara considerations in other communal leadership positions (such as shul presidency and elected political positions), and they may well feel the same about Rabbinic positions)." They also penned an extensive footnote listing those Poskim who disagree in their more complete Hebrew article. I have made a similar claim in my own treatment of the broader question.

stand certain language from the *Rishonim*, it does not reflect the lived experience of many Jews in the twenty-first century.[8] The Rav is one very important voice among many poskim who have addressed this question. He happens to have concluded in a restrictive manner based on an unconvincing read of Rambam.

Claim III: מנהג בשב ואל תעשה—A Negative Custom

This brings us to the first approach outlined in the Rav's essay. Here the Rav develops an idea that he calls a "מנהג בשב ואל תעשה (a negative custom or a custom of abstention)." Although the Mishnah (Eduyot 2:2, Zevahim 12:4) states explicitly: "לא ראינו אינו ראיה, (not seeing something cannot serve as evidence)," there are instances of communal decisions to abstain from a certain behavior that can develop a kind of negative custom.

The Shakh, in a number of places, develops the idea, based on a teshuvah of the Maharik (Siman 171), that within the context of customs it is possible that not seeing or not doing something (לא ראינו) can serve as evidence (ראיה) of a negative custom (See Yoreh De'ah 1:1). The Rav points out a few examples from the laws of mourning in which customs of abstention developed after the Talmud (See Rema Yoreh De'ah 381:1, 389:3).

The Shakh, in his comment on Hoshen Mishpat (37:38) explains that the a negative minhag can only be created in the context of something that "arises regularly," שכיח טובא. The Shakh himself wrote in the beginning of Hilchot Milah (264:2) that the practice to not have women serve as mohalot cannot

8. Rabbi Michael Broyde and Rabbi Shlomo Brody in a lengthy footnote in their article on Orthodox Women Rabbis (p. 44n.21) responded to the claim of Rabbi Aryeh Frimer that based on this shiur, the Rav would obviously forbid the granting of semikhah to women. They are not convinced at all that this shiur was meant to be a statement about halakhah, but that it appears rather to be an in-depth shiur in lomdus. In addition, it is just as likely that a synagogue president could be a problem of serarah but a shul Rabbi perhaps may not because the rabbi can be fired. They quote a tradition from Rav Ahron Soloveichik to that effect.

be considered a minhag with obligatory force because it is so unusual: "דבר שאינו מצוי אין בו מנה—a matter that is uncommon is not subject to [the force] of minhag." At the end of this comment he refers to a comment he made in Hilchot Nidah (Siman 190:3): "ועוד דהדבר ידוע שדבר שאינו מצוי אין שייך בו מנהג—and it is known that [the concept of] minhag does not apply regarding something uncommon."[9]

The Shakh then refers to a similar comment made by Rambam towards the end of the 11th chapter of Hilchot Shehitah. In Halakha 13 Rambam is dealing with the question of what happens if an organ gets taken away before it can be inspected for treifot. He says that we can rely on a presumption that the organ was healthy and that the animal is therefore kosher. He concludes by saying, "ואין בזה מנהג שדבר שאינו מצוי אין בו מנהג—and this is not a matter of custom, because customs are not instituted regarding cases that are not commonplace."

Rabbi Yonatan Eibescheutz, in his commentary on Hoshen Mishpat wrote (Urim ve-Tumim, 37:22):

> ואני איני מבין בזה דבריו, דודאי במקום דהדבר תלוי וידוע דיש מקומות שנהגו כך או כך, או דיש מחלוקת בפוסקים, שפיר הוי לא ראינו ראיה.
> And I do not understand [the Shakh] in this matter. For certainly in a place where some matter was unsettled and it is known that some places behave like this and some like that, or there is a debate among the poskim, then we can say that 'not seeing' can serve as evidence.

Rabbi Eibescheutz concludes his comment in support of the Beit Yosef and leaves the Shakh with a need for further analysis (צ"ע). He may not be rejecting the Shakh entirely, but even if he does not

9. See the Peri Megadim, Siftei Da'at 2 who points out that the creation of a custom of abstention can only be done in an area that is commonly found (שכיח טובא). The Mahatzit ha-Shekel (1) assumes as well that women must have been asking explicitly to serve as shohatot and then be turned down in order for the negative custom to develop.

go that far, he is clearly not convinced by the Shakh's application of this rule.

In his shiur, the Rav only referred to the Shakh's comment in Yoreh De'ah (1:1) in which he relies on the teshuvah of Maharik. While the Shakh does say that minhagim of abstention or withholding can be created, he explicitly says that this only possible in a manner that is common or regular. Given the unusual nature of a panel of esteemed rabbinical scholars convened on behalf of this OU, one is hard pressed to claim that this is a "common" question. It is, in fact, the unusually sensitive nature of this question, that necessitated this entire panel. The issue of the granting of ordination to women and their appointment as members of clergy is a thoroughly new and uncommon question.

Three Decades of Women Learning

It is hard to overstate just how different the reality of women's advanced learning is today than it was twenty-five or thirty years ago. In the universe of the Orthodox community pre-1990, it would have been unreasonable to imagine a group of women learning for semichah. There were, no doubt, over the course of Jewish history individual women who excelled in learning and who perhaps deserved to receive semikhah. However, until:

1. Modern Orthodox High Schools began teaching Gemara to girls on par with their male colleagues and;
2. those same women had places to learn in Israel that could extend their skills and;
3. shiurim to attend at Stern or on a college campus;

no one could even have asked the question.[10]

10. This argument was already made explicitly by Rabbis Broyde and Brody (p. 45) of their above-cited article: "Given the lack of formal education for women, the question of women rabbis, quite simply, did not arise on a regular basis. There is no basis for a mesorah which would assert that women were regularly qualified to serve as rabbis, but did not do so for some halakhic reason."

To claim that the Rav would apply the notion of a negative minhag to an idea that existed only in the abstract is untenable. The year that the Rav passed away was also the first year of the Drisha Scholars' Circle. The only place in America where women could learn Gemara and/or Halakhah in a full-time setting was Drisha. There were fewer than a dozen women who had those skills. It is not reasonable to assert the creation of a minhag of abstention in a world in which no one was asking the question.

There were of course non-Orthodox women who were being ordained as Rabbis by the mid-1980s. For the purposes of defining a custom of abstention, the group of Jews who must be seeking semikhah is the Orthodox community. We do not define the parameters of minhagim based on Jews who do not observe Halakhah in accordance with our worldview.

Conclusion

What emerges from this careful reading of the Rav's Yoreh De'ah lecture is that there are different ways to read these same sources. At a fundamental level, the OU panel has chosen a specific approach to a certain set of mekorot. However, there are other voices from within the mesorah that lead to a different understanding of this very sensitive issue. This debate is extremely important for the Modern Orthodox community. Future discourse should be based on careful reading(s) of the sources of our tradition. We all need to raise the level of discourse to reach the outcome most in tune with Ha-Kadosh Baruch Hu.

Rabbi Jeffrey S. Fox serves as the Rosh Yeshiva of Yeshivat Maharat, the first yeshiva to ordain women as Orthodox clergy. He was the first graduate of Yeshivat Chovevei Torah Rabbincal School. Rabbi Fox served as a pulpit rabbi for nearly seven years and has taught at YCT, Drisha, the ALEPH Rabbincal school, the Florence Melton Adult Educational Center as well as Yeshivat Hadar.

APPENDIX III: WANTED: PRECISION, NUANCE, AND AVODAT HASHEM

Jeffrey R. Woolf

AFTER THE *TSUNAMI* OF REACTIONS TO THE RECENT OU statement on Orthodox women clergy, one wonders what more there is to say on the subject. The issue is so explosive, and the discussion often so extreme, that though there is much more to say, it would appear that discrete silence is presently the better part of valor; at least until the present wave of passionate intensity recedes. Perhaps then, after the adrenaline driven protestations have entered the blogosphere, that people who only seek the greater glory of God and His Torah will be able to listen to one another. Perhaps then, the moderates who fully support the study of Torah by women, yet oppose the ordination of women as rabbis (in its present iteration), will also have their turn to offer an opinion.

In the interim, I would like to offer a few observations concerning the OU paper and some of the published reactions thereto. I hope, thereby, to introduce an element of precision and a degree of nuance to a discourse that has been frequently lacking in both.

Owing to the fact that it has been invoked by both sides, with varying degrees of imprecision, I would like to concentrate here on the term *Mesorah*.

Mesorah has a long and venerable history, though it might be called by other names. It also refers to very different things, though one would hardly know that from many of the articles and social media posts of the past few weeks. So, in full cognizance of the limitations of a *Lehrhaus* essay, here are several salient examples.

(1) *Mesorah* is an important factor in verifying *realia* or skills. The question of *Mesorah* looms large in *kashrut* (e.g., the permissibility of fowl (among Ashkenazim), allowing consumption of new types of animals, or the proper method of removing prohibited portions of an animal [*nikur*]). It is not, however, restricted to *kashrut*. Much of the discussion concerning wearing *tekhelet*, or identifying the exact site of the *Beit Ha-Mikdash*, revolves around the existence of a living tradition. Opinions are sharply divided as to the possibility of restoring a living tradition, once it has disappeared. [For the record, my personal conviction and practice aligns with those who believe this to be possible.]

(2) *Mesorah*, more importantly, refers to the *corpus receptus* of Jewish practice. The 'Burden of Tradition' is a very potent, and frequently determinative, factor in Traditional Judaism. One expression of this is the absolute authority of the Babylonian Talmud. From the time of its redaction and ratification, the Talmud is the foundation of all *Halakhah*. Its explicit rulings are set for all time, and all subsequent rulings must pass muster with the Talmud in lie with the broads lines of traditional interpretation thereof (*Bi'ur ha-Gra al Hoshen Mishpat,* sec. 25 s-p. 6).

At the same time that the authority of the Talmud cannot be impugned, established halakhic consensus, otherwise known as *sugya de-alma*, also represents a formidable portion of *Mesorah*. *Halakhah* is cumulative, as anyone who has studied *Rosh*, *Sanhedrin* 4:4 and *Hoshen Mishpat* 25 knows. Its cumulative wisdom is self-perceived as binding. It is not, of course, static and can change over time. However, as *Rosh* and *Rema* (*ad loc.*) note, halakhic consensus can only be overturned when two factors are at play: an overwhelming, halakhically defensible objection (*kushya mefursemet*) and advocates of change who possess towering scholarship and piety.

(3) Millennia of usage demand that it be addressed with rev-

erence and deference, for the collective wisdom of the Jewish People has a certain *vox populi, vox Dei* quality to it (as long as the 'People' are God-fearing and observant). As Hillel the Elder once declared, 'Rely upon Israel. If they be not prophets, they are the sons of prophets.' This is the reason that the observations of the Shakh (themselves rooted in the normative discussion of the fifteenth century scholar, Rabbi Joseph Colon Trabotto in *shoresh* 172) figure in the statement of the rabbis who signed the present statement. Yet, as with the first iteration of the term, in this sense *Mesorah* does not have an absolute veto on proffered changes. Its valence, however, is formidable. Depending upon the weight of the question at bar, one can easily affirm that 'He who would proffer change (especially tectonic change), must prove his/her case beyond any reasonable doubt.'

(4) *Mori ve-rabi, Rabban shel Yisrael*, Rabbi Joseph B. Soloveitchik *zt'l* invoked the concept of *Mesorah* on many different occasions, and it is appropriate that his teachings and authority stand in the center of the present discussion (though, for some reason, his halakhic and talmudic *oeuvre* is nowhere to be seen). Anyone who either had the privilege of studying with the Rav (as I did for almost a decade) or who has studied his writings, knows that he was very deferential and reverential towards received tradition. Thus, he opposed altering elements included in the above understandings of *Mesorah*. At the same time, more than anyone else, it was he who advanced the notion that women must serve God through Torah study in the fullest sense.

Nevertheless, when he discussed the definition of *Mesorah*, he consistently described the character of Torah Study, in its wider sense. Torah study, and by extension halakhic decision-making, is an encounter with God and must be enveloped with awareness of that fact. The Torah is not a 'text.' It is the Word of the Living God, and must be treated as such. *Talmud Torah* is carried on from a posture both of deep and abiding humility, alongside great empowerment since He invites man (and woman) to join in the exploration and applications of its endless vistas. Creativity and

Initiative are balanced by Deference not only to God, but to the collective wisdom of Hazal and the great post-Talmudic authorities. In a recently published essay, found in the volume *Halakhic Morality*, the Rav expands upon this last point by discussing the intimate and loving relationship between Teacher and Disciple, which is the manifestation of *Mesorah*, literally, 'passing on.' I must register my deep dismay that *Mesorah* in this sense, in its most important sense, is almost totally absent from the present discussion. That, I assert in deep pain, is a serious indictment of the state of 'Orthodox' Judaism in the United States.

(5) Rabbi Soloveitchik explicitly asserted that there is a methodological component of *Mesorah*. On more than one occasion, he emphasized the autonomy of Torah Study and the existence of a unitary dialogue that unites generations and spans the centuries. Even though there are clearly different schools of Law and Commentary within Rabbinic Tradition, it remains a fact that the *Texti Recepti* provided the fulcrum for talmudic and halakhic study and decision-making. The encounter between protean reality and the Talmud and Codes was effected by the imminent study of the latter, and its application to the former. As a result, one can certainly see the 'signs of the times' in responsa and Law Books. However, these are limited and modulated by the accepted canons of Torah study and halakhic decision-making. Only in extremis did the greatest of Rabbis deviate from this approach, and only then using tools that Tradition itself provided and through consultation with colleagues of equal, or greater, stature.

It was for this reason that Rabbi Soloveitchik categorically rejected the application of Historicist reductionism and psychological analysis to Talmud and Halakhah (and we could add Lacan-based Literary Analysis). History and all the disciplines of Western Culture have a legitimate interpretative, yet ancillary place, in the *Santum Sanctorum* of *Talmud Torah*. However, the Rav taught that these remain essentially speculative and materialist atheist approaches, which corrode Tradition and raise the dangerous prospect of turning the Torah into nothing more than a Jewish ornament on value systems that are in many ways at odds with the Torah.

Each of these (*pace*, the first) different, but related, meanings of *Mesorah* directly impact upon the serious question of creating Torah leadership structures for learned women, who thirst for the contests of Abaye and Rava. Personally, I am deeply committed to the position that we owe it to them, to ourselves, and to our forebears to develop such structures. However, for those structures to be meaningfully Orthodox, they must emerge out of the methodology of *Mesorah* and be expressed, above all, as a deep and abiding yearning by Jews (of both genders) for the Greater Glory of God and His Torah.

Rabbi Dr. Jeffrey R. Woolf serves as an Associate Professor in the Talmud Department at Bar-Ilan University in Israel, where he specializes in the History of Halakhah, Medieval and Renaissance Jewish History, and the inter-action between Judaism, Islam and Christianity. His latest book, The Fabric of Religious Life in Medieval Ashkenaz (1000–1300): Creating Sacred Communities, *appeared in 2015. He is presently working on a study of the leading Halakhist in Renaissance Italy, R. Joseph Colon, as well as a book (in Hebrew) of essays on Israeli Orthodoxy and its encounter with modernity.*

Originally published February 28, 2018 on Lehrhaus
https://www.thelehrhaus.com/timely-thoughts/wanted-precision-nuance-and-avodat-hashem/
Excerpted with permission.

APPENDIX IV: WHAT IS "MESORAH"/TRADITION?

What Is "Mesorah"/Tradition?

In a somewhat heated controversy over the issue of women's ordination to the clergy, the OU issued the rather extensive statement cited above, with the main message being:

> Accordingly, we note that the Rabbinic Panel has made clear that women serving in clergy roles or holding clergy titles is at odds with halacha and our mesorah . . . . [President Moishe Bane's and Chairman of the Board Howard Tzvi Friedman and Executive Vice-President/Chief Professional Officer Allen I. Fagin's statement.]

This statement made no attempt to define the nature of "mesorah" or its parameters.[1]

---

1. For a penetrating analysis of this concept, see the comprehensive treatment of the subject by Edward Shils, *Tradition*, Chicago, 1981. But just as an example of his descriptive analysis I shall quote a key sentence from p. 3 of his Introduction:

> As a temporal chain, a tradition is a sequence of variations on received and transmitted themes, in the contiguity of presentation and departure, and in descent from a common origin.

And he adds (ibid., p. 14):

> A sense of identity and a sense of fixation with earlier recipients of a tradition are different things from the actual reception of a tradition.

And see especially chapters 5 and 6, pp. 213–261, entitled "Why Traditions Change: Endogenous Factors," and "Why Traditions Change: Exogenous Factors."

And on p. 42 he makes the following meaningful comment:

> .... when a disposition is formed and aroused – within the frame set by some preexisting and acquired perception and assessment of certain features of society or of nature – the person so disposed finds ready to hand a more differentiated picture and a more differentiated plan already in being. This picture and this plan are intellectual traditions. He becomes a possession as well as a possessor of the tradition. If he is very imaginative, curious, ratiocinative, and studious, he will modify the picture and plan to suit his own more idiosyncratic intellectual and moral powers. If he is weak intellectually, he will accept it as it stands, to the extent that he can assimilate it; he will add nothing to it, he might even simplify and impoverish the tradition of the idea or complex of ideas which he receives. As the situation to which the idea refers changes, the ideas might change too; the ideas change as their possessors attempt to improve them by making them more consistent, by taking into account ends other than, for example, the elimination of poverty, or by correcting the factual assumptions of the programmatic part of the idea.

Of course, one may argue that there is a distinct difference between an "intellectual tradition" – in his words – and a religious/ideological one. Yet his comment still makes us take pause to reflect upon the nature of "mesorah" and its reception.

And for a somewhat different formulation of this basic position we find in Hans-Georg Gadamer's major work, *Truth and Method*, New York, p. 1975, p. 263:

> Every age has to understand a transmitted text in its own way, for the text is part of the whole of the tradition in which the age takes an objective interest and in which it seeks to understand itself. The real meaning of a text, as it speaks to the interpreter, does not depend [solely] on the contingencies of the author and whom he originally wrote for. It certainly is not identical with them, for it is always partly determined also by the historical situation of the interpreter and hence by the totality of the objective course of history ... Not occasionally only, but always, the meaning of a text goes beyond its author. That is why understanding is not merely a reproductive, but always a productive attitude as well.

"Tradition" is, then, eisegetical, and not merely exegetical – this approach as

The Rabbinic Panel's statement[2] was far more explicit, explaining the "Halakhic Methodology" (pp. 1 et seq.) whereby it reached its conclusion that:

> For the reasons stated above we believe that a woman should not be appointed to serve in a clergy position. (p. 12)

The reasons expounded are summarized as "precedent and halakhic concerns" which "preclude female clergy" (p. 10).

I have discussed the halakhic aspects elsewhere (in this book); it is the "precedent" aspect that I would like to examine here.

The panel wrote as follows on this particular part of their argument (pp. 3–4) (cited above in Appendix I, p. 122, with footnotes):

> . . . The Torah community's historical and widespread observance of a particular practice establishes a default position for halakhic decision-making. The Talmud resolves halakhic questions by examining the prevailing normative practice, instructing younger students, "*puk chazi mai amma dabar*" – go out and observe the common practice." (*Eruvin* 14b) Time honored traditions of the Torah community are revered, and *Chazal* have attributed a level of Divine sanction to those who sustain its practice: "*Im einam nevi'im – b'nei nevi'im heim*" – "if they are not [actually] prophets, they are sons of prophets." (*Pesachim* 66a)

---

opposed to Dilthey's hermeneutical principle that the meaning of a text is to be discovered by uncovering the original intentions of the author. (See Wilhelm W. Dilthey, *Selected Writings*, ed. and transl. H.P. Rickman, London, Cambridge, 1976, pass.)

For various attitudes to tradition over the last millenium, from Saadya Gaon to Shimshon Raphael Hirsch, see Daniel Eidensohn, *Daas Torah: A Jewish Sourcebook*, Jerusalem, 2005, index s.v. Tradition (p. 29).

2. The statement is signed by seven distinguished Rabbis: Rabbi Daniel Feldman, Rabbi Yaakov Neuburger, Rabbi Michael Rosensweig, Rabbi Ezra Schwartz, Rabbi Gedalia Dov Schwartz, Rabbi Hershel Schachter, and Rabbi Benjamin Yudin.

This is not to say that an established practice can never be altered: it must be assumed, however, that normative practice reflects a baseline truth that must be grappled with when innovations are suggested. Great caution must be employed before altering *mesorat Yisrael*. This deep respect for established communal norms can be found throughout the works of the Ba'alei HaTosafot whose writings often invoke the validity of communal practice even in the face of apparently conflicting Talmudic texts. This is true regarding *minhagim* (customs),[3] and all the more so regarding matters that are dependent on the application of Jewish law. In fact, many practices that currently find expression in textual sources, and are thus understood to be textually based, were actually resolved based on the authority of precedential practice.

Not only is there enormous significance in the Torah community's manner of observing a particular custom or behavior; equally significant is the community's failure or refusal to practice a certain custom or adopt a particular behavior. Although the *Mishnah* (*Eduyot* 2:2) states that "*lo ra'inu – aino raya*" (the fact that something has not been observed cannot be brought as a proof to one side of a legitimate halakhic dispute rooted in *pesukim* or *sevara*), the nonperformance of a particular practice does constitute a *minhag*, and such a *minhag* attains binding status. In addressing the implication of a community practice, the Maharik (quoted by the Shakh at the beginning of *Yoreh Deah*) rules that, by inference, the community's failure to adopt a particular practice can be understood to reflect an objection to that practice.[4]

---

3. [See my *Minhagei Yisrael*, vol. 3, p. 23 note 17. D.S.]

4. [But see Yitzhak Zeev Kahana, *Mehkarim be-Sifrut ha-Teshuvot*, Jerusalem, 1973, p. 364, citing R. Yitzhak Isaac Yehudah Yehiel Safrin, of Komarna, in his *Otzar ha-Hayyim*, Yitro 20, Lvov 1858, Mitzvah 39, for a permissive approach. And for a comprehensive discussion on this subject, see Richard I. Cohen, *Jewish Icons: Art and Society in Modern Europe*, Berkeley, Los Angeles, London, 1998, especially chapter 3, entitled "The Rabbi as Icon," pp. 114–153.

So the basic argument here is that precedent, and even absence of precedent which in itself constitutes precedent, is formative in that it creates an obligation to preserve both practice and/or non-practice. Absence of practice creates a *minhag of prohibition* – a negative *minhag*.

Let us look at the proof text which is used to contradict the Mishnah in *Eduyot*'s (2.2) clear formulation that "*lo ra'inu – aina raaya*" ("the fact that something has not been observed cannot serve as proof to one side of a legitimate halachic dispute . . .") as cited above.

The *Shulhan Aruch* in *Yoreh Deah* 1:1 writes

> All may slaughter in the first instance, even women and slaves and any person, even if one is not acquainted with them that they are capable of slaughtering without fainting. . . .

On the Mehaber's statement, the Rema (R. Mosheh Isserles) remarks:

> There are those who say that one should not permit women to slaughter, *for already they have been accustomed not to slaughter* (שכבר נהגו לא לשחוט), and so is the custom that women do not slaughter (וכן המנהג שאין הנשים שוחטות).

We have here a controversy between the Sefaradi *Mehaber*, R. Yosef Karo, and the Ashkenazi Rema, the former permitting women *shochtot* – slaughterers, the latter forbidding it.

The *Shach* (*Siftei Cohen*, by R. Shabtai Katz, one of the major super-commentators to the *Shulhan Aruch*) writes ad loc. that the custom not to permit women to serve as slaughterers is the view of the *Agur* (sect. 1062), but the *Beit Yosef* (*Tur Yoreh Deah* 5 – i.e., R. Yosef Karo) disagreed with him, for *lo ra'inu*

See also Aviyad ha-Cohen, "Images of Scholars - Between Halachah and Reality" (in Hebrew), *Mahanayim* 7, 1995, pp. 100–121. D.S.]

aina raaya. The *Shach* continues to explain that the *Agur*'s view is consistent with that of the Maharik (R. Yosef Kolon), *Shoresh* 171 that in such a case the *minhag* follows the view that *lo ra'inu raaya*, referring us to *Shulhan Aruch Hoshen Mishpat* 37 (22), where we find an extended discussion on this subject in a different halachic context.

The *Turei Zahav* (by R. David ha-Levi) would seem to disagree with the *Shach*, noting that the *Mehaber*'s view is based on the Tosafot in *B. Hulin* 2a; and see the numerous discussions in the various commentaries ad loc.

The *Shach* has a very lengthy discussion on this very issue in his commentary to *Hoshen Mishpat* 37:22. We shall not examine it in full detail, but nonetheless introduce the main elements in his argument:

> Nowadays it is our custom (*minhag*) to accept witnesses from the community in accordance with their regulations and agreements[5] concerning dedications (*hakdashot*) and other issues, and they are eligible [to give testimony] even to their relatives, since they look up on themselves [to accept such manner of testimony].
>
> *Hagah*. Everything is dependent upon the custom of the community (*minhag benei ha-ir*). We do not say that two are as a hundred, but rather we go according to the majority, and in all such similar cases we do not require real testimony. Similarly, we do not say in such cases, that which we have not seen does not constitute evidence, but that *it does constitute evidence*.

The *Shach* ad loc. again refers to the *Agur* (1062) referring to

5. See Louis Finkelstein, *Jewish Self-Government in the Middle Ages*, New York, 1964. See further *Shulhan Aruch Even ha-Ezer* 152:4, contra R. Yeruham in the name of the Rashba, and *Yam shel Shlomoh* to *Ketubot* chapter 2, sect. 34, while R. Isserles in his *Hagah*ad loc. rules like the Rashba. See also Menasheh Cohen, *Leket Kelalei ha-Gemara*, vol. 2, Jerusalem, 2013, pp. 300–301 (which needs some correction). [D.S.]

Yoreh Deah ibid., and continues to mention the *Maharik* (171) concluding that "in the case of *minhag*, that which we have *not* observed *does constitute* evidence." He then has a very lengthy discussion, in which, inter alia, he argues that "since the custom is so and this is the practice, if the matter had been permitted it is impossible that we would not have seen at some time or other that people are accustomed to permit it. Hence, it is certain that the custom to forbid was intentional, and so too vice versa." He brings proof to his view from *B. Eruvin* 41a, where R. Yohanan ben Nuri rejects R. Yehoshua's attempt to change an earlier ruling of Rabban Gamliel, arguing "We do not listen to you, [Yehoshua], (for the law has already been fixed) in accordance with [the view of] Rabban Gamliel, and there was no one who questioned that ruling." The *Shach* then concludes that R. Yehoshua did not respond that "we have not heard is not evidence," thus bolstering the *Maharik*'s argument, and rejecting the *Shiltei Gibborim*'s attempt to refute the *Maharik* (see *Baba Metzia* 52a, in the pagination of the *Rif*). (See further *Darkei Mosheh Hoshen Mishpat* 7:18.)

At this stage we should like to highlight one specific point in his argumentation, namely that "it is impossible that we would not have seen of some time or other 'such a practice,' hence, it is certain that the custom to forbid [or to permit] is intentional." However, here we must note the fact that in communities (such as France, Spain) women did act as slaughterers (in accordance with the *Mehaber*'s view), and we even have records of the licenses that were accorded them giving them rabbinic authority to carry out *shehitah*.[6]

6. See my *Minhagei Yisrael* vol. 4, Jerusalem, 1995, pp. 9–12; vol. 6, Jerusalem, 1998, pp. 260–263; vol. 7, Jerusalem, 2003, pp. 401–402; vol. 8, Jerusalem, 2007, p. 268. To the above we may now add: *Shut Shoel U-Meishiv*, by R. Yosef Shaoul Natansohn, 4th edition, vol. 3, sect. 41, in the name of R. Arieh Leibush, apud A.Y. Bromberg, Ha-Gaon R. Y.S. Natansohn, in the series *Mi-Gedolei ha-Torah ve-ha-Hassidut* vol. 16, Jerusalem, 1960, p. 72. See most recently David Golinkin, in Responsa in a Moment 12/1 (December

Now clearly, even according to the *Shach* it is manifoldly evident that the concept of "mesorah" cannot create an halachic paralysis, obviating all manner of innovation. The history of the halachah is replete with innovation, as the panel of Rabbis was fully aware, expressed in their statement that "this is not to say that an established practice can never be altered. . . ." But they added, "However, normative practice reflects a baseline truth that must be grappled with when innovations are suggested." With this I am in full agreement; but the question is what are the parameters permitting innovations. This basic question has not been effectively answered by the panel of Rabbis. Indeed, the right to halachic innovation is expressly stated in numerous rabbinic sources. Thus, in *B. Berachot* 10b we are told of the six "innovations" of the king Hezekiah, three of which were accepted and three of which were rejected. One of them was the destruction of the brazen serpent that Moses had created in the wilderness (*Numbers* 21:9). And the Talmud in *B. Hulin* 6b–7a relates the following:

> Rabbi [Yehudah ha-Nasi] permitted the whole of Beit Shean [with regards the law of Sheviit]. They said to him: "A place where your fathers and your forefathers regarded it as forbidden, you see it as permissible? He expounded to them this verse: He [i.e., King Hezekiah] removed the high places, and broke the images, and cut down the groves, and broke in pieces the brazen serpent that Moses had made; for unto those days the Children of Israel did burn incense to it: and he called it Nehustan" (2 *Kings* 18:4). Can it be that [King] Asa came and did not eradicate it?
>
> [Can it be that King] Yehoshafat came and did not eradicate it? Surely, all the idolatry in the world Asa and Yehoshafat erad-

2017), article entitled "Is it Permissible for Women to Serve as Shohatot (Ritual Slaughterers)?" who brings a wealth of halachic and historical material to show that this was an accepted practice in many communities.

> icated! However, our forefathers left us a place to distinguish oneself (להתג[נ]דר בו); So, I too – my forefathers left me a place in which to distinguish myself, i.e., to arrogate to myself the authority even to destroy that which Moses himself had created!

Similarly, in *Y. Demai* 2:1, 22c we read:

> Rabbi [Yehudah ha-Nasi] permitted the use of grass at the end of the Sabbatical year, and all were murmuring against him. He said to them: Come, let us discuss [the matter]. It is written "and he broke in pieces the brazen serpent." Was there no righteous person from the time of Moses until that of Hezekiah who could not have broken it in pieces? However, the Holy One blessed be He placed before him a crown with which to distinguish himself. We too have been granted by the Holy One blessed be He such a crown with which to coronate ourselves.

The crown here symbolized a form of sovereignty, which grants the independence to act in an innovative fashion.[7] The interesting point to note here is that this "innovation," which might be regarded as a stringency, was actually a leniency permitting the destruction of something that Moses himself had created. In the first case the leniency is patently apparent. The absence of such leniency in the past did not create a non-permissive "mesorah," or *minhag*. Apparently, where there is a true necessity, the "tradition" can be revoked.

It is true that at times, in order to avoid dissension and controversy, one may forego one's opinion. Thus, in *B. Pesahim* 51a we read:

---

7. We might add that the community has the right to accept such innovations, in accordance with the principle of *Kiblu alaihem*, ("they accepted themselves"). See on this concept Abraham Hirsch Rabinowitz, *The Jewish Mind in its Talmudic Expressions*, Jerusalem, 1978, pp. 207–225. We shall not expand on this issue here, as we have done so elsewhere.

> It once happened that Rabban Shimon ben Gamliel sat on a bench of a non-Jew on Shabbat in Acco, and the whole community criticized him (*laazu alav*). They said, "We have never seen such [behavior]." He slipped down [off the bench] onto the ground. And he did not want to tell them. "You, to inhabitants of the sea-board, are permitted to do so."

So their negative evidence, was not evidence of a prohibition: *lo rainu aina raaya*.

When might we argue that, following the *Shach*, the absence of evidence constitutes evidence? Perhaps, this might be the case when a certain activity could have taken place earlier, but did not – presumably because at some stage it had been forbidden (see above). Hence, *lo ra'inu* in such a case may be a *raaya*. And again, let us stress, this is only according to the *Shach* (for Ashkenazim). But if a certain kind of activity was unavailable in the past, a technology had not been developed, or the sociological situation did not admit of a certain type of activity, then surely its absence cannot constitute evidence of a prohibition. Would we forbid the use of electricity[8] because for thousands of years in the past it was not used because it had not yet been discovered? Surely not. But slaughtering by women had been possible, as we know from the Talmud and the *Rishonim*, but apparently was not practiced in Ashkenaz. Hence the *Shach*'s position. In the case of women becoming clergy, this was obviously not possible in medieval times, given their known sociological status. They were only granted the right to vote in the twentieth century – and this against the wishes of Rav Kook.[9]

Perhaps the learned Rabbis should have limited their ruling

---

8. See what I wrote in *Minhagei Yisrael* vol.3, Jerusalem, 1994, p. 17, that the *Hafetz Hayyim* would not permit the use of electricity in the synagogue, even on weekdays, because this constituted an "innovation" (*hit'hadshut be-minhag ameinu*)!

9. See my *Darchah shel Torah: Keriyat Nashim ba-Torah: Perakim be-Mediniut Pesikah*, Jerusalem, 2007, pp. 79–80, 110, for a discussion of this issue.

to Ashkenazi congregations. Or do they see those congregations also as subservient to their decisions? Rav Ovadiah Yosef *z"tl* recorded in his *Yabia Omer* vol. 6, sect. 43, pp.143–144, that in the year 1969, when he was Chief Rabbi of greater Tel-Aviv, he permitted the registration of marriages and the ceremony of marriage from the 17 Tammuz to *Rosh Hodesh Av*, excluding *Rosh Hodesh*, in accordance with the rulings of Maran (the *Beit Yosef*) and the custom in Jerusalem.

He continues to relate:

> And I have heard that there are those who claim that since the Chief Rabbis of Tel-Aviv Yafo who preceded me continued the custom of stringency – i.e., not permitting marriage during this period – one may not change the custom. And this is not the case, for a place was left to me in which to distinguish myself (*B. Hulin* 7). And even more so, since it is known that the Sefaradi Chief Rabbi who preceded me was subservient (*kaifei*) to their Ashkenazi Chief Rabbi colleague. (And it is [also] known that because of his great love and desire for unifying the communities [i.e., Ashkenazi and Sefaradi], he supported doing away with Sefaradi *Shehitah*. However, it was R. Zvi Pesach Frank who opposed this . . . , for each community must continue to preserve its specific tradition as followed throughout he generations, and each "tribe" (*shevet*) must hold on to the customs of its forefathers . . .) . . .
>
> But we, who are not subservient, praise be the Lord, "I will stand upon my watch" (*Habakuk* 2-1), to return the crown to its former [glory], to rule according to Maran (R. Yosef Karo) whose rulings we have accepted. . . .

Of course, for him, as a Sefaradi, *lo rainu* remains *aina raaya*. However, I contend that also in the case we are discussing, the *Shach* would agree that the absence of women clergy in the past is in no way evidence of its being prohibited.

The principle of "mesorah," one of the central aspects of the distinguished panel's tripartite argument against women's rabbinic ordination, would seem to me to be largely irrelevant. The panel waxed eloquent on the nature of "mesorah":

> The idea of *mesorah* is often mistaken as a mere historical record of Jewish practice. That misunderstanding, combined with both the absence of historical uniformity of normative practice, and the gradual evolution of *halakhah*, can be misconstrued as compromising the authenticity of *mesorah*. Authentic *mesorah* is rather an appreciation for, and application of, tradition as the guide by which new ideas, challenges and circumstances are navigated.
>
> Our precious *mesorah* has thereby been the cornerstone of not only the preservation, but also the development of our religious and spiritual heritage. *Mesorah* is the bridge between our past and our future. When studying a proposed innovation, in addition to considering its immediate implications and whether it is consistent with Torah principles, attention must be paid to the potential impact of such changes on generations through the distant future. Each and every generation confronts an ever-changing social, cultural and technical environment. Halakhic leadership must, therefore, continually probe whether proposed changes and accommodations will enable the community to advance the objectives of an authentic Torah ethos, or simply accommodate prevailing values and expectations, often in opposition to the Torah worldview (ibid., pp. 6–7).

I fully concur with these sentiments. It is all too true that every generation confronts an ever-changing social, cultural and technical environment, and must carefully consider proposed changes and their danger implications. These changes must be in accord with certain basic ethical principles hallowed by *tradition*, such as the dignity of the individual, *kevod ha-beriyot*, and an halachic framework that engenders pleasantness (*darchei noam*) and brings more and more people under the canopy of the *shechinah*.

Our "innovations" seek not to fracture our society, but to unify them, bringing the disparate parts closer to one another. It is OU's "prohibition" which is further fracturing our community, and it is for precisely this reason that אנו לא כייפינן ליה, we do not see ourselves as subservient to their leadership. As to the halachic discussion (ibid., pp. 7–9), I have discussed it earlier, and need not duplicate my responses.[10]

Finally, I would most respectfully request of the learned members of the panel, to seriously consider whether their ruling benefits the Orthodox community as a whole or does it considerable damage. Does *their* understanding of the notion of "mesorah" outweigh the enormous benefits of this and other feminist innovation, religious revival, spiritual fulfillment, and a sense of belonging, to mention but some examples? Can they in all due honesty justify their attempt to stifle this spirit of renewal, one that clings to Orthodoxy and thus places its own claim on the understanding of "tradition"? Is this the way to move along the path of peace? Let us together work to achieve an actualization of דרכיה דרכי נועם וכל נתיבותיה שלום – "Her ways are the ways of pleasantness, and all her paths are peace" (*Proverbs* 3:17).

10. See what I wrote in *Black Fire on White Fire: Essays in Honor of Rabbi Avi Weiss*, ed. Daniel R. Goodman, Ktav, Brooklyn, New York, 2017, pp. 149–152.

APPENDIX V

THIS STUDY, IN A CERTAIN SENSE, REVEALS THE STRUGGLE and the tension between tradition and innovation. This was a subject of deep concern to my late father, Rabbi Samuel Sperber *zt"l*. That our tradition is one of constant innovation was a fundamental premise in his religious thought. The necessity of innovation and research, on the one hand, and the inherent dangers thereof, on the other, were the source of his deep concern – concern and fear, a fear lest the innovation break from and stray away from tradition. This he expressed in his classic essay, *Masoret ve-Hidush* (pp. 359–365) that was published in his volume of articles, *Maamarot* published in Jerusalem in 1978. The style is richly associative – almost every line relates to either a biblical verse or a rabbinic statement – and the full richness in this style cannot be fully conveyed in translation. I have therefore included the original Hebrew version (in a slightly abbreviated form) together with the excellent translation, so kindly carried out by my friend and colleague, Rabbi Shimon Altshul. The reader who peruses this Appendix will perhaps get some sort of feeling from where I come, and to where I hope I am going. . . .

TRADITION AND INNOVATION

by R. Samuel Sperber zt"l

The nature of the Torah and the nature of the creation are similar. The world was created with fixed laws of heaven and earth, laws that will never change. Nonetheless, a place in creation was allotted to the control of man. In this world, the earth does not give forth ready-made delicacies, but man must exert much effort and perform many labors before he can recite the blessing of "*Ha-Motzi*" over his daily bread. Moreover, through these labors man resourcefully transforms, separates and assembles the elements of creation – so that he may enjoy the bread of his sustenance.

Constant Renewal

The world was created in six days by means of ten acts of speech. Even so, the Creator, Blessed be He, continuously renews the work of creation in His goodness. It would seem that there is nothing new under the sun, but in truth everything is created anew, with worlds being added, improved and elevated. The entire creation is created again every day.

What is the nature of the Torah? The Torah was given from Heaven, fully arranged and organized. Its every aspect is firm and established, like fixed nails, engraved on tablets of stone. God will not alter or change His law for eternity. Is it possible that it can never contain anything new? We are taught: [Moses was instructed to engrave the words of Torah] *herut* – engraved on the tablets; [this teaches that] there is a place for man to create his own domain, by interpreting the Torah, by discerning the new meanings that emerge from it every day. Generation after generation contemplates its letters and discovers the hidden light contained in them, lights that no eye has ever gazed upon before.

Questions arise continuously – and they find their solutions in new Torah discoveries, innovative ideas which bestow upon man the greatest joy imaginable, which is characteristic of Torah study.

Innovative Torah ideas have two faces: the face of the person engaged in them and the face of the Torah itself. One who is engaged in Torah study for its own sake experiences the undeniable feeling that the Torah he studies is brand new, not some ancient edict. He finds endless fulfillment and pleasure in the new meanings that are constantly being added. "Every day (the words of the Torah) should be seen as if they are new." How does this feeling of innovation express itself? It is as if the Torah was given and received during the life of one who studies and sustains it. His living, subjective, direct emotional relationship to the Torah makes it seem as if it has been given anew, and he cleaves to it with great joy, identical to the joy that was experienced when it was given at Mount Sinai.

What is the face of the Torah? Problems arise continuously, demanding solutions, demanding that scholars and sages intensify their efforts at "the New Gate of [the House of] the Lord" (*Jeremiah* 26:10) where the scribes of old revitalized the halachah (*Y. Eruvin* 5:1). Through their determination to understand the perplexities of the *halachah* [scholars of today] will uncover its hidden secrets, never before revealed. Every new discovery radiates new light in the world of Torah, as bright as the light of Creation.

These discoveries are *sui generis* and incomparable in their sweetness and appeal. ("Had I been worthy I would have learned this originally – the difference is in respect to the knowledge acquired in one's youth" . . . [*B. Shabbat* 21b.]) There is an unquestionable distinction between learning something immediately when it is discovered, for then it is more powerful and logical, and between learning it at a later point in time. That is the meaning of "knowledge acquired in one's youth" (*Mei Hashiloach, Likutei HaShas*). Such an exceptional learning experience not only enlightens us with its own light, but enlightens all aspects of reality. Original ideas in Torah have their source in the world of *Binah*; so that the world of *herut* – freedom influences the world of *harut* – engraved and permanent, and all rejoice in the experience.

Herut and Harut: Permanence and Freedom

The dual principles of *herut* – freedom and *harut* – permanence, together create the world of Torah. But apparently not all periods are identical, for there are times when the principle of *harut* – permanence dominates and then there are times when *herut* – freedom and originality are the rule. There are times when [students] who are like "a plastered well who never lose a drop" thrive, and then there are times when students who are like "an ever-flowing spring" proliferate. Originality comes to the fore when change occurs in both the world of action and the world of ideas. Practical developments stimulate innovation in the paths of Torah, and changes in our ways of thinking require us – indeed grant us the privilege – to take a new look at the vast repositories of Torah. There are often matters which seem impenetrable and unclear, and go lying about unnoticed, which suddenly emerge as the building blocks of new and original ideas. [When this occurs] great joy descends upon all, the joy of innovation which is an integral part of the given Torah.

The Sages taught that the world was created by using the letters of the Torah: "God looked into the Torah and created the world." The Hassidic masters further explained that even though the Holy One, blessed be He, continuously renews the work of creation in His goodness, He does so solely by means of authentic original Torah ideas which are parallel to the discoveries in the natural world. While we are not privy to cosmic mysteries, nevertheless, we are entitled to examine this concept that descends to the world of *asi'a* and declare that when Israel stands at the brink of an era of historical renewal, then the desire to create original Torah ideas is parallel to the newly emerging events. When the generation is worthy of them, righteous leaders who are imbued with emotional sensitivity and intellectual brilliance, grow to maturity and reveal themselves; leaders who sit at the "New Gate of [the House of] the Lord" to forge pure and original pathways that repair the soul of the generation. However, if [unfortunately] the generation is not yet worthy, then the soul sighs with despondency and has no strength to create new ideas, and people are lost and perplexed and thirst for the word of God. But [in such a situation] it is better for Israel to endure with a lowly and broken spirit rather than to become caught up in the snares of new ideas which lack the time-honored, tangible, certainties of the Torah.[1]

Hassidism – Innovation from Within

The basic principle of innovation and the demand for it becomes stronger in those who have sensitive souls, whose feelings are perceptive and individual. Striving for innovation grows within them and they desire to independently experience our age-old tradition, and want it personally adapted for them. This inner demand controls their serenity as they ponder and advance to reveal new meanings in the given Torah. If they are grounded in the eternal truths of the tradition then they will be worthy of seeing new illuminations of the Torah heritage. Innovations of this sort come totally from within, and are enwrapped in holiness. Hassidism is a classic example of innovation from within. It is written in the Torah that "Moses undertook to expound (*be'er*) the Torah" (*Deut.* 1:5). [The Hebrew letters *beit alef resh* can refer either to the verb "to explain" or the noun "a well."] One

1. Cf. *Hazon Ish* on the Ramban, p. 838; S. Leiman, *Tradition* 14, 1981, pp. 301–310; my own *Legitimacy and Necessity: Scientific Disciplines and the Learning of Torah*, Jerusalem, 2006, pp. 23 et seq.; idem, *Darkah Shel Halakhah*, Jerusalem, 2007, p. 122. [D.S.]

of the great Hassidic masters explained that the words "*be'er Moshe*" – "Moses expounded" mean that Moses transformed the Torah into a well of living water. How indeed does the Torah become a well of living water? When one explains and interprets the Torah from within one brings about innovation to the world. Moreover, such original Torah ideas constitute the body of the Torah itself. "The phrase in *Leviticus*: *darosh darash Moshe*, which marks the midpoint of the letters of the Torah, alludes to the idea that the interpretations (*derashot*) of the Sages make up only half of the Torah . . . **and so in every generation the [rest of the] Torah must be completed, for the Torah is to be expounded in every generation** according to what it requires and in keeping with the source of its soul. Therefore the Almighty, may He be blessed, enlightens the eyes of the sages of the generation with his holy Torah, and one who denies this principle is as if he denies the Torah, God forbid . . ." (*Degel Machaneh Ephraim, Breishit*, p. 3).

The Teaching of R. Pinchas of Koretz

However, if the generation is not worthy, and original Torah ideas do not descend from heaven, then the soul [of the nation] enwraps itself in mourning and a chill descends to the earth, a chill that cannot be withstood without heavenly mercy. The following profound and daring ideas were expressed in this regard by a great Elder of the early days of the Hassidic movement, R. Pinchas of Koretz, *zt"l*, ideas which cause fear and trembling. "King David was now old, advanced in years, and though they covered him with garments, he never felt warm" (*I Kings* 1:1). King David represents the Oral law, and this verse alludes to a time when original Torah new ideas are not being created and people just go on studying the same old material, even though they dress it up differently, elaborating it with a piece of Talmud here and there . . . This is comparable to King David being covered in his bedclothes but never feeling warm. In other words, Torah study lacks enthusiasm, since the material is old even though it is presented in a different way. If R. Pinchas (in *Parshat Vayetzei*) had not made this audacious statement, then it would have been forbidden to say it; however it illustrates the [tragedy] of what happens when the overwhelming demand for originality and the need for individual enthusiasm are not satisfied. [But there is another aspect to this lesson as well.] Just as the rewards of individual experience, personal renewal, and enthusiasm are numerous, at the same time, they can bring about a very dangerous situation, which can lead one down a blind path of terrible failures, may the All-Merciful protect us.

If we consider them carefully, this lesson and others like it, should cause us serious concern. For they clearly show the attraction of the personal and the desire for innovation [and its potential negative consequences]. It is a wonder how Hassidism was able to prevail, and fulfill the [intention of] the verse: "Both [the] freshly picked and the long-stored [fruits] have I kept [the new and the old] my beloved, for you" (*Song of Songs* 7:14). This is only because it was rooted in holiness and purity, and more importantly, in the fear of heaven and the fear of sin which protects man from \.cutting off the branches of the Torah. The creative freedom it stimulated was permanently affixed in tablets of stone – and therefore it was worthy of creativity – and did not disappear. From this we learn how important it is to be wary of the desire for enthusiasm,[2] personal experience and originality, for they must be surrounded with the true fear of God, for those who fear God do not reject or destroy [His Torah].

Holy and Secular

Halachah does not allow for variable and equivocal standards. However, there was a sincere longing by those who wished to grasp the rope by both ends: on the one hand, they were not able to relinquish wondrous and original ideas, but on the other hand,

2. See the *Netziv* commentary to *Song of Songs* 6:5 [D.S.].

they were not willing to sacrifice the fixed nature of the given Torah. *Aggadah*, however, responded and set a variable standard and therefore many of its teachings are difficult to explain. (See what R. Zvi Peretz Chajes wrote in his *Torat HaNevi'im*, Section *Hukat Olam*. After citing a number of difficult aggadic sayings, he comments: "When you find *aggadot* which contradict this principle, it is in this connection that the Rabbis wrote that we do not question aggadic sayings [for their logic]; and moreover, these may be regarded as individual opinions.") See also the addenda at the end of his book and the introduction to the book *Ezor ha-Emunah* on the Thirteen Principles of Faith, by the Admor R. Moshe of Kossov and the notes thereon by my revered father and teacher, HaRav HaGaon R. David Sperber, *zt"l*.

Lest you say that [if] the world goes on as usual and nothing changes – then [is] the vision is stripped and emptied entirely [of its significance] so that it lacks imagination and glory of innovation? That is not the case, for even if the world carries on as usual the vision is still retained, and it is the vision that the prophets foresaw (Maimonides, *Hilchot Teshuvah* 8:7 and *Kesef Mishneh* and *Lehem Mishneh* ad. loc.).

All Maimonides writings on this subject are pure and true poetry (Hilchot Teshuvah 9:2 and the Hilchot Melachim), a vision of amazing new ideas – but they are an innovation from within, a song of ascent to the renewal and progress of man as an individual and society, positive relations between men and nations, and the elevation of the desire and potential to know the true God. The Messianic Era itself is an era [which will be characterized by] Torah that emanates from man's originality.

The principle of *harut-herut*, heritage and innovation, both contribute to the living tradition of Israel of Old. In the nexus between these two principles, Israel creates a living nation, by presenting its Torah and producing new true ideas. Just as the laws of nature make it impossible to abrogate any element of creation, but allow for elements to be combined, so no aspect of the Torah can ever be abrogated and no new idea can be created which does not have a firm basis in tradition, so that no one can create a new Torah and still imagine that he remains within the bounds of the given Torah.

A person desires to elevate and redeem his soul through individual experience and *devekut* – deeply rooted in the fear of heaven and the fear of sin. This tension between the two principles and the care which must be exercised is expressed beautifully in the words of the Holy *Zohar*: R. Abba said: One verse writes "You shall not make for yourself a graven image or any likeness" and another verse writes "Carve two tablets of stone," that is to say, do not make a graven image, do make another Torah which you did not know and have not been taught (*Zohar Shemot*, Chapter 7). This statement may reflect the polemic alluded to in the verse "the daughter rose up against mother" [the rise of Christianity] which brought another idolatrous religion into the world. (See Maimonides, *Hilchot Melachim* 11:5 "he imagined that he was the messiah but was put to death . . . For has there ever been a greater stumbling than this? . . . He was instrumental in changing the Torah and causing the world to err and serve another besides God.)

In conclusion, the main thing is to recognize the value of innovation in Torah, as the *Zohar* writes "Carve out for yourself" while at the same time remembering the serious caveat "not to make a graven image." This is a profound matter, suitable for all generations.

מסורת וחידוש

מאת הרב שמואל שפרבר ז״ל

מידותיה של תורה ומידותיה של בריאה דומים הם זה לזה. משנברא העולם ניתנו בו חוקות שמים וארץ, חק צוה ולא יעבור. ועם זאת, מקום ניתן בבריאה לתפיסת ידי אדם. בעולם הזה, אין הארץ מוציאה גלוסקאות מן המוכן, אלא אדם טורח כמה טרחות ועושה כמה מלאכות עד שהוא מברך המוציא לחם מן הארץ ולא עוד אלא שבמלאכות הללו אדם משנה, מפריד ומרכיב, במעשה בראשית – עד שהוא מוצא לחם למזונו.

התחדשות מתמדת

בעשרה מאמרות נברא העולם בששת ימי בראשית. ואף על פי כן הוא הבורא, ב״ה, מחדש בטובו בכל יום תמיד מעשה בראשית, לכאורה, אין כל חדש תחת השמש ולאמיתו של דבר הכל מתחדש, עולמות מתווספין, משתפרים מתעלים והיצירה כולה היא בריה חדשה בכל יום.

מידתה של תורה מהי? ניתנה תורה מן השמים, ערוכה בכל וסדורה. הכל בה קבוע, כמסמרות נטועים. חרות על הלוחות. לא יחליף הא-ל ולא ימיר דתו לעולמים. שמא תאמר אין בה מן החידוש? תלמוד לומר: חרות (חית צרויה) על הלוחות, מקום ניתן לאדם להתגדר בו, בפירושיה של תורה, בפשטות המתחדשין בכל יום. דורות על דורות מסתכלין באותיותיה של תורה ומגלים בהן אורות גנוזים, עין לא שזפתם.

בעיות מתחדשות תמידין כסדרן – והן מוצאות פתרונים בגלויי תורה מחודשים ואין שמחתה של תורה אלא בחידוש, שהוא טבע קיים בה.

וחידוש תורה שתי פנים לו. פנים שבנפש העוסק בה ופנים שבתורה עצמה הא כיצד? העוסק בתורה לשמה מרגיש הרגשה וודאית שהתורה חדשה היא לו ואינו מואס בה כבדיוטגמא ישנה אלא מתוספים לו טעמים על טעמים ומוצא בה קורת רוח והנאה שאין בה כילוי. בכל יום יהיו בעיניך כחדשים. הרגשת חידוש זו מה משמעותה? יש בה **בהרגשה זו מעין מתן תורה וקבלתה** בחיי העוסק בה והמשמרה. הגישה האישית החיה והיחס הנפשי הישיר אל התורה הנתונה מחדש את תנינתה ומיד הוא שמח ודבק בה כבשעת נתינתה מסיני.

פנים שבתורה כיצד? בעיות המתעוררות חדשים לבקרים דופקות על פתחי הלב ותובעות את פתרונן. תביעות הללו מחייבות את הסופרים והחכמים לקבוע ישיבתם ב״שער ה׳ החדש״ (ירמיה כ״ו כ׳) ששם חדשו סופרים את ההלכה (ירושלמי עירובין פ״ה ה״א). מתוך שהם חותרים לנבכיה של תורה מעלים הם

צפונות-ספונות של הלכה שלא נתגלו מקודם. כל גילוי חדש מעלה **אור חדש כאור בראשית** בעולמה של תורה.

גילוי זה חד-פעמי הוא ואין שני לו בנועמו ובטעמו. ("אי זכאי גמירתא לשמ־עתנא מעיקרא – נפקא מינה לגירסא דינקותא".... היינו שיש חילוק בין הלומד דבר תומ"י כשנתחדחש בעולם, אז יש בו **יותר כח וטעם** מאשר כבר נתחדש. וזהו פירוש גירסא דינקותא... מי השלח, ליקוטי הש"ס עיש"ה). וחידוש זה כשהוא בא לעולם לא ללמד על עצמו בלבד יצא אלא ללמד על הכלל כולו יוצא. יסוד החידוש הבא מעולם הבינה, מעולם החרות (חית צרויה) משפיע בהתחדשותו גם על עולם החרות (חית קמוצה) והקבוע והכל שש ושמח.

חרות וחירות

החרות (חית קמוצה) והחרות (חית צרויה) שניהם יחד בונים את עולה של התורה. ודומה, לא כל העתים שוות, יש עתים שיסוד החרות והקבוע גובר בהם ויש עתים הקבועות במזל החרות והחידוש. יש עתים ונפשות שהן בבחינת בור סוד שאינו מאבד טיפה ויש עתים ונפשות שהן בבחינת מעין המתגבר. יסוד החידוש נתבע ועולה עם חלות שינויים והתפתחות בחיי מעשה ובעולם המחשבה. כל התפתחות מעשית מחדשת גם בשביליה של תורה ותחולתם של שינויים במערכת המחשבה מחייבת ומזכה אותנו לראייה חדשה בגנזיה של תורה. יש ודברים שהיו סתומים וחתומים, מונחים כאבן שאין לה הופכים, שהולכים ונעשים לאבן-הראשה ובנין המחשבה מתבסס ומתבשם בריח החידוש. ושמחה יורדת ללבות, שמחת חידוש שיש בו מאתתה של התורה הנתונה.

חז"ל אמרו כי העולם נברא באותיותיה של תורה, הסתכל בתורה וברא את העולם. באו גדולי החסידות ואמרו אף כשהקב"ה מחדש בטובו בכל יום תמיד מעשי בראשית, אינו מחדש אותם אלא על ידי חידושי תורה אמתיים המתחד־שים חדשים לבקרים. זאת אומרת, חידושי תורה אמיתיים הם אלה המקבילים לחידושים במעשי בראשית. אנו אין אתנו יודע עד מה בנסתרות הקוסמיות אלא רשאים אנו להסתכל בגילוי רעיון זה כשהוא יורד לעולם העשייה ולומר כי בשעה שישראל עומדים בפרקי זמנים שיש בהם מן ההתחדשות ההיסטורית מתעוררת התשוקה לחידושי תורה שיש בהן מן התקבולת למאורעות המתחדשות ובאות. לכשהדור זוכה צומים ומתגלים צדיקים גדולי לב גאוני עיון והרגשה היושבים בשעה ה' החדש ומפלסים שבילים טהורים וחדשים ועושים תיקון לנפש הדור. עד שלא זהכה הדור – הנפש קודרת ונאנחת ואין כח לחדש חידושים של אמת אלקית ובני אדם תועים ותוהים בצמאות לדבר ה', **ומוטב להם לישראל שיעמדו ברוח שפלה ונמוכה ובלבד שלא יתפסו במכמורת של חידושים שאין בהם מן הישן, מן המובהק ומן הודאי של תורה.**

החסידות – חידוש מבפנים

יסוד החידוש והתביעה אליו גובר בבני אדם בשעה שנפשם רגישה, כשהרגשתם חריפה ואינדיבידואלית. הכמיהה להתחדשות מתגדלת בהם והם נתבעים ותובעים חויה אישית, וסיגול אישי לכל מה שניתן במורשה. תביעה נפשית זו מדריכה את מנוחתם והם מתלבטים ומעפילים לגלות פנים חדשות בתורה הנתונה ואם מעורים הם בקרקע עולם של המסורת זוכים הם ורואים אור חדש באורה של תורה-המורשה. התחדשות מעין זו כולה מבפנים, כולה בקודש. החסידות היא דוגמה אפיינית לחידוש מבפנים. אמרה תורה הואיל משה באר את התורה הזאת ובא אחד מגדולי החסידות ופירש שמשה באר כלומר עשה את התורה לבאר מים חיים. וכיצד באמת עושים את התורה לבאר מים חיים? על ידי הביאור והפירוש מתוכה ובתוכה המביא חידוש לעולם. ולא עוד אלא שחידושי תורה הללו הם מגופי תורה ממש "וזה י"ל שבא הרמז דרש דרש משה הם חצי אותיות שבתורה, היינו עד שדרשות חז"ל אינה נקראת התורה שלימה רק חצי ... **וכן בכל דור דור ודורשיו הם משלימין התורה כי התורה נדרשת בכל דור ודור** לפי מה שצריך לאותו דור ולפי שרש נשמתו של אותו הדור, כך מאור השי"ת עיני חכמי הדור ההוא בתורתו הקדושה והכופר בזה כאילו כופר בתורה חו"ש ..." (דגל, בראשית ד"ה א"י ע"ד אברם אינו מוליד).

מימרתו של ר' פנחס מקוריץ

אמנם אם עדיין לא זכה הדור ואין חידושי תורה יורדין מן השמים הנפש מתעטפת בעטיפה של אבל וצנה יורדת לעולם, צנה שאין בני אדם יכולים לעמוד בה עד שמרחמין עליהם מן השמים. ודברים נוקבים ונועזים נאמרו בזה על ידי אחד זקן גדול בראשית תקופת החסידות רבי פנחס מקורין זצ"ל, שיש בהם כדי להרעיד את הנפש. "והמלך דוד זקן בא בימים ויכסוהו בבגדים ולא יחם לו", שהוא רמז, כי ידוע שדוד הוא תושבע"פ, וכשאין בה התחדשות התורה בכל יום ובכל עת, רק שעוסק בדברים ישנים, אע"פ שבכל פעם מלביש אותם הדברים בלבושים אחרים, פעמים בגמרא זה ופעמים בגמרא אחרת ... וזהו ויכסוהו בבגדים, ועל כל זה לא יחם לו, **היינו שאין לו התלהבות מזה**, כיון שתוכם דברים ישנים אע"פ שהלבוש משתנה, **רק עיקר שיהיו חדשים לבקרים**, כמאמרם ז"ל בכל יום יהיהו בעיניך כחדשים ... (דגל, ויצא ד"ה, אם יהי,). ודברים הללו אלמלי אמרם זקן לא היו רשאים לאומרם כלל אלא שהם מגלים את הגורם העצום לבתיעה זו לחידושים, זאת אומרת התביעה **לחויה אישית של התלהבות שלא באה על סיפוקה.** תביעה זו לחויה אישית, והתחדשות אישית שבהתלהבות כשם שברכתה מרובה,

כך סכנתה עצומה שהיא יכולה להביא את האדם לידי תהו לא דרך של נפילות נוראות, רחמנא ליצלן.

הדברים שהבאנו לעיל, הם וכיוצא בהם, יש בהם להרעיד אותנו, אחרי העיון והניתוח: מראים הם בעליל עד כמה התגבר היסוד האישי, חפץ החידוש ואנו תמהים כיצד זכתה החסידות ונתקיים בה מקרא שכתוב: חדשים גם ישנים, דודי צפנתי לך? אין זאת אלא מפני שהיתה כולה נטועה במקום קדושה וטהרה ובעיקר **במקום יראת שמים ויראת חטא** השומרים על האדם שלא יבא לקצץ בנטיעותיה של התורה הנתונהף החירות היוצרת שבה אחוזה היתה אחיזת עולם של קבע בגופן של לוחות הברית – ומשום כך זכתה וחידשה – ולא ביטלה חו"ש. **מכאן אנו למדים כמה עלינו להזהר בכל תביעה להתלהבות, לחויה אישית ולחידוש שתהא מסוייגת בסייג על גבי סייג של יראה אמיתית** , שכל הירא אינו בועט ואינו הורס.

חול וקודש

נהר כי יגאה שוטף ועובר הוא על גדותיו וברכת המים הופכת לקללה. צמיחה גדולה מעלה עמה עשבים רעים, ציצים וספיחים שיש בהם כדי לסכן את כל ברכת האדמה. במידה שיגדל כוחו ואיכותו של החידוש המתגלה בעולם, ככה תגדל גם סכנתו.

דברים לשיעורין

לא נתנה ההלכה את דבריה לשיעורין אלא שהלבבות היו כמהים ולהוטין לאחוז את החבל בשני ראשין, לא יכלה הנפש לוותר על יסוד הפלא והחידוש ולא לוותר על הקבע שבתורה הנתונה. באה האגדה ונתנה דבריה לשיעורין, מכאן כל אותן המאמרות שקשה ליישבן (עי' תורת נביאים, מאמר חוקת עולם למוהר"ץ חיות שהביא כמה אגדות ומסיק ואומר: ואף אם תמצא אגדות סותרות זה העיקר, בכגון זה אין מקשין באגדה והמה דברי יחידים. עי' גם בהוספות שבסוף הספר וכן עיין בהקדמה לספר אזור האמונה על י"ג עיקרים לאדמו"ר מוהר"ם מקאסוב זי"ע ובהערותיו של אאמו"ר הרב הגאון שליט"א . . . . וינעם לך.

שמא תאמר אם עולם כמנהגו נוהג ואין כל שינוי – אם כן נתערטל החזון ונתרוקן כולו ושוב אין בו מן המעוף וההוד של חידוש? אין הדברים כן. אף אותו עולם כמנהגו נוהג הוא משא וחזון וכל הנביאים לא נתנבאו אלא לו (רמב"ם ה' תשובה פ"ח ה"ז ועי' כס"מ ובלח"מ שם).

וכל דבריו של הרמב"ם עצמו בזה (ה' תשובה פ"ט ה"ב ובהלכות מלכים) הם מיטב השיר ואמיתו, חזון של חידוש מופלא – אלא שהחידוש הזה הוא מבפנים, שיר למעלות ולהתחדשותו ולהתקדמותו של אדם ביחיד ובחברה. ביחסים שבין

אדם לאדם, בין עם לעם ובהתעלות החפץ והיכולת לדעת את אלקי האמת. **ימות המשיח הם תקופת קיומה של תורה מתוך חידושו של אדם.**

יסוד החרות והחירות, המורשה והחידוש, שניהם בונים ומצמיחים את המ־סורה החיה של ישראל סבא. במתח זה שבין שני היסודות הללו חי ויוצר לו ישראל, משמר את תורתו ומחדש בה חידושי-אמתף כשם שאין אדם מבטל דבר במעשה בראשית אלא מצרף צירופים במערכת חוקים נתונים, כך אין מבטלים לעולם בתורה ואין מחדשים בה חידוש שאין לו בית-אב כדי שלא יהא אדם נמצא עושה לו תורה חדשה תוך כדי אשליה שהוא עדיין בתחומה של התורה הנתונה; שואף אדם להתעלות, לגאולת נפשו תוך כדי חויה אישית ודביקות – תוך כדי שהוא מעורה ביראת-שמים וביראת-חטא. מתח זה שבין שני היסודות האמורים והזהירות בו מצינו לו הבעה נפלאה בדברי הזוהר הקדוש: "אמר רבי אבא כתיב הכא לא תעשה לך פסל וכל תמונה וכתיב התם פסל לך שני לוחות אבניםף כלומר לא תעשה לך פסל, לא תעבד לך אורייתא אחרא דלא ידעת ודלא אמר לך רבך" (זוהר שמות פ"ז ע"א וע"ב עיש"ה). יתכן כי מאמר זה יש בו מן ההתפלמסות עם אותה "בת הקמה באמה" שהעמידה תורה אחרת וגרמה לעבודה זרה (השוה לשונו של הרמב"ם ה' מלכים פי"א ה"ה בציללום דפוס רומי הוצ' הנ"ל, "אף . . . שדמה . . . שיהיה משיח ונהרג . . . וכי יש מכשול גדול מזה . . . וזה גרם ולהחליף התורה ולעבוד אלוה מבלעדי ה'"). אלא שעיקרן של דברים הוא ההרגשה וההכרה בזכותו של החידוש וערכו, בחינת פסל לך, עם האזהרה החומרה של לא תעשה לך פסל. והדברים עמוקים, יפים לשעתם ויפים לדורות-עולם.

SUBJECT INDEX

NAME INDEX

BIBLICAL SOURCE INDEX

OLD TESTAMENT

MISHNAH

JERUSALEM TALMUD

BABYLONIAN TALMUD

MIDRESHE HALACHAH VE-AGGADAH

RAMBAM AND COMMENTARIES

ADDITIONAL SOURCES FROM THE RAMBAM

TUR AND SHULCHAN ARUCH AND COMMENTARIES

RISHONIM AND AHARONIM

ADDITIONAL TEXTS

ABOUT THE AUTHORS

Rabbi Professor DANIEL SPERBER is a leading scholar of Jewish law, customs, and ethics. He taught in the Talmud Department of Bar-Ilan University, where he also served as dean of the Faculty of Jewish Studies and president of the Jesselson Institute for Advanced Torah Studies. In 1992, he was awarded the Israel Prize for Jewish Studies. Prof. Sperber currently serves as rabbi of the Menachem Zion Synagogue in the Old City of Jerusalem.

The descendant of a line of distinguished Orthodox rabbis, Prof. Sperber was born in 1940 in a castle in Ruthin, Wales, and studied in the Yeshivot of Kol Torah and Hevron in Jerusalem. He earned a BA in art history at the Courtauld Institute of Art and received a PhD in classics, ancient history, and Hebrew studies from University College, London.

Prof. Sperber has published more than thirty books and four hundred articles on the subjects of Talmudic and Jewish socio-economic history, law and customs, classical philology, and Jewish art. Among his major works is a well-known, eight-volume series, *Minhagei Yisrael*, on the history of Jewish customs. More recently, he has written books on halachic methodology and rabbinic decision-making in confrontation with modernity, and has established an independent *beit din* dealing with a*gunah* issues. He is the author of *On Changes in Jewish Liturgy: Options and Limitations*; *On the Relationship of Mitzvot Between Man and His Neighbor and Man and His Maker*; and *The Importance of the Community Rabbi: Leading with Compassionate Halachah*, all published by Urim Publications.

* * *

Rabbanit Dr. MICHAL TIKOCHINSKY heads the Women's Beit Midrash and Halachic writing program at Herzog College as well as the Halachah program for Rabbaniot at Migdal Oz. Previously, she headed the Beit Midrash program for women at Beit Morasha. She also lectures at Shalem College, and is a widely published author of Torah and halachic research articles that appear in scholarly Torah journals. Rabbanit Tikochinsky has a Bachelor's and a Master's degree in Law and a PhD in Talmud from Bar-Ilan University. Her book on the scholarship of the Minchat Chinuch is set to be published soon. She and her husband, Yakir, live in Nof Ayalon, where they are raising their seven children.